The SOCIOLOGY of CHILDREN, CHILDHOOD and GENERATION

The
SOCIOLOGY of
CHILDREN,
CHILDHOOD and
GENERATION

Madeleine Leonard

Los Angeles | London | New Delhi
Singapore | Washington DC

Los Angeles | London | New Delhi
Singapore | Washington DC

SAGE Publications Ltd
1 Oliver's Yard
55 City Road
London EC1Y 1SP

SAGE Publications Inc.
2455 Teller Road
Thousand Oaks, California 91320

SAGE Publications India Pvt Ltd
B 1/I 1 Mohan Cooperative Industrial Area
Mathura Road
New Delhi 110 044

SAGE Publications Asia-Pacific Pte Ltd
3 Church Street
#10-04 Samsung Hub
Singapore 049483

Editor: Chris Rojek
Editorial assistant: Delayna Spencer
Production editor: Katherine Haw
Copyeditor: Sharon Cawood
Proofreader: Camille Bramall
Indexer: Charmian Parkin
Marketing manager: Michael Ainsley
Cover designer: Shaun Mercier
Typeset by: C&M Digitals (P) Ltd, Chennai, India
Printed and bound by CPI Group (UK) Ltd,
   Croydon, CR0 4YY

Library of Congress Control Number: 2015942702

British Library Cataloguing in Publication data

A catalogue record for this book is available from
the British Library

ISBN 978-1-4462-5923-8
ISBN 978-1-4462-5924-5 (pbk)

CONTENTS

ABOUT THE AUTHOR

Madeleine Leonard is a Professor of Sociology at Queen's University, Belfast, where she teaches a course on Sociological Approaches to Understanding Children and Childhood for the Doctorate in Childhood Studies. She is particularly interested in creative and participatory approaches to including children in the research process. She employs a range of mainly qualitative methods in her research with children and their childhoods. Her main research interest is in teenagers' everyday experiences of growing up in politically sensitive societies, and she has carried out research into the perceptions and experiences of Catholic and Protestant teenagers growing up in Belfast as part of an Economic and Social Research Council (ESRC) project 'Conflict in Cities and the Contested State' (www.conflictincities.org). She has also carried out research with Greek Cypriot and Turkish Cypriot teenagers growing up in Nicosia funded by the British Council. She is a founder member of the Research Network for Sociology of Children and Childhood of the European Sociological Association's Research Network for the Sociology of Children and Childhood, and she is involved in planning and organising the childhood sessions of the Association's bi-annual conferences. She is also secretary of the International Childhood and Youth Research Network (ICYRNET) based at the European University, Nicosia.

ACKNOWLEDGEMENTS

I would like to express my thanks to the following individuals as, without their support, this book would not have been written: Chris Rojek and Gemma Shields from SAGE, the former for initiating and stimulating my involvement in this project and the latter for her help at various stages throughout the production process; my colleagues from Research Network 4: Sociology of Children and Childhood network of the European Sociological Association, particularly for stimulating conversations in Modena, Italy during the mid-term symposium held in 2014; my colleagues from Queen's University, who are part of the School of Sociology, Social Policy and Social Work's writing group; my son Christopher Leonard and his colleague Paolo Pirroni for their help in constructing the diagram used in the book to illustrate the concept of Generagency; my colleague Professor Liam O'Dowd, who continues to give me ongoing support and encouragement, which is always appreciated; and, finally, my three children – Cathy, Christopher and Colin – for the wonderful ways in which they have enabled me to come to terms with the death of my husband in 2012, and, as always, Martin, this book is dedicated to you.

I

INTRODUCTION

In recent years, there has been a strong movement towards establishing childhood studies as a multi-/inter-disciplinary subject. Childhood researchers from sociology, psychology, law, education, anthropology, geography, medicine, and the list is ever growing, all subscribe to outlining the complementary fit within and between disciplines and their contribution to enhancing understanding of children and their everyday lives. But it remains unclear whether childhood studies is a newly emerging academic field or simply the gathering together and rebranding of what is already known, albeit in diverse disciplines, about children and their childhood (Kehily, 2008). While the wide-ranging perspectives that characterise childhood studies are laudable, at times, the role of specific disciplines gets somehow lost. The particular contribution of sociology to childhood studies tends to become engulfed within the myriad inter-disciplinary approaches, making it difficult to ascertain the core contribution of sociology to current thinking on children and childhood. Alanen (2012), for example, argues that we need a robust base strongly embedded in existing disciplines such as sociology to effectively contribute to genuine inter-disciplinary understandings of childhood, while Prout (2005) reminds us that inter-disciplinarity does not mean non-disciplinarity, hence prioritising certain disciplines over others becomes a worthwhile exercise.

The purpose of this book is to firmly acknowledge and illuminate the distinctive contribution of sociology to debates on children and childhood. The influential Danish sociologist Jens Qvortrup (2009: xiv) argues that the sociology of childhood continues to pose and debate the following questions: 'should we talk about the sociology of children or the sociology of childhood; how should we balance agency and structure in our analyses; is childhood mainly to be seen as a small-scale phenomenon or are children and childhood interesting also for and as a part of the larger social fabric?'. The aim of this book is to address these questions and outline and critically evaluate the body of sociological theory and empirical research which attempt to answer these questions. While these issues have been individually dealt with by the plethora of books on childhood studies, few have attempted to bring together these questions within the one volume.

This does not mean that the book will simply focus on work produced by sociologists. In an ever-increasing inter-disciplinary climate, such a narrow focus would not take us very far. Hence, the book will draw on work from a range of disciplines, including development psychology, anthropology, history and geography, but evaluate these contributions through the lens of sociology and privilege accounts which demonstrate the usefulness of sociological approaches to children and childhood. Sociological theories of childhood reflect discourses on children and their childhoods and how these feed into social, cultural, economic, political and legal definitions, and indeed how these discourses are context- and time bound. While childhood is commonly defined by age, various sociologists have illuminated the fallacy of simplistically reducing childhood to chronological age through their comparisons of the competing and contradictory meanings of age across different societies and cultures. As Thorne (2007: 150) puts it, 'age is an embodied form of difference that is both materially and discursively produced and embedded in relations of power and authority'. Hence, age should not be reduced to a biological process. Rather, different societies structure and order age differently and use a range of formal and informal processes to define and regulate acceptable age-related behaviour. For example, the age at which a child can legally smoke, drink alcohol, have sex, get married or commit a crime varies across different societies. The UK has one of the lowest ages for criminal responsibility in the world, as 10-year-old children can be arrested and taken to court if they commit a crime. The age of criminal responsibility is much higher in other European countries, set at age 13 for France, 14 for Italy, 15 for Denmark and 16 for Spain. The age of consent for sex also differs, with Austria, Germany, Portugal and Italy setting the age at 14, France, Denmark and Greece at 15 and the UK, Cyprus, Finland, Norway and Switzerland at 16. These examples suggest that age is as much a social construction as it is a biological process. In line with the United Nations Convention on the Rights of the Child (UNCRC, henceforth referred to as CRC), the age range applied to children in this book is 0–18 years. However, for the most part, the research that the book draws on relates to children under 16 years of age. There are a number of terms that can be applied to describe children, including infants, toddlers, tweens, teens and adolescents. 'Children' is a more generic term as is the term 'young people', and these two terms are the ones that will be used most frequently throughout the book, and, for the most part, the term young people will be applied to older children.

The book is structured around three core concepts – children, childhood and generation – and underpinning these conceptualisations is the relationship between structure and agency. In relation to the term 'children', some commentators have put forward the view that there are characteristics common to all children and these universal traits mean that children are broadly similar in a number of core respects. Others argue that there are no normative characteristics pertaining to children, rather these traits take on particular meanings in specific historical, social, economic and cultural settings. Hence, childhood is experienced differently across time and space and indeed it might be more accurate to talk about 'childhoods' rather than typical children. The term 'generation' draws out the relational aspects of childhood. This concept does not make sense without the associated twin concept of adulthood. Each is defined in relation to the other and each takes on significance because of the existence of the other. Indeed, traditionally, adulthood has been the norm against which childhood has been understood and measured. Children and adults have been commonly portrayed as possessing different traits and capabilities, with children being seen as immature while adults are seen as mature, and children being seen as irrational and closer to nature compared to the cultural, reflective, rational adult.

Understanding children and childhood necessitates unpacking the structural location of childhood in relation to adulthood. This brings to the fore the usefulness of dualisms in understanding children, childhood and generation. The core dualism between structure and agency continues to pose epistemological and ontological concerns within sociology. In relation to education, Shilling (1992) argues that dualistic ways of thinking about structure and agency lead to accounts of the social world that are often framed in terms of being strong on structure and weak on agency or vice versa. Prout (2000: xii) argues that more work needs to be done to bridge the gap between theoretical approaches that divide childhood as a 'large-scale structural order from the small-scale interactions and perspectives of children'. In a later publication, Prout (2005) cautions childhood theorists to move beyond oppositional dichotomies, suggesting that modern childhood is characterised by the weakening of boundaries between adulthood and childhood, rendering dichotomous positions obsolete. While acknowledging that the ongoing positioning of both childhood and adulthood and relationships between the two are likely to be dynamic rather than fixed, nonetheless the core argument adopted throughout the book is that there remains validity in maintaining an interest in the dichotomies that continue to characterise some aspects of childhood and adulthood, provided that these dichotomies are presented as messy, ambiguous, uncertain and interrelated rather than stable, durable and separate. An ongoing problem with dualisms is that, in attempting to critically unpack and question their applicability, there is a danger of reifying their existence. Yet dualisms continue to provide a useful lens for understanding sociology's contribution to childhood. This does not just apply to the ever-present debate between structure and agency but also to other fundamental ways of understanding contemporary childhood. Hence, critically examining dichotomous ways of thinking about children and childhood involves unpacking and outlining a range of dualisms while, importantly, demonstrating their interpenetration, hence rendering these dualisms artificial and questionable. However, in order to discuss the mechanisms and processes which link the two, one needs to acknowledge the presence of these dualisms in the first place. This will be a key feature of the book's overall structure. As Adrian James (2010: 490) puts it, 'Dichotomies are valuable heuristic devices: they enable us to compare and contrast important structural and theoretical concepts, to highlight their key features and to map out their interrelationships and interdependencies'. But, once again, to re-emphasise my position here, the overall aim of the book is to illuminate how the social construction of childhood and its multiple forms impact on these dichotomies and enable us to see multiple connections between seemingly polarised positions and locations.

All books involve omissions. Decisions have to be made about what to include and what to exclude. The sociology of children and childhood is so vast that some selection is necessary. The spatial focus of the book, for example, draws on children and childhood as they are perceived and experienced in a number of societies located in what has been referred to as the 'developed world' (also referred to as minority countries). Drawing on global childhoods, particularly lived childhoods in so-called 'developing societies' (also referred to as majority countries), brings in further complexities around how childhood is defined, perceived and inhabited by children subject to very different historic, economic and cultural contexts. Even across and within the societies covered in this book, various types of childhood are not included, for example those of children with disabilities, or who are in care and various forms of custody. The intention is not to imply that these aspects of childhood are not important, but in trying to present an overview of sociology's contribution to childhood studies, choices have to be made and this inevitably results in absences. The core strength of the book is its focus on the ongoing relevance of key issues such as rights, citizenship, structure, agency, macro childhoods, micro worlds, and how these are underpinned by notions of generation.

Chapter 2 sets the scene by looking at the somewhat dichotomous relationship between development psychology and sociology. The chapter will review how 'western' developmental psychology promoted a particular construction of childhood linked to the life course and how this influenced sociology through its articulation of socialisation. The chapter will chart how this focus was subsequently challenged by a paradigm shift referred to loosely as the 'new' sociology of childhood. This approach to the sociology of childhood implies a dichotomous relationship between 'traditional' and 'new' ways of thinking about children and their childhood. This 'new' way of conceptualising children and childhood opened up space for asking different questions about children and their childhoods, articulated how the concepts themselves varied considerably across time and space and addressed questions which were overlooked, excluded or marginalised by the focus on socialisation. The chapter will explore how rather than being treated as a focus in their own right, children were largely sidelined in mainstream sociology to areas such as the family, education or deviance. Within these fields, socialisation was the core conceptual framework for thinking about children and their childhoods. Writing in North America, Ambert (1986) argued that children were only visible in sociology in respect of their progress along the path to adulthood, and that the research agenda largely focused on effective and ineffective processes of socialisation. Similarly, Qvortrup (1994) argued that traditional sociology largely concerned itself with children as 'human becomings' rather than as human beings, focusing on how their future potential could be effectively developed through socialisation while, for the most part, ignoring their lives in the present.

Drawing on theoretical advances from sociologists working in Nordic countries, the chapter will outline how this 'new' sociology of childhood has influenced debates about children and childhood in a variety of European countries and the USA. For example in the UK, James and Prout (1997) produced a range of work which marked a departure point for thinking sociologically about children and childhood, drawing on the perspective of social constructionism and advocating new methodological approaches to the empirical study of children's everyday lives. In the USA, sociologists such as Corsaro (1985) and Thorne (1993) developed and applied social constructionist approaches to the lives of American children, outlining how they apply meaning to their everyday lives and in the process create peer cultures, thus presenting children as active agents who create meaning through their interactions with others. Collectively, social constructionist approaches repositioned children as active social actors and emphasised their capacity for agency. They advocated a renewed research agenda aimed at seeing children in the here and now, rather than in terms of what they would become as adults. They called for more active engagement of children in the research process and advocated a set of techniques whereby children's own experiences of the social world, their own meanings and interpretations should be central to the data collection process. The chapter will review some of the most influential theorists who locate children within this social constructionist approach and whose work frames children as active social actors. This does not mean that socialisation is now rendered obsolete. Baraldi (2010), for example, argues that Italian sociology remains preoccupied with socialisation theory and that Italian social policy continues to fail to engage with children as active agents. The chapter will also present critiques of the claims made by 'new' sociology of childhood theorists. Ryan (2008), for example, argues that a more thorough engagement with the history of children and childhood suggests that there have always been interconnections between the concepts of socialisation and agency, rather than the agency approach being 'newly' linked to the 'new' sociology of childhood. Underpinning these debates are wider sociological concerns about the relationship between structure and agency, and the chapter sets the scene for rendering problematic this relationship in later chapters.

New ways of thinking about children and their childhoods stimulated a flurry of empirical studies aimed at subjecting and extending children's everyday micro lives to academic scrutiny, but this was at the expense of a corresponding focus on broader structural understandings of childhood. While the focus on the plurality of childhoods and the diversity of children's experiences is justifiable, Qvortrup (2011) reminds us that the idea of childhood developed as a structural form, irrespective of children themselves. Hence, as a permanent, structural form, a focus on childhood necessitates unpacking the manifestations of structural childhood – in other words, the macro processes which interact with and shape how children live their day-to-day lives. Chapter 3 will explore the work of those theorists whose thinking contributes to a broader structural understanding of childhood, including Zelizer in the USA, Qvortrup in Norway and Sgritta in Italy. Adopting a structural approach, Zelizer (1985), for example, illuminates how the modern child became transformed from being 'economically useless' to 'emotionally priceless'; Qvortrup (2011) outlines how compulsory mass schooling changed the landscape of childhood as, for the first time, large numbers of age-specific children were brought together institutionally with the object of transforming them into literate adults; and Sgritta (1994) illuminates how society construes childhood and outlines how children inhabit and interact with institutions differently from adults because they hold a child status. In order to make sense of the impact of macro structures on children and their childhoods, the chapter will focus on four areas: work, family, education and play. The intention is not to provide a comprehensive overview of these four themes but to construct a framework which will elaborate on how macro processes have impacted on children's involvement in the labour market, their family life, their education and their play and leisure. Collectively, these four topics cover a significant part of children's childhoods and will enable the reader to effectively see the extent to which almost every aspect of childhood is influenced by macro forces.

Chapter 4 turns attention to the micro worlds of children. The 'new' sociology of childhood stimulated the development of a rich and multifaceted body of empirical research, exploring and unravelling children's everyday lives in a variety of different contexts. The chapter will review some of the most important contributions in this field, showing how such work uncovers the heterogeneity of children and their childhoods. While the volume of output on the micro worlds of children is vast, in keeping with the structure of Chapter 3, the focus will be on the same four areas: work, family, education and play. Each theme has produced a burgeoning amount of research and one chapter cannot do justice to the quantity available. Hence, as in Chapter 3, the four areas will provide a framework whereby the reader can gain insight into how children interpret, reinterpret, reconstruct and reformulate the various discourses offered to them through multi-dimensional socialisation processes in order to create and categorise their own culture-laden social worlds. These four topics provide a scaffold for illuminating children's active agency. The chapter will draw on a body of work which collectively demonstrates how, rather than being shaped by adult culture, children actively and creatively appropriate, transform and reconstruct information, processes and practices from the adult world to produce their own understandings of that world. The chapter will outline how children position themselves in particular social contexts and how they attribute meanings to age, gender, class and ethnicity. By drawing attention to the diversity of roles that children construct in daily interactions within various social contexts, the chapter will demonstrate the complexity of children's lived experiences and the diversity of meanings children attribute to recurring social practices. In myriad ways, children make a significant contribution to cultural reproduction and the resulting strategies they implement effectively show how socialisation is not a matter of adaptation and internalisation but an ongoing process of negotiation and reinvention. The chapter will provide a context for demonstrating the agentive role that children play in cultural reproduction.

Chapter 5 highlights how theoretical challenges outlined in the 'new' sociology of childhood paralleled changes in national and international arenas where new spaces were opening up to facilitate and acknowledge children as subjects in their own right. To the forefront of these wider developments was the CRC, which is regarded as a watershed in the movement towards the recognition of children as rights bearers, particularly around the right to be consulted about decisions which directly affect their everyday lives. The chapter will review how children came to be politically positioned, particularly with respect to the increasing emphasis on children's voices and their capacity to be active social actors. This involves examining the background to the CRC, its implications in setting a global framework for improving the conditions of children and exploring the ways in which ratifying countries have (or have not) incorporated its values into their national plans, programmes and legislation. The chapter will also review how this debate has evolved into one on creating an effective balance between rights and responsibilities and how this has been applied to and rendered problematic in relation to children.

Positioning children as rights holders is a fundamental step in advancing their pathway to citizenship. While citizenship may be simplistically defined as being born in a state, in reality it is linked to issues of inclusion and exclusion, including children's core exclusion from voting. Marshall (1950), for example, argued that although children had some social and civil rights, they could not be regarded as full citizens because they had no political rights. The chapter will review key debates on citizenship, focusing in particular on how the lack of voting rights dilutes citizenship, and will review a number of creative proposals for extending voting rights to children. The chapter will also outline how a number of childhood researchers have attempted to define what citizenship might mean for children, including suggestions that citizenship needs to be seen as a 'lived' practice rather than being narrowly reduced to its formal dimensions. The chapter will also articulate the ways in which many societies prepare young people for exercising the rights and responsibilities of citizenship through involving them in school councils. Finally, the chapter will review the arguments around creating a complementary balance between children's positioning in society and potential need for protection with their entitlement to be considered as rights-holding citizens, and how this may involve confronting and critiquing how citizenship is commonly defined.

The penultimate chapter turns to the problematic relationship between structure and agency, which is a recurring theme throughout the chapters presented thus far and continues to influence theoretical and empirical articulations of children and childhood. This reflects wider debates in sociological theory whereby the relationship between structure and agency continues to vex social theorists. Structure refers to the recurring patterned arrangements which make up macro society and its various institutions such as the economy, the legal system, politics, religion and culture. Structural variables such as class, ethnicity, gender and age also impact on how individuals produce and reproduce these structures. People's everyday routine, repetitive actions produce and reinforce a set of expectations about these institutional features of society and their location within them. These expectations influence or limit the opportunities available to individuals and indeed the choices they subsequently make. However, society is not just determined by social forces, rather individuals have the capacity to act independently. In other words, individuals are able to reflect on and change their behaviour. People do not passively respond to structures but, as reflective agents, they can act intentionally to change structures and their positioning within these structures. Hence, while the various institutions and positions that make up the structure of society often produce established ways of doing things, these are not effortlessly reproduced. As reflective agents, individuals can consciously alter their place in the social structure and the traditional expectations attached to their positioning. However, a fundamental problem remains concerning the extent to which structures impact on individuals' behaviour and, concurrently, the extent to which individuals' behaviour impacts on structures. While the 'new' sociology of childhood sought to reposition children as active agents, their location within the structural component of childhood calls into question their scope for autonomous action. Hence, childhood is both structured and structuring. Childhood sociologists draw heavily on Giddens' (1984) 'structuration' theory, which emphasises the duality of structure and agency. As James et al. (1998: 202) put it, childhood becomes 'a magnificent testing ground for the dichotomy between agency and structure ... it is adult society which constitutes the structure and the child, the agent'. By revisiting how childhood theorists and researchers treat the relationship between structure and agency, the chapter questions and renders problematic the extent to which children's agency can ever be fully activated by children themselves. While children are undoubtedly agents, nonetheless they continue to be widely influenced by adults' ideas about childhood, and these ideas and the structural generational framework set limits on children's agency and actions, thereby calling into question their status as autonomous agents. What children can and cannot do continues to be influenced by adults' conceptions of childhood, and this fundamentally dilutes the impact that children have on shaping the societies in which they live their daily lives. The chapter will review how the concept of generational order was an important advance in sociological thinking around adult–child relations. Theorists such as Alanen (1994), Mayall and Zeiher (2003) and Qvortrup (2011) analyse generation as a core element of social structure which is bound and linked to other structural variables such as gender, ethnicity and class. These theorists outline how children can be considered as a minority group conditioned by resilient power relations based on generation. The chapter will elaborate on the body of work which outlines how children and adults are holders of specific social positions that are not only defined in relation to one another but are also defined within specific social structures. The chapter will review these debates and suggest that children's agency needs to be framed within and between generations.

This argument will be developed through the author's conceptualisation of generagency, which is further sub-divided into inter-/intra-generagency. Generagency brings together the mutually reinforcing and interdependent relationship between generation and agency. Inter-generagency refers to existing hierarchal, structural relationships between adults and children and thus sheds light on the macro framework within which children's agency is expressed and practised. Children continue to be located in historically durable, generational relationships based on power, and it is within this framework that their agency is practised. In other words, agency takes place against a backdrop, where existing hierarchies between adults and children structure the conditions under which children practise their agency, calling into question the extent to which participating in these recurring forms of social interaction makes children agents. Yet, recognising the constraints under which agency is practised does not necessitate dismissing the potential impact of agency on social structures and this will be discussed and illustrated in the chapter.

The concept of intra-generagency will also be introduced to suggest that children do not simply internalise adult society but actively select, dilute, contest and challenge aspects of the adult world through creating their own peer cultures. These peer cultures do not exist independently of the adult world and, at times, they may become appropriated by the adult world, but they also have the ongoing, ever-present potential of directly and indirectly influencing that adult world. While these arguments are not new, generagency enables the construction of a tighter framework within which to examine and illuminate how structure and agency become activated within relationships influenced by generational positioning.

The author will draw on and revisit her previous research and re-evaluate this work through the lens of generagency in order to examine the usefulness of this model as a tool for understanding how children engage with the adult world and with each other, and how the blurred boundaries between the two show how structure and agency are fundamentally interconnected generationally. By eluci-dating the theoretical and empirical importance of inter-/intra-generagency, the book emphasises the importance of generation in understanding the relationship between structure and agency and in accounting for the commonality and diversity of children and childhood.

The concluding chapter will bring together the core themes of the book and remind the reader of its main arguments. The book's overall aim is to present a wide-ranging account of some of the core concepts that continue to challenge sociology and of how these dilemmas feed into and influence the work of childhood theorists.

2

BECOMING AND BEING: DEVELOPMENTS IN THE SOCIOLOGY OF CHILDHOOD

Chapter Aims

1. To explore the similarities and differences between psychological and sociological approaches to children and childhood.

2. To outline and critically evaluate the contribution of socialisation theory to sociological approaches to understanding children and childhood.

3. To set out the principles of the 'new' sociology of childhood.

4. To critically evaluate the 'newness' of the 'new' sociology of childhood.

Learning Outcomes

By the end of this chapter, you should be able to:

1. Understand some of the core ways in which psychological and sociological approaches to children and childhood differ.

2. Understand the contribution of socialisation theory to the sociology of childhood and the criticisms the concept generated.

3. Describe and illustrate the six features of Prout and James' 'new paradigm for the sociology of childhood'.

4. Demonstrate awareness of the criticisms of the 'newness' of the 'new' sociology of childhood.

The purpose of this chapter is to explore the similarities and differences between psychological and sociological approaches to children and childhood. This focus draws attention to some key dichotomies in the social sciences around the relationships between biology and society, nature and nurture and the individual and society. The chapter will commence by exploring how development psychology dominated the field of childhood studies for most of the 20th century. Childhood was considered as consisting of a set of predetermined stages, the end point of which is adulthood. Children were located along different age bands within this temporal journey and, for the most part, childhood was considered natural and universal. Child development was seen as 'an inevitable and invariable process driven by a biologically rooted structure which the child inherits' (Archard, 1993: 35). These concepts were incorporated into sociological theorising on childhood during the 1950s in the form of socialisation. Through socialisation, children acquire and internalise the norms and values of the society into which they are born. The early years of life were considered particularly important, hence the family was accorded a key role as a major agent of socialisation, with other key agents such as the education system playing an important role as children get older. The chapter will outline the contribution of socialisation theory to sociological understandings of children and childhood. Within this paradigm, children were largely viewed as passive objects unable or unwilling to respond actively to the range of influences external to them. This approach was challenged by the 'new' sociology of childhood which gained gradual academic legitimacy and influence from around the 1980s onwards. The chapter will outline this 'new paradigm' and explore its impact on the sociology of childhood. Central to this approach is an acknowledgement that children are active agents who are not simply shaped by the world around them but actively shape and change that world. The final part of the chapter will bring together the core themes explored throughout the chapter and question the extent to which a simple dichotomy exists between development psychology and sociology, and between 'traditional' and 'new' sociological approaches to children and childhood.

Development Psychology

Child development psychologists are concerned with how certain behaviours develop, how and when they develop and to some extent the influence of the environment on development. Traditionally, development was seen as having typical or average components, hence children became incorporated into standard measures of development, with their progress continually contrasted against the yardstick of a 'normal' child. In this vein, a normal, all-encompassing childhood was constructed even though in reality it was based on 'normal' expectations of childhood within western societies, particularly Europe and the United States (Woodhead, 1999). Moreover, adults were deemed to be experts on childhood. As Woodhead and Faulkner (2000: 11) put it: '"Child Development" is a body of knowledge constructed by adults for other adults to use in order to make sense of, regulate and promote children's lives and learning. Most often, children's actions and thoughts are interpreted against models of psychological processes, stages of relative competence, and/or deviations from "normality".' Hence, child development produced a body of adult experts on childhood. Woodhead (2011) outlines how this was facilitated by the introduction of universal birth registration and universal schooling whereby children were increasingly defined in terms of age-related competencies. Hence, age impacted on school starting and leaving age, when a person could legally have sex, marry, vote, commit crime and enter work, and while this varied slightly from one country to another, overall it was based on using age as an indicator of universal traits. A host of adult professionals charted children's journeys through age-specific periods and provided advice to parents, carers, teachers, lawyers, health workers and policy makers on 'normal' expectations and what to do in cases where children deviated from the norm.

This top-down approach produced a universal child against which individual children could be measured, assessed, praised or problematised if they deviated from what was considered 'normal'. While environmental influences were taken into consideration, the focus was on the positive or negative impact of wider forces in facilitating or interrupting 'normal' development and, in the case of the latter, the potential role of interventions in getting the child back on the proper path to development. Woodhead and Faulkner (2000) outline the research implications of this approach to child development, whereby children were seen as the objects of research and research was done to children rather than with children. They outline a range of experiments which had a significant influence on child psychology as a discipline. For example, the 'stranger situation' procedure observed infants' reactions (from behind a one-way screen) to a situation where mothers would leave the room and be replaced by a stranger who would proceed to interact with the infant while the child psychologists, hidden from view, measured the infants' reactions and subsequently categorised these reactions across four dimensions: 'secure', 'anxious/avoidant', 'anxious/ambivalent' and 'disorganised'. Woodhead and Faulkner state that, while this methodology is now seen as ethically unacceptable, in order to get published in leading journals, aspiring attachment researchers risk having their papers rejected if they do not make reference to these classic experiments or indeed include the methodology in their range of research tools. This has also resulted in a body of knowledge being constructed around the importance of the mother as the primary carer of children and the psychological damage that could result from maternal deprivation. Sommer (2012) argues that developmental psychology was thus mother-centric, reducing the social world of the infant to the mother–child relationship and leaving little room for other significant adults.

Piaget (1932, 1936, 1957) also had a significant impact on the psychology of child development. He was the first influential psychologist to undertake a systematic study of cognitive development in childhood. Piaget sought to demonstrate how children think in different ways to adults. His goal was to describe the staged journey whereby reasoning becomes developed during childhood. He studied children from infancy to adolescence, and indeed his own three children and their peers were core research participants. He made detailed observations of young children's cognitive behaviour and carried out interviews in a clinical setting with older children. He identified four key, distinct stages in child development, each marked by shifts in how children understand the world. His work had a profound impact on educational policy, intelligence testing and teaching practice, particularly in Europe and the USA during the 1960s and 1970s (Walkerdine, 1984). His theory of how intelligence develops through a series of progressive stages impacted on the standardised testing of children on the basis of age, even though his theory was more nuanced and emphasised that children's performance should not be equated with same-age peers but rather judged in relation to their own previous standard of development. Moreover, Woodhead and Faulkner (2000) argue that his methodology, which encouraged children to talk freely, albeit within clinical settings, was innovatory at the time and his core goal was to treat seriously young children's ways of thinking. Nonetheless, his focus on stages captured the imaginations of later psychologists, who tended to limit their studies to observing how the immature child performed against adult standards of thinking and reasoning.

To recap, a number of implications stemmed from psychological approaches to child development, such as child development being seen as essentially biologically based. Children's cognitive abilities were linked to a set of stages which served as a set of benchmarks to determine 'normal' childhood and, while individual differences were observable in the rate at which children progressed through these stages, the overall process was considered universal, linear and based on age, hence where children differed, these were seen as deviations from the norm. Development therefore represented a ladder-type progression with each step being seen as qualitatively unique. The child starts at the bottom rung of the ladder and progresses through a series of fixed, universal stages to the top rung. Childhood was therefore viewed as a transitional period. Throughout this journey, childhood was defined as an age-specific period of life and children were seen to possess distinct characteristics which separated them from the adult world.

Adulthood was seen as the end point of childhood and, since the child had not yet reached adulthood, she/he was seen as not fully developed, as incomplete, as not fully 'being', but rather subject to a set of processes whereby she/he would learn and internalise how to become an adult. Drawing on these insights, sociology sought to bring in the wider environmental impact of this journey through the concept of socialisation.

Socialisation

By the 1950s, underlying themes in development psychology around the natural, universal, irrational, immature child had fed into sociological accounts of childhood in the form of theories of socialisation. Sociologists argue that what is important in becoming an adult is not our biological nature but the process of learning, whereby society teaches the young the norms and values crucial to maintaining social order. The dominant paradigm was functionalism, which emerged in the USA after the Second World War. Talcott Parsons (1954) was one of the most influential exponents of this paradigm, and he viewed the family and the educational system as two of the most significant sites for socialising the young into adult norms and values. The implication here was that the child was somehow non-social or not fully social and had therefore to be moulded into a social person through interaction with influential adults through the process of primary and secondary socialisation. In order to elaborate on this approach, the chapter turns to briefly examine socialisation processes within the family and the school. The intention here is not to reduce socialisation to these two spheres as socialisation (whether accepted or rejected) is part and parcel of all social relationships and therefore operates across multiple social domains. However, a focus on the family and the educational system enables us to see how accounts of societal institutions were largely adult focused with little attention being paid to how these institutions were experienced by children.

Successful Socialisation within the Family

The family is the first human group that an individual usually belongs to, hence it was seen to clearly play a key role in socialisation. However, the approach was based on a particular family type – that is, a traditional nuclear family – which was thought to be prevalent at the height of the dominance of socialisation theory during the 1950s and 1960s. Within this family type, the child would see how adults have learned distinctive patterns of behaviour and Parsons illustrated this through his focus on the expressive traits of mothers concerned with the personal and intimate aspects of social life, compared to the instrumental traits of fathers concerned with aspects outside the family, such as politics and work. We can see here how during this period, human characteristics were seen as partly driven by biology and were gender specific. Indeed, feminists such as Mitchell (1971), who criticised this male-focused view of the family and sex roles, went further, suggesting that some sociologists seem to imply that 'biology is destiny'. Marxists also criticised the consensus view of social order outlined by Parsons. They argued that the shared societal values outlined by Parsons were little more than a smoke screen for inculcating individuals into accepting patterns of authority and power. However, they also focused on how children learn obedience within the family and how this obedience is fundamental to maintaining the status quo and unequal relationships on which capitalism depends. Althusser (1988), for example, argued that through socialisation, the family was one of the best institutions for encouraging individuals to think and behave in ways conducive to the continuation of the capitalist system. Hence, while Marxists and functionalists had different views on family life, none of them paid much attention to the actual internalisation of norms and values by children themselves. Instead, the family was seen, particularly by functionalists, as the sine qua non for the child's socialisation, with socialisation being largely seen as a one-way process.

Successful Socialisation within School

The school takes over from the family as a key site for socialisation. Young people spend a considerable amount of their childhood in educational institutions and indeed become defined in relation to their status as school pupils. Within school, children meet a wider circle of people and learn not just formal subjects such as English and History but also the importance of competition and reward – values crucial for wider society. Testing is a fundamental aspect of school organisation and children come to accept that, while ability is partly natural, it can be developed and strengthened through hard work. Parsons (1954) argued that within school, children learn to accept the unequal distribution of reward and status in wider society. Within school, children learn to accept the authority of adults and, for Parsons, this ensures the smooth functioning of present and future society. Children learn to view adults as superior and to accept this superiority. In all these ways, education becomes part of the process of preparing children for their adult roles, particularly for their lives as future workers. Continuing this theme of passive children, Marxists argued that within school children are divided into specific categories essential to the needs of capitalism. Children gradually internalise the view that they have different 'natural' traits, making them suited to one type of work rather than another, and of course with these different types of work being differently rewarded so that people who work with their hands will be paid less than people who work with their heads. As Bowles and Gintis (1976) put it, education is little more than a 'giant myth-making machine' whose core purpose is to encourage the oppressed to accept their inferior position within society. Through sites of secondary socialisation such as the school, children begin to develop a sense of wider social structures and their place within them. While there was some recognition of class impacting on structural positions, children's capacities to engage with and negotiate wider social structures were largely muted in these discourses, and in the case of functionalism their resistance was often interpreted as evidence of faulty socialisation.

Faulty Socialisation

While there was some consideration given to conflict in the socialisation process and to the idea that competing ideologies may be at play, there was little interest in children as actual social beings and in how they might accept, resist or challenge whatever norms and values were on offer. Where socialisation was seen as going wrong, this often involved constructing new categories of 'children', particularly around juvenile delinquents and youth subculture. Hence, most introductory textbooks throughout the 1950s to 1970s limited discussions of children and childhood to specific chapters on the family or school, mainly centring on successful socialisation, or juvenile delinquency and youth subculture as examples of unsuccessful socialisation. Referring to American sociology, Johnson (2001) argues that sociological studies of children up until the 1970s were dominated by a focus on deviancy and delinquency. Pearson (1983) also articulated how older generations often view young generations with suspicion and how each existing adult generation looks back to a 'golden age' of well-behaved young people with whom to compare the 'hooligans' of the present.

Underlying these discourses are notions of children and young people as needing strong discipline from adults to ensure that they don't stray from the path of acceptable behaviour. This approach found expression in the case of the murder of James Bulger in the UK in the early 1990s. Bulger, a 2-year-old child, was led away from a shopping centre, where he had been with his mother, by two 10-year-old children who were truanting from school. He was subsequently brutally murdered. Security cameras captured images of the 2-year-old being led away by the two 10-year-old boys who were holding his hands. The incident confronted society's privileging of childhood as a period of innocence, although attempts to keep this image intact were secured by treating the boys as adults in the ensuing court hearings. Dominant discourses of contemporary childhood were severely challenged by this incident, and exiling these children from childhood and according them adult culpability allowed the dominant images to co-exist. However, Franklin and Petley (1996) outline how media reporting of the case gradually became generalised into the notion that all children had the dangerous potential to be 'evil'. Ensuing debates on the need to protect children from society were extended to suggest that society needed to be protected from children. These conflicting images are presented by Jenks (1996) as the Dionysian and Apollonian models of childhood, positioning children as naturally evil or naturally innocent. These natural traits could be encouraged or suppressed through interaction with significant adults. Children were largely viewed as separate from adults but subject to adults determining their nature through socialisation processes.

Moving beyond Socialisation

The concept of socialisation dominated theory and research about children and their childhoods. Speier (1976) argued that this perspective highlighted the power of adults to define children. It reflected an 'adult ideological viewpoint', whereby children were regarded as dependents in a range of adult structures, rather than being considered as individuals in their own right. Childhood was regarded as a period of dependency and indeed subordination and children were thus rarely considered as a distinct social entity. In relation to North American sociology, Johnson (2001) outlines how children and their childhoods received scant and indirect attention. Where they were included in mainstream theoretical or empirical research, it was usually to demonstrate other social processes such as the family, schooling or deviance. In a similar vein, Ambert, writing in 1986, outlined the 'near absence' of studies of children in mainstream sociology. She briefly reviewed the work of Comte, Marx, Pareto, Durkheim, Weber, Simmel, Mead, Merton and Parsons, who either ignored childhood altogether or discussed the concept in a highly limited way. Likewise, Jenks (1982), in an introduction to a collection of articles from influential sociologists, suggests that the child was considered only in relation to adults. The child was a person devoid of adult competencies and traits. Hence, as Alanen (1988: 56) put it, 'a conception of the child is reached only by leaving the child side of the relationship empty'. Mainstream sociology journals, such as *The American Journal of Sociology*, reflected the marginalisation of children and childhood, with only 5% of the articles published from 1895 to 1980 referencing children (Shanahan, 2007).

Ambert (1986) argued that sociology textbooks by the mid-1980s did not fare much better, with children and childhood still relegated to the margins of the discipline. Where children were included, it was under the framework of socialisation. This future-looking perspective continued to consider children as passive recipients of a homogeneous adult culture and sought to unpack how the key agents of socialisation, such as the family or educational system, were charged with transmitting the core norms and values of mainstream society to children, who were, as yet, incomplete members. While resistance to socialisation, particularly in relation to youth subcultures and deviancy, was at times articulated, along with other examples of faulty socialisation, the child, for the most part, was not considered a fully active co-constructor of this process.

In an influential collection of readings on socialisation, Waksler (1991) discusses the need to move beyond socialisation. The collection brings together a number of core sociological readings on socialisation theory, with Waksler providing commentaries on the various chapters. At the outset, Waksler acknowledges the huge contribution socialisation makes to the study of childhood and suggests that 'studies of socialization are certainly worthy of serious attention by anyone interested in understanding the social worlds that children inhabit' (1991: 1). However, she identifies a number of core problems with the concept. First, she questions whether socialisation is a recognisable process. What is it that distinguishes socialisation from other processes? How, for example, would one set out to empirically study socialisation? What would be considered as evidence? Second, rather than a binary focus on adults socialising children, Waksler asks, are adults also socialised and if so, how and by whom? Are there similar processes at work or are the processes different? Returning the attention to children, Waksler asks what the child is doing when she/he is being socialised. This brings to the fore her fourth criticism, around whether or not the child should be viewed as a 'blank slate', existing as a kind of sponge, soaking up the attitudes and experiences of others. If not, and the child has some prior knowledge of society, how does this existing knowledge impact on what is being undertaken during any particular incident of socialisation? For example, the concept of secondary socialisation implies that some socialisation has already taken place. How does primary socialisation impact on secondary socialisation? These questions were rarely asked or even contemplated. Following on from this, Waksler considers whether socialisation is a one-way process or a reciprocal process. This involves returning to her earlier criticism and asking not just what is happening to children during socialisation but also what is happening to adults. There is an implicit assumption that socialisation ends with adulthood. However, socialisation exists throughout the life course. Adults are constantly and continuously socialised into the ongoing acceptance of established roles, changing rules associated with these roles or new roles that come into play during adulthood, such as grandparenthood. This locates both children and adults as recipients and agents of socialisation. How then and in what ways are these agents successful in their endeavours and how do we judge success?

Throughout this critique, Waksler underlines the need to illustrate socialisation as an 'empirical feat' rather than a statement of 'fact'. By emphasising the need for an empirical basis for understanding socialisation, Waksler argues that questions need to be asked around who it is that commonly socialises children. Traditionally, the focus has been limited to a set of influential primary and secondary agents of socialisation, such as the family and school, as outlined above. But transforming socialisation into a more serious empirical question may uncover a whole range of additional relationships at work. Indeed, Waksler, reiterating Speier, argues that socialisation theory is often little more than adult perspectives on childhood. Hence, the concept of socialisation produces 'data' rather than 'theory' about children. Moreover, if one considers the myriad activities that adults and children engage in together, is it sufficient to label all these interactions as aspects of socialisation? Might other processes be taking place? If this seems a reasonable assumption, how then do we identify what kinds of activities involve socialisation and which activities are immune? In other words, should every single interaction between adults and children be seen through the lens of socialisation, and indeed is there only one group (society) into which children are socialised? Reducing everything to socialisation is likely to produce 'an over-socialised conception of man' (Wrong, 1961). If socialisation is likely to be a messier process, a non-lineal process, a reciprocal process, indeed one process among many, then how are we to study socialisation? By asking these questions, Waksler moves beyond considering socialisation as the 'be all and end all' underpinning all parent–child relationships. Her critique views socialisation as a far less certain set of processes than is commonly envisaged. Understanding these broader processes might involve suspending the concept of socialisation (which implies suspending adult beliefs about children) and at the very least subjecting the assumed processes involved to empirical investigation, rather than reducing the concept to a singular, taken-for-granted accomplishment.

The gradual realisation that the categories of children and childhood might have social and cultural significance and are likely to differ across time and space paved the way for a renewed concern with how children themselves might experience their childhood in the here and now and how their experiences might impact on both childhood and adulthood. This is reflected in James' (2013) recent work where she outlines a child-centred perspective on socialisation. Her work draws on children's narratives on their everyday lives at home, at school and in their neighbourhood, and she illustrates how children participate in, contribute to and shape their experiences of socialisation. This focus on how children conceptualise and experience the process of becoming social is central to the so-called 'new sociology of childhood'. It is to this 'new' paradigm that we now turn.

New Paradigms? A Childhood Psychology and a New Sociology of Childhood

Paradigms provide frameworks for observing and understanding the world we live in. They shape both what we see and how we understand and interpret what we see. They rely on shared preconceptions made prior to and impacting (often unconsciously) on the collection of evidence. Kuhn (1962) discusses how paradigms reflect a set of practices that define a scientific discipline at a particular time, based on often untested assumptions about the nature and behaviour of individuals. Paradigms provide 'convincing' accounts of social reality that close off alternative versions. Development psychology and socialisation theory positioned children in particular ways with reference to how they were viewed and how they related to the world around them. They were seen as passive dupes of biology and/or socialisation. While their lives in the present were subject to a great deal of research, the frameworks for interpreting their attitudes and responses were future-orientated, based on a specific understanding of the adult society into which they would eventually become incorporated. The limitations of this approach became increasingly apparent as childhood researchers turned their attention to uncovering the myriad ways in which children's everyday lives seemed to produce anomalous results. Simplistic unidirectional models of biological and social development seemed unable to capture the diversity of children's everyday lives and the ways in which they responded to such taken-for-granted overarching frameworks, ways which at times supported and at other times challenged, contested, negotiated and reworked these existing taken-for-granted paradigms. This led to what Kuhn (1962) called a paradigm shift, whereby conceptual frameworks and basic assumptions for understanding a phenomenon go through a crisis, resulting in a call for a re-examination and re-conceptualisation of the existing paradigm. Central to this shift was an increasing awareness that children were social actors in their own right, and both disciplines sought to address and explore the subsequent theoretical implications of this shift in how children were traditionally viewed. This involved a reassessment of previous positions and it is to this issue that the chapter now turns.

A Childhood Psychology

By the latter end of the 20th century, the universal psychological principles that shaped children's development towards adulthood were being increasingly questioned. The 'normality' of the child's journey to fully developed adulthood seemed ill equipped to deal with actual children's progression or to capture the widespread societal changes within which movement took place. Rather than child development being seen as universal and static, there was an acknowledgement that childhood could be perceived and experienced differently across time and space. While Woodhead (2011) argues that the wide range of diverse theories and perspectives that characterised child development make it misleading to condense into a single paradigm, Sommer (2012: 231–2) outlines what he calls a pre-paradigm psychology of childhood with a post-paradigm position termed 'a childhood psychology'. This paradigm shift has a number of elements. First, there is a move away from universal top-down knowledge drawing on grand theories relating to human development towards an approach which recognises that knowledge is culturally and historically situated and that inter-disciplinary approaches may more aptly capture the diversity of children's childhoods. This also involves acknowledging that child psychologists are part of the world they are researching. As Woodhead (1999: 12) points out, 'they are subject to the same psychological processes they seek to describe; there may be a connection between the "inner" child of their own autobiography and the "outer" child they seek to describe … their scientific claims to objectivity rest on assumptions that their own theories of human cognition cannot sustain'. The early simplistic focus on socialisation as a one-way process was also challenged and the notion that socialisation could operate in both directions became acknowledged. Alongside this was a move away from the mother as the centre of the child's personal world towards the notion that the child resides in an increasingly complex and changing world which involves a range of multi-personal and inter-personal relationships. Sommer (2012), for example, outlines how wider societal changes make top-down general, universal psychological theories more difficult to apply. He outlines how widespread changes in female employment outside the household, the rise in the number of children in out-of-home care, falling birth rates, rising divorce rates, coupled with myriad changes to family types, fundamentally transform the context within which children live their early, everyday lives. Focusing in particular on women's increasing role as waged employees, Sommer argues that this has led to an increased separation of young children's daily lives into family time and childcare time. He argues that approximately 80% of 3–5-year-old children in the developed world are subject to some form of childcare. This means that families are less and less likely to act as key sites for children's primary socialisation. Instead, a diverse range of adults are likely to routinely and repeatedly interact with young children. Hence, growing up in today's changed world is qualitatively different from the experience of previous generations, necessitating an unpacking of the taken-for-granted assumptions on which the previous paradigm rested.

Rather than the typical child living their early years in mother-dominated contexts, modern children interact with a whole range of adults including fathers (with fatherhood being seen as a more active role), peers, siblings, grandparents and childcare staff, each contributing to the socialisation context in which the child is located. Socialisation is therefore seen as being more than a simple one-way process and is rather the result of reciprocal interactions, occurring between these various agents and the child, with the child playing an active part in this process. The fragile, incompetent, passive child was increasingly called into question by a range of studies on how children accomplish their everyday lives and this promoted more nuanced conceptions of childhood, whereby children exhibit resilience and competency and in myriad ways are active meaning makers. These new insights underlined the need to reassess previous paradigms. As Sommer (2012: 35) succinctly articulates, 'altered living conditions for children not only challenge old paradigms but require new ones'. This revolution in thinking also impacted on sociology, where a similar process of questioning old paradigms and rethinking new ones began to take shape.

The 'New' Sociology of Childhood

The emergence of the so-called 'new' sociology of childhood sought to unpack children's experiences of childhood in the here and now rather than in terms of the future adults they would become. It sought to give 'conceptual autonomy' (Thorne, 1987: 103) to children, to see them in their own right without reference to adulthood. Hence, the perspective moved beyond seeing children as the 'cultural dupes' of socialisation theory. Prout and James (1997) have been at the forefront in articulating what they call 'a new paradigm for the sociology of childhood'. This paradigm fundamentally challenged the notion of a 'natural' or 'universal' child. It sought to illustrate how childhood is socially constructed and therefore varies across time and space. This 'new' paradigm had a significant impact on the development and theorising of childhood studies. It forced a reassessment of previous understandings and it is therefore worth outlining the core tenets of the 'new' sociology of childhood, as outlined by Prout and James.

There are six core aspects of the new paradigm (1997: 8):

1. Childhood is a social construction.

2. Childhood is a variable of social analysis.

3. Children's everyday lives are worthy of study in their own right.

4. Children are not passive subjects of social structures but active actors.

5. Ethnography may be the most useful methodological approach to understanding children and childhood.

6. Childhood theorists and researchers also play a role in reconstructing childhood.

It is worth unpacking these six features in more detail.

1. Childhood is a social construction

Of primary importance to the new paradigm is the need to underline the point that childhood is a social construction. Indeed, the book in which James and Prout (1997) outline the 'new' paradigm is entitled *Constructing and Reconstructing Childhood*. This position challenges the notion of childhood as a universal, biological stage of life by emphasising that biology may be played out differently in different contexts and across different time periods. It suggests instead that childhood may be shaped and constructed by historical, cultural and social factors. This means that everyday structures such as the family, education, what is meant by work and play, and so on, may differ across and within different contexts. Indeed, a global focus on childhood suggests that childhoods rather than childhood may be a more accurate term to capture this diversity. While the focus of this book is limited to 'western childhoods', these are also characterised and shaped by widespread diversity. Within specific cultures, there may be a multiplicity of childhoods leading to huge differences in how individual children experience family, school, play and work, and some of this diversity will be outlined in subsequent chapters.

2. Childhood is a variable of social analysis

The second aspect of the paradigm seeks to articulate the importance of age as a serious dimension of analysis. However, while childhood is a variable of social analysis, it is by no means the only variable. It does not exist independently of other variables such as class, gender and ethnicity, and the interplay between these variables and age may play out differently for different groups. It is therefore up to sociologists to explore these intersections and their implications for children and their childhoods. This necessitates questioning childhood as a homogeneous stage of life and challenging interpretations of childhood as an 'undifferentiated category' (Morrow, 1996). Gender, class and ethnicity, among other variables, impact on how childhood is experienced.

3. Children's everyday lives are worthy of study in their own right

The move from becoming to being led to a renewed focus on children's lives in the here and now. Understanding childhood in the present necessitates talking to children about their everyday lives, acknowledging their expertise in articulating their everyday experiences and prioritising areas deemed important by children themselves rather than imposing adults' interpretations and concerns on their everyday lives. Hence, this necessitates conceptualising childhood, both theoretically and methodologically, as independent of adulthood. This has led to a burgeoning amount of research on previously hidden aspects of childhood and on topics prioritised by children themselves as important to them in their daily lives.

4. Children are not passive subjects of social structures but active actors

While childhood may be constructed for children, it is also constructed by children. Children do not merely replicate and perpetuate the social processes they are subjected to, but actively make sense of these processes, which may result in these processes being contested, negotiated, challenged and reinterpreted. Lee (1982) charts the evolution towards considering the child as a person capable of acting at some level independently of the adult generation. He identifies 'three paradigms of childhood'. In the first, children were considered the property of adults. In the second, children were located as dependents in need of protection by and from adults, while, in the third, the child emerges as an active actor. This latter component is one of the most significant contributions of the Prout and James' paradigm as it relocates children as persons in their own right with the ability to act in and influence the world around them. This notion of the child as an active agent underpins all the components of the new paradigm.

5. Ethnography may be the most useful methodological approach to understanding children and childhood

While a discussion on methodology lies outside the remit of this book, it is worth emphasising here the enormous impact that the 'new' sociology of childhood has had on research methods. Prout and James made a case for ethnographic methods having the ability to get closer to the 'truth' about what childhood is like and how it is experienced. Ethnographers are concerned with seeing the social world from the point of view of research participants. Hence, they seek an insider's perspective. This means that rather than start out with a clear idea of what the research is about, ethnographers learn what is important and significant by talking to research participants. It then follows that this is a potentially useful approach to adopt when researching children and their childhoods. It allows children a more direct voice in research and privileges the insider's point of view.

6. Childhood theorists and researchers also play a role in reconstructing childhood

Prout and James (1997: 9) also remind us that 'childhood is a phenomenon in relation to which the double hermeneutic of the social sciences is present ... that is to say, to proclaim a new paradigm of childhood sociology is also to engage in and respond to the process of reconstructing childhood in society'. In other words, sociologists are not neutral, impartial observers of society but are products of their own environment. Through their theorising, they also contribute to recreating the categories they set out to deconstruct. Indeed, Prout (2005), in reflecting on the contribution of the 'new' paradigm, suggests that in retrospect the social construction of childhood was over-emphasised to the extent that it allowed no scope for biological or psychological factors and thus narrowed rather than expanded the field of childhood studies. This will be returned to at the end of the chapter.

What's So New?

Of course, the 'newness' of the 'new' sociology of childhood can be questioned. Indeed, Prout and James (1997) admit that their paradigm, rather than being a radical break from the past, drew on insights from interactionism and phenomenology where the child was located not just as a product of social processes but also as an active agent capable of impacting on wider structures. Mead (1934), for example, attributed to children a core role in creating and developing their own social identity. On this view, socialisation, rather than being a one-way process, is seen as a site of negotiation between adults and children, whereby the child interprets and actively, rather than passively, responds to the attitudes and actions of adults. Similarly, within childhood psychology Vygotsky (1962) was influential in highlighting how culture and social context play a fundamental role in cognitive development and stressed the importance of interaction in the development of cognitive abilities in children. Since the main purpose of this book is highlighting sociology's contribution to these debates, the discussion will now centre on unpacking the 'newness' of the 'new' sociology of childhood. While a paradigm shift may be too great a claim, nonetheless the 'new' sociology of childhood brought together the arguments of a range of researchers working across a variety of countries, including Qvortrup in Norway, Alanen in Finland, Jenks in the UK and Thorne and Corsaro in the USA. Their work was groundbreaking in terms of underscoring the importance of studying children/childhood as a subject in its own right. Their criticisms of influential theories in psychology and sociology around child development and socialisation led to more attention being paid to how childhood is shaped by wider historical, social, economic and cultural factors. Hence, childhood is not a universal age-specific period with children possessing general traits that separate them from adults. Rather, childhood is perceived and experienced differently not only across but within specific societies. Uncovering these wider processes and their impact on how children live their childhoods spearheaded a host of empirical research that provided an evidence-based body of work that made the traditional paradigms no longer tenable.

However, the question remains: to what extent does the 'new' sociology of childhood represent a significant change in theorising about children and their childhoods? A number of recent commentators have questioned the 'newness' implied by recent childhood sociologists. Ryan (2008) argues that every single issue of the journal *Childhood*, ever since its origin in 1993, outlines the 'new' sociology of childhood as the overarching theoretical framework to which the journal is committed, while King (2007) states that the 'new' sociology of childhood has established itself, particularly in the English-speaking world, as the dominant theoretical framework underpinning sociological understandings of children and childhood. Yet in unpacking this framework, Ryan (2008: 553) exposes what he sees as 'the myth of a paradigm shift'. What Ryan views as particularly problematic is the claim embedded in the 'new' sociology of childhood of moving beyond the dualism of the adult–child distinction. In order to demonstrate the shift away from this dualism, Ryan argues that 'new' childhood theorists make two further claims. The first is to view childhood as a permanent structural feature of modern western societies and the second is to consider children as active agents operating within this wider structure. However, Ryan argues that these two principles only make sense within the framework of adult–child distinctions.

In a similar vein, King (2007) outlines how the 'new' sociology of childhood's raison d'être is to uncover and illuminate how similar children are to adults. Hence, like adults, children are competent. Like adults, children have agency, although they are often denied opportunities to practise their agency, because of adults' misguided focus on their child-like attributes. Counter claims such as those coming from psychology which outline children's biological and psychological immaturity are subsequently dismissed as being adultist. To legitimate these claims, King argues that 'new' sociology of childhood theorists select evidence to support this perspective and communicate findings to other enlightened followers. The elevation of the child to the status of active agent is core to the 'new' sociology of childhood. However, the child as an active agent fundamentally depends on an adult–child distinction being brought into play in the first place. If modern society is structured around legitimating differences between the adult and the child, and if the child is to move to the status of active agent who accepts, rejects, challenges or negotiates these wider processes, it is clear that the status of the child as active agent depends on the existence of these boundaries.

King (2007) is also critical of the methodological implications of this 'new' perspective. He argues that 'new' sociology of childhood researchers have developed a toolkit of methods which claim to get closer to the truth of what childhood really means for children themselves. They do this by emphasising the artificial divisions that exist between adulthood and childhood and how these divisions endorse power differentials between adults and children so that research on children reflects adults' concerns and priorities around what to research and indeed how to research. King questions the extent to which a reliance on the perceptions and beliefs of children themselves is any more capable of producing a reality of modern children than other versions. He outlines how the 'new' sociology of childhood is premised on the assumption that it is possible to capture the authenticity of childhood by prioritising children's voices. Through developing a range of supportive methodologies that enable children to articulate their attitudes and experiences, childhood researchers seek to demonstrate children's competency. The validity of the evidence produced depends on an acceptance of the basic assumptions outlined in the 'new' sociology of childhood's creation of a 'new' paradigm. Hence, the communications produced are those by adults working in adult institutions and communicating their 'authentic' knowledge of children to other adults. The upshot, according to King, is that childhood theorists produce 'information' rather than 'facts' about children and their childhoods.

Likewise, Gallacher and Gallagher (2008) question the superiority of the participatory research methods advocated by 'new' sociology of childhood thinkers as the best way of capturing and understanding children's everyday lives while simultaneously empowering them and enabling them to practise agency. Here, agency appears limited to merely taking part in research. The epistemological framework for this approach rests on children being considered as experts on their own lives, knowing more about childhood in the present than adults, and with this self-knowledge producing 'authentic' accounts of childhood. However, Gallacher and Gallagher argue that, in practice, most participatory methods are adult designed. While advocates claim to empower children, for the most part children are empowered by adults to create knowledge about their lives which is subsequently used to further regulate them, with the altruistic aim of improving their circumstances. Drawing on Lancaster and Broadbent (2003), Gallacher and Gallagher question whether children are the only experts. In doing this, they are not advocating that adults (including researchers) are mature and knowledgeable while children are immature and amateurish. On the contrary, they call for 'methodological immaturity' in research. Such an approach acknowledges that there is no 'real' world out there waiting to be discovered by the utilisation of the right techniques. It recognises that all humans and not just children are in a process of becoming, and the role of research is to capture the complex, messy, contradictory ways in which adults and children move through stages of becoming. By extending and challenging the binary between becoming and being to adults, Gallacher and Gallagher (2008) blur distinctions between maturity and immaturity and force a rethink of the binary frameworks on which distinctions between adult and child research rest.

This reflects Lee's (1998) call for an 'immature sociology' based on what he identified as limits to 'new' theorising on children and childhood. He argues that at the outset, the discipline of sociology has to decide on children's ontology. Indeed, to decide on children's ontology also involves deciding on adults' ontology, as outlining in theoretical terms that there are children and there are adults implies that passing from one stage to another is to pass from one ontological order to another (Mackay, 1991: 29). Ontology refers to the subject of existence. It relates to the nature of being. Hence, a decision must be taken in relation to whether children are 'becomings' or 'beings' (the decision has already been made on behalf of adults). As outlined earlier, traditional theories of socialisation positioned children as in a process of becoming, while the 'new' sociology of childhood sought to reposition children as beings in their own right. To move to this position, 'new' childhood theorists have to reconceptualise children as interpretative agents. Indeed, as outlined earlier, the focus on agency is one of the most significant distinguishing features of the 'new' sociology of childhood. However, Lee questions the substance of this re-conceptualisation. According to Lee (1998: 460):

To enter the world of sociology, unaccompanied by an adult, the image of children must be 'matured'. This tells us that sociological theory presents us with a model of the social world that is peculiarly 'mature'. The young cannot figure in their own right in sociological theory unless they are understood as 'mature' in their possession of agency.

By emphasising the competency, the rationality, the agentic being of the child, 'new' sociology of childhood theorists, in Lee's view, continue to privilege rather than challenge completeness and maturity over incompleteness and immaturity. Lee points to other consequences of this framework. He argues that it tends to result in childhood theorists and researchers fitting children into existing forms of sociological theory rather than advancing a sociological theory that is fit for children. To make children fit for sociological theory, as outlined above, decisions have to be made concerning their ontology. While considering children as beings rather than becomings may be considered an advance, the new conceptualisation necessitates taking as given a theory based on a world of 'completed beings' (1998: 458). To respond to this fallacy, Lee calls for an 'immature' sociology. This immature sociology should move beyond binary states of becoming and being to recognise that all persons, whether adults or children, are likely to move between and across these dimensions. This means that both children and adults move in and out of states of competency, maturity and rationality. These are not fixed states possessed by persons located in a particular age hierarchy. Immature sociology moves children and adults into an incomplete world but an unfinished world for both, and one in which the grounds on which difference is based no longer hold up. This creates new possibilities for theorising. It necessitates acknowledging that independent action often occurs within dependent relationships. The implications of this in terms of how agency is defined will be discussed more fully in Chapter 6.

Competing or Complementary Perspectives

In its early stages, development psychology and sociology conceptualised children as 'incomplete – immature, irrational, incompetent, asocial, acultural' compared to adults who were regarded as 'complete – mature, rational, competent, social and autonomous' (Mackay, 1991: 28). However, the growing recognition that childhood is socially constructed led to an increased emphasis on the social context in which child development takes place. This led to a new awareness of wider social processes within which psychological and social development occurs, although Ingelby (1986) argues that much more work is needed to critically unpack the links between the psychological and social contexts. Nonetheless, progress has been made in terms of an increasing recognition and acceptance of the fact that dependency cannot be reduced to biology but needs to take account of the ways in which dependency is socially determined, hence attention needs to be paid to the structurally dependent relationships involving differential access to power within which children are placed and the social, economic and political policies which uphold the dependency of children on adults and adult structures. These debates will form the core of Chapter 6 where children's agency will be critically unpacked.

Through socialisation, sociologists sought to theorise how children gradually internalise and reproduce the norms and values of society. This concern with the reproduction of social order rendered children as little more than passive recipients of adult norms and values (which were also universalised). When norms and values were unreflectively reproduced, this was referred to as successful socialisation, whereas instances where these processes were challenged were considered failed socialisation, with the children concerned being labelled as deviants. Moreover, while adults' role as agents of socialisation received extensive coverage, how children accept, reject, resist or transform processes of socialisation remained under-theorised and under-researched. This necessitates understanding socialisation as a process involving both adults and children. It is a process which is continually challenged and negotiated, rather than a simple process of internalisation. Moreover, socialisation occurs throughout the life course. It is not a process that ends in adulthood. Adults experience various life transitions as they pass through adulthood such as getting jobs, losing jobs, buying houses, relocating, getting married, divorced and re-married, becoming parents and grandparents. All these life events introduce new norms and values and involve adult and child adaptations.

The divisions between psychology and sociology and indeed between the 'traditional' and 'new' sociology of childhood may have been to some extent overstated. Indeed, according to Woodhead (2011), development psychology has always been messier, more complex and nuanced than some childhood sociologists imply in their often simplistic critiques. At the same time, Woodhead (1997) cautions against ignoring the 'fact' that children do indeed have specific needs and hence calls on development psychology to reframe rather than reject this position by situating needs within the particular social, political, cultural and economic contexts in which they are defined and responded to. In a similar vein, Boyden (1997) argues that the trend towards establishing global standards for children's rights, while needing to pay more attention to the local, regional and national contexts, also needs to incorporate some acknowledgement of the roles of biology and psychology in child development. As outlined earlier, this leads Sommer (2012: 4) to argue for a childhood psychology rather than a psychology of children. He argues that while child psychology can no longer be simply equated with stage development, 'elements of traditional stage theories may be adapted and incorporated into a comprehensive understanding of children's everyday life in society and culture'. However, he warns against paying so much attention to wider historical, social, cultural and economic factors that the child's actual psychological development is rendered invisible and meaningless.

The separation of the biological child of development psychology from the social child of sociology remains largely intact. Lee and Motzkau (2011) use the term 'bio-social dualism' to refer to the continuing inability of childhood researchers to bridge the gap between psychological and sociological explanations relating to children. Each views childhood either through the lens of nature or of culture. In reflecting on 'The Future of Childhood', Prout (2005: 3) argues that we need to move away from reducing childhood to either biological or social factors. Modern childhood is too complex, in his view, to be reduced to a single over-arching framework. His solution is to regard childhood as a 'hybrid form' which transcends both nature and culture. Drawing on Foucault's notion of bio-politics, Lee and Motzkau (2011) introduce the notion of 'multiplicities' as a way of negotiating the bio-social divide. Rather than childhood being reduced to either nature or culture, they suggest that a multiplicity of childhoods exist or are possible. In particular, they argue that the pervasive capacity of technology to intervene in life processes dismantles and merges traditional biological and social boundaries. To illustrate the bridge between technology, biology and culture, Lee and Motzkau discuss the application of a gadget called the 'Mosquito Teen Deterrent' in the UK. The device is aimed at disrupting the possibility of young people congregating in public places and potentially acting in an anti-social manner. The contraption can be placed on exterior walls and emanates a high-pitched noise that can be heard by teenagers but not by adults. In other words, the device provides a technological response to real, biological differences between adults and children in terms of hearing ability.

Lee and Motzkau employ the concept of multiplicity as a navigational tool to enable the crossing of disciplinary boundaries for researching the deployment of Mosquito devices, and suggest this example could pave the way for a more comprehensive and fruitful adaptation of the concept in theory and research in childhood. The usage of Mosquito appliances brings into play different conceptions of childhood, merging together different interests from biological to psychological to technological to social and cultural. Core customers for Mosquito devices are local government departments and shopkeepers. However, using Mosquito devices is problematic as children are a valuable resource, providing the rationale for the setting up of leisure facilities by local government agencies or providing customers for retailers. The Mosquito device provides a solution in that it doesn't deter children from using public premises all of the time but only some of the time, as with the press of a button the device can be activated. This enables local government departments and shopkeepers to merge two competing accounts of children's potential – that is, their economic potential as customers with their cultural potential for perceived, peer-influenced anti-social behaviour. No verbal exchanges come into play here, rather interaction is shaped remotely through the device. Users merely press a button while recipients engage with the device through their age-specific, biological, hearing ability. Lee and Motzkau point out that usage of the device brought other voices into play, in that the mechanism created a backlash from children's advocacy groups opposed to use of the device and to the treatment of children as non-social beings. This reflects social and cultural challenges to the notion of children as a species apart and also reflects the growing cultural trend of seeing children as rights holders. Hence, the device is an example of where biology meets technology meets the social child. For Lee and Motzkau, examining the impact and significance of Mosquito devices needs collective input from across various disciplines, stretching from the biological to the social, but from the starting point of multiplicity, rather than emanating from the interests of specific disciplines. The concepts of 'hybridity', used by Prout (2005), and 'multiplicity', used by Lee and Motzkau (2011), are presented by Ryan (2012) as a move from a 'new paradigm' to a 'new wave'. However, Ryan (2012) questions whether this 'new wave' presents anything radically new and is suspicious of whether these recent approaches have the capacity to dismantle ongoing boundaries between psychology and sociology. Thorne (2007: 150), for example, laments what she sees as the 'continuing wall of silence' between the two disciplines and appeals to both to engage in more fruitful mutual dialogue to transcend the ongoing divide, although she acknowledges that conceptual difficulties around ontology render this a difficult task.

The Sociology of Childhood and Sociology

It is worth briefly outlining the contribution that the 'new' sociology of childhood has made to sociology more generally. In the journal *Current Sociology* in 2010, various childhood researchers from a number of different countries, including the USA, Australia, the UK, France, Germany, Italy and Finland, were asked to reflect on the relationship between childhood sociology and 'mainstream' sociology. I want to draw on their reflections to illustrate the significant contribution of childhood sociology to the discipline, but also to call attention to the ongoing marginalisation of the study of children and childhood and how it continues to exist at the peripheral edges of the discipline. Buhler-Niederberger (2010: 155) argues that childhood remains a 'young branch of the discipline' and, while there is now a wealth of studies on previously neglected aspects of young people's lives, nonetheless, at the level of sociological theory, children remain largely invisible. This is despite the range of theoretical advances that the 'new' sociology of childhood has brought to our attention. For example, the location of childhood as a permanent structural feature of society opened up interest in the generational order, and theorists such as Qvortrup and Alanen argue that this generational order is as important as other structural variables, such as class and gender, and should be subject to a similar level of scrutiny. At the same time, the acknowledgement that childhood is socially constructed called for a comparative framework which would illuminate how childhoods are experienced across time and across different societies rather than existing as a fixed universal state. The location of the child as social actor necessitated detaching the child from mainstream sociological interest in the family or education system and considering children in their own right, living their lives in the here and now. This led to a renewed focus on how daily life is accomplished in the present, thus challenging the often overwhelming focus on the child in terms of future potential. All these observations opened up space for new questions and new perspectives to emerge but the impact across different societies has been variable. Reflecting on Italian sociology, Baraldi (2010: 285) argues that children still tend to be seen through the primary lens of socialisation theory, with sociological interest in children's agency remaining 'weak in Italy compared to other European countries'. In the UK, Moran-Ellis (2010) argues that mainstream sociology has yet to engage in any systematic way with many aspects of children's lives. For example, the sociology of work continues to marginalise the formal and informal work activities of children. The sociology of sexuality is guilty of a similar neglect, while mainstream research on class and gender still tends to position children in terms of socialisation theory, albeit within frameworks outlining socialisation as a messier process. In relation to France, Sirota (2010) argues that much French sociology continues to see children through the lens of socialisation and in terms of their location in family and educational systems. She cautions against the danger of 'a sociological field closing in upon itself' and argues that more mainstream sociological engagement is necessary to 'consider the child in socially structured relations such as social classes, gender or generation relationships' (2010: 263). These relationships are central to mainstream sociology.

Hence, while the burgeoning field of childhood studies has significantly contributed to challenging the invisibility of children, and children within sociology, its impact remains piecemeal. Childhood sociology has emerged as a new, somewhat trendy, sub-discipline, leading to a range of special options within sociology degree programmes, rather than being integrated into the mainstream concerns of the discipline.

For example, in relation to Germany, Zeiher (2010: 293) argues that childhood sociology can be seen as a 'progressively developing sub-discipline' but one that exists on the fringes of mainstream sociology rather than being viewed as an integral part of the discipline. The major sociological associations have special thematic groups in the field of childhood sociology. For example, the International Sociological Association's Research Committee, RC53, specifically relates to The Sociology of Childhood. The European Sociological Association has a similar thematic group relating specifically to children – Research Network 4. While, of course, both these organisations arrange and classify the divergent interests of members around specific themes, a review of plenary and semi-plenary sessions and keynote speakers during the annual/biannual conferences aimed at showcasing central sociological debates and concerns would suggest that childhood remains low on overall agendas and in their identification of the important overarching themes that sociology currently needs to engage with and debate. The American Sociological Association had a Children's Section from 1992 to 2000 but since then, childhood has been merged with youth studies to form a children and youth section of the organisation (Bass, 2010), while The Australian Sociological Association has a section on youth but none on childhood (van Krieken, 2010). This brief review suggests that childhood sociology still has some way to go towards establishing itself as core to the mainstream discipline.

The move within universities to promote inter-disciplinary research units and centres, together with an increasing need to demonstrate research 'impact', has led to a mushrooming of inter-disciplinary perspectives on childhood, and this has further weakened the potential of childhood sociology to impact significantly on core sociological theorising. Indeed, Strandell (2010) suggests that there has been more commitment to adopting core sociological concepts and approaches to children and childhood by other disciplines rather than within sociology itself. Within sociology, as outlined above, childhood is often conceived as a separate, narrow, specific theoretical and empirical research topic rather than a core component of the overall discipline. Efforts to illustrate 'impact' often lead to a narrow focus on 'problem children and children's problems' (Qvortrup, 1994), and funding opportunities often become reduced to identifying the necessary inputs to produce successful outcomes for children, particularly those from disadvantaged or problem backgrounds, to enable their effective inclusion in future society. In the process, how 'ordinary', 'everyday' children live out their 'ordinary', 'everyday' childhoods gets somewhat lost. It is against this background that this book centres on sociology's contribution to understanding 'ordinary', 'everyday' children and their childhoods by demonstrating the importance of generation as an overarching concept and subsequently applying this framework to the core sociological themes of structure and agency.

Conclusion

This chapter sought to critically unpack the neat binary divisions between psychology and sociology and between traditional and newer versions of each. The debates raised in this chapter are central to the core arguments that will subsequently be developed throughout the remainder of the book. The discussion thus far suggests the ongoing importance of dualisms in understanding children's and adults' attitudes and experiences and the relationships between them, although, as the chapter demonstrates, these dualisms are messy and overlapping rather than distinct. The next two chapters bring to the fore additional dualisms between the macro and micro contexts within which adults and children live out their daily lives. While the division of the macro and micro into separate chapters could be considered as reinforcing a false dualism, the intention is to explore these two positionings of childhood and children in detail to set the scene for Chapter 6, which brings to the fore the messy relationship between structure and agency that emerges from and operates within the boundaries of the macro and the micro and the border between adulthood and childhood. The relationship between structure and agency underpins these divisions and remains an unresolved tension within the 'new' sociology of childhood. Chapter 6 will put forward the concepts of inter-generagency and intra-generagency as a potential framework for illuminating but not resolving these ongoing debates.

QUESTIONS FOR DISCUSSION

1. Outline and critically evaluate the main differences between psychological and sociological approaches to children and childhood.
2. Discuss and critically evaluate the contribution of socialisation theory to sociological accounts of children and childhood.
3. To what extent is childhood a social construction?
4. Outline and discuss the contribution of the 'new' sociology of childhood to promoting new ways of thinking about children and childhood.
5. Have divisions between the traditional and the 'new' sociology of childhood been overstated? Give the reasons for your answer.
6. Evaluate the arguments put forward by Lee and Motzkau (2011) to bridge the gap between technology, biology and culture.

Recommended Reading

Ambert, A. (1986) 'Sociology of Sociology: The Place of Children in North American Sociology', in Adler, P. and Adler, P. (eds) *Sociological Studies of Child Development*, 1, 11–31.

Lee, N. and Motzkau, J. (2011) 'Navigating the Bio-politics of Childhood', *Childhood*, 18, 1, 7–19.

Prout, A. and James, A. (1997) 'A New Paradigm for the Sociology of Childhood? Provenance, Promise and Problems', in James, A. and Prout, A. (eds) *Constructing and Reconstructing Childhood: Contemporary Issues in the Sociological Study of Childhood*, London: Falmer Press.

Ryan, P. J. (2008) 'How New is the "New" Social Study of Childhood? The Myth of a Paradigm Shift', *Journal of Interdisciplinary History*, XXXVIII, 4, 553–76.

Waksler, F. C. (1991) *Studying the Social Worlds of Children: Sociological Readings*, London: Falmer Press.

3

MACRO CHILDHOODS: PRIORITISING STRUCTURE

Chapter Aims

1. To outline and illuminate how macro structures impact on children and childhood.

2. To illustrate the impact that the Industrial Revolution had on how childhood was conceptualised.

3. To explore how wider structural processes have impacted on family life and relationships.

4. To account for the impact of compulsory education on children's positioning in society.

5. To understand how the consumption practices of children have been shaped by wider transformations in childhood.

Learning Outcomes

By the end of this chapter you should:

1. Be able to understand the arguments in favour of considering childhood as a structural component of contemporary societies.

2. Comprehend the significant impact that the Industrial Revolution had on how childhood was conceptualised.

3. Know how wider structural forces impact on children's experiences of family life.

4. Be able to reflect on and evaluate the significance of the introduction of compulsory education for childhood.

5. Be able to give specific examples illustrating how children's consumption practices reflect wider transformations in childhood.

Social structure is a key concept in sociology. It refers to the social institutions and relationships that together form society. These institutions and relationships are ever present and they impact on all aspects of human experience in society. The economic system, legal system, political system and so on are all examples of social structures. Individuals are also grouped into structural positions, including class, ethnicity, religion, gender and age. These structural features of society are considered as enduring and relatively stable. Social relations result from these pre-existing structures. Through processes of norms and sanctions, individuals accept, perform and sometimes challenge expected roles in society. However, where structures are challenged, they are often replaced with new structures that once again regulate social action. According to Firth (1971: 47), social structure is 'concerned with the ordered relations of parts to a whole; with the arrangement in which the elements of the social life are linked together'. While Parsons (1954: 32) argues that social structure refers to 'the particular arrangements of the inter-related institutions, agencies and social patterns, as well as the statuses and roles which each person assumes in the group', these roles are seen as more durable than the occupants of roles. For example, in Chapter 2, I outlined how traditional accounts of socialisation suggest that society is ruled by norms, values and beliefs that are transmitted from one generation to the next. On reviewing the importance of the concept of social structure in sociology, Bernardi et al. (2006: 165), while recognising the complexity and ambiguity of the concept, nonetheless suggest that most definitions shared some common generic traits. Social structure refers to organised, ordered, patterned relations that are constituted and reconstituted through regular, recurrent, repetitive behaviours that influence choice and behaviour, thus enabling structures to achieve an element of permanence in time and space.

Some sociology of childhood theorists argue that it is important to view childhood as one of the core structural elements around which society is organised, producing roles and expectations based on and divided by generation. Hence, reducing children's everyday lives to their everyday micro experiences risks ignoring the extent to which these everyday practices are shaped by wider macro structures. This chapter is thus concerned with illuminating childhood as a structural form. Its intention is to explore how wider macro changes impact on childhood. In order to illustrate these changes, the chapter will focus on a number of core areas of children's everyday lives, namely work, family life, education and play. These are by no means exhaustive but they are useful in highlighting how changes at the macro level brought into being core notions of childhood (and adulthood) which subsequently impacted on children's everyday lives. The next chapter will focus on the micro effects of these macro changes using the same broad topics. While the topics will be discussed separately, this does not imply that each area had specific effects. Rather, these topics are interrelated so that changes in one impacted on others. These interrelationships will be discussed at the end of the chapter.

While Chapter 2 outlined the emergence of a body of work on child development, according to Qvortrup (2011: 23) it is important to move beyond these narrow confines by enlarging the focus to consider the development of childhood. Childhood is a permanent structural feature of 'developed' societies. Its membership may change as children are born into and leave childhood, according to the legal definitions of adulthood in their respective societies, but the segment itself remains (Hardman, 2001: 504). Qvortrup is one of the most significant exponents of how macro-societal transformations have impacted on childhood. He argues that to understand childhood necessitates unpacking macro historical changes in the economy. These changes fundamentally shaped the parameters of childhood and continue to have significant effects on how childhood is experienced. Qvortup argues that changes in the mode of production that accompanied the Industrial Revolution are pivotal for understanding how childhood increasingly became separated from adulthood and formed the basis for the shape of childhood in the present. As Bradley (1996: 176) puts it:

> the development of modern industrial capitalist societies brought increased awareness of age as a basis of social distinctions and greater segregation of age groups. While most societies have elements of age stratification, capitalism has promoted a distinct form of age inequality which rests on the socially dependent status of the young and the old.

The chapter will focus on this period as a convenient starting point for examining the structural nature of childhood. However, it is worth alluding here to the importance of Aries' (1962) seminal account of childhood and his thesis that locates the discovery of 'childhood' as occurring in the late 16th and early 17th centuries and being fundamentally linked to the development of the modern education system and the formation of the nuclear family. His provocative thesis, that 'in medieval society the idea of childhood did not exist' (1962: 125), continues to capture the attention of scholars in various academic disciplines. Aries argued that in medieval society, children from about the age of 7 were incorporated into adult society and were generally viewed as miniature adults. Hence, childhood was not recognised or valued as a separate phase of existence. Since then, Aries argues, there has been a transition in society's ideas about childhood. He relates this transition to a number of factors including: the decrease in infant mortality; the introduction of compulsory schooling; and a gradual privatisation of the family. These transformations led to the discovery of childhood as a distinct and separate phase of life. While Aries' methods have been widely criticised (Pollock, 1983; Wilson, 1980), and he has been accused of 'presentism' (Archard, 1993) in that he views the different treatment of children in the past from how they are now treated as evidence that there was no childhood, nonetheless most commentators agree that his main thesis remains justifiable, which is that childhood is not a universal or natural category but is constructed differently according to prevailing economic, political, social and cultural processes. The remainder of this chapter focuses on the impact of these wider processes during the period of industrialisation which brought to the fore fundamental differences between childhood and adulthood.

Work

In this section, the discussion focuses on the enormous impact the Industrial Revolution had on work and family life. The section will concentrate on the Industrial Revolution which began in Britain in the late 18th century and gradually spread throughout the 19th century to Western Europe and the USA. Changes in the system of production under capitalism separated home from work and the accompanying widespread urbanisation fundamentally impacted on family life. The Industrial Revolution changed the nature of both adulthood and childhood and indeed relations between the two. It also spearheaded new relationships between the family, economy, state and polity. In order to demonstrate the significance of this period, the discussion will centre mainly on major transformations in the world of work in British society as a result of the Industrial Revolution. The trends that emerged in Britain rapidly spread to other advanced economies.

Prior to the emergence of industrial capitalism in Europe, the family was an important economic unit. Children worked alongside parents in the production of a range of goods and services which were central to economic survival. With the onset of industrialisation, the family lost control over the production process, which moved to the mills, mines and factories of the rapidly emerging and expanding urban towns and cities. For the first time, the workplace became separate from the family. This is not to say that no child had experience of work outside the household, as sending children to work as servants and apprentices in other people's households was common practice. But what the Industrial Revolution did was to make it more economically viable for children to remain within the household, as the era opened up opportunities for children to gain income and contribute to the family economy through paid work. Cunningham and Viazzo (1996) draw on a range of historical sources that suggest that children were preferred as wage earners to mothers. In the USA and five European countries, children's contribution to the family budget was greater than that of their mothers. Moreover, as the male in the household got older, children's contributions to household income increased. In European countries, children were contributing a third of household income by the time their fathers reached their 40s and this increased to over 40% when their fathers were in their 50s. The age at which children entered employment varied according to industry. Lace making, the textile industries and coal mining relied heavily on the labour of young children. For example, in British coal mines in the 1840s, the average age of entry was just under 9. Work was regarded as good for children and idleness was abhorred. Children without employment were regarded as a potential threat to society, even though the supply of workers often exceeded demand.

Drawing on research in Belgium, De Herdt (1996) outlines the negative health consequences of work for children and argues that these trends were observable in a number of European countries. In the coal-mining industries, children had to work in cramped conditions, leading to posture problems. Some worked very long hours with up to 36-hour shifts and rarely saw daylight. Coal dust produced lung problems. Girls working in sewing shops and at lace making often developed curvature of the spine, and tuberculosis was prevalent in these industries. Some children died from exhaustion, while others experienced severe health problems that culminated in reduced life expectancy.

Over time, the horrors of child labour in factories, mills and mines prompted philanthropists to press for regulations to protect children from labour. Hendrick (1994: 25) outlines how child work came to be seen as an abomination:

> There was nothing new about children working in the Industrial Revolution, for it had long been established that they should contribute to the family economy. ... However, it was their working in textile mills, mines and as chimney-sweeps which most dramatically captured the imagination of reformers and philanthropists who campaigned against this form of exploitation. Many contemporaries were appalled, not only by the scale and intensity of the exploitation, but also by the brutalization of the young workers, and the violence which it was felt was being done to the nature of childhood itself.

Working children came to be regarded as 'children without a childhood'. Various Factory Acts restricted the types of jobs children could undertake, limited working hours and set a minimum age for starting work. Cunningham (2012) argues that while these policies took shape in Britain, as other countries industrialised, they also began to legislate to protect children from labour. His analysis outlines how during the second half of the 19th century, France, Prussia and New England introduced laws to protect and segregate children from the world of work. These initiatives, stemming from philanthropy, gradually opened up 'huge areas for public intervention into working-class life' (Cunningham, 2012: 360). They necessitated bringing to the fore new images of childhood based on children's dependency on adults and separation from the adult world. Childhood was idealised and romanticised.

A growing body of experts and professionals became involved in defining, monitoring and regulating childhood. The spread of compulsory schooling further entrenched this trend. Families were subject to increased surveillance and if they were deemed not to be fulfilling their responsibilities, the state had a right to intervene to ensure that children experienced a proper childhood. The dependency of children on a range of adults increasingly characterised children's everyday lives and this dependency was largely motivated by children's right to a childhood characterised by innocence and play. While considerable disparities continued to prevail for many children between their actual everyday lives and the ideology of a care-free childhood, the separation of childhood from adulthood, along with notions of different adult–child characteristics and traits, found expression in a range of emerging social policies, aimed at endorsing and legitimising this division.

While the period 1880–1918 is often considered to represent the end of child employment in Britain, Lavalette (1999) argues that it is more accurate to consider the period as one during which child labour was restructured and increasingly marginalised. Children became involved in a whole range of part-time informal work activities that continued to be essential for their families' survival but which could be structured around educational commitments. Child employment was not eradicated but transformed so that many children combined employment with education and this trend continues in many contemporary societies. Quoting OECD statistics, Loudoun and McDonald (2014) argue that in most developed countries (the trends are even more prevalent in majority world countries), the employment of children, particularly from the age of 13 upwards, is widespread. However, their involvement in the labour market is subject to legal regulation and control, reflecting idealistic notions of childhood as a dependent stage of life. Global frameworks recommend that states should play a crucial role in determining when and under what conditions children can become involved in the labour market. The International Labour Office (ILO) Convention 138 set up a standard principle that no child under 15 should be employed. The CRC advocated under Article 32 that states had a duty to protect children 'from economic exploitation and from performing any work that is likely to be hazardous or to interfere with the child's education or to be harmful to the child's health or physical, mental, spiritual, moral or social development'. The sentiments expressed by these frameworks are laudable and, of course, children should be protected from exploitation in its myriad forms. Indeed, many abuses of children's labour are ongoing but, while acknowledging this, my intention here is to show how these frameworks sought to promote a 'globalisation of childhood' (Boyden, 1997), reflecting 'western' adult views of childhood as a period separate from adulthood and ideally free from the adult world of paid employment. Where children cross these boundaries by entering the labour market, adults are accorded the right to make all sorts of judgements around what kind of work is and isn't appropriate for children to do. Local and national legislation has been adopted by the majority of developed societies to regulate and control children's entry into and engagement with the labour market. The detail of the law differs – indeed, even within specific countries, such as the USA, Australia and the UK, there may be some state, local or regional variations. But, for the most part, a number of common themes are prevalent.

To illustrate these common themes, I will draw on some examples from the legislation in Australia, the USA and the UK. With the exception of the entertainment industry and children working for parents on family farms or in family businesses, all three countries recommend a minimum age at which children can be employed. In Australia, the minimum age is 13, although this is lowered to age 11 for children delivering newspapers and advertising material or making deliveries for registered pharmacists. In the UK, the minimum age for children starting work is 13, while in the USA the starting age for employment is 14 and, as in Australia, a lower starting age rate is set for children delivering newspapers. Hence, age is used as a general category for determining children's entry into the labour market, and, with some exceptions, this is usually set at when children enter their teenage years.

Most states also recommend the hours during which children can work and the maximum hours that they can work in one day and the maximum hours over 1 week. The legislation emphasises that school is the proper place for children by banning children from working during school hours. In Australia, children can work for up to 3 hours per day and 12 hours per week during term time and up to 6 hours per day and 30 hours per week during school holiday periods. In the UK, children cannot work before 7.00 a.m. or after 7.00 p.m. and for more than 1 hour before starting school, in case their work impacts on their education and they turn up for school too tired to learn. They also cannot work for more than 2 hours during a school day or on Sundays, which are defined as family time, and the overall working week must not exceed 12 hours. During school holidays, children may work up to 25 hours per week but no more than 5 hours on any particular day. In the USA, children can work up to 3 hours on school days and up to 18 hours per week during term time and this rises to 8 hours per day and up to 40 hours per week during vacation periods. If these hours were added to the hours children must spend in compulsory education, many children will have more time commitments than adults in full-time employment.

States also stipulate the kinds of occupation children can and can't be involved in. In most cases, general statements are made. For example, in Australia, the legislation relates to 'all industries' but elsewhere this is specified as 'retail, hospitality and delivery'. But within these industries, children cannot operate heavy machinery, work on fishing boats, work on building sites, sell things door to door, work in gaming or serve alcohol. Similarly in the UK, children cannot work in pubs or betting shops or on industrial sites. In the USA, the legislation is more complex, but what is apparent across all three countries is that states make moral judgements about the types of work children can undertake. Serving alcohol, for example, is not a strenuous task, nor a difficult one, but it is seen as bringing children into contact with behaviour that is only normalised for adults.

States also have different provisions when work is performed for one's family or where children work alongside family members. For example, in Australia, children need a permit to work which stipulates various conditions, however no such permit is required when children work for parents. White (1996) argues that this reflects wider international approaches to children and childhood, which locate parents as natural protectors of children and their interests, and assume that working for one's parents at home, usually without pay, is more acceptable than working for others outside the home for payment. The legislation in the USA is particularly complex relating to family labour, as in southern states, in particular, whole families may be employed as migrant labourers, and where children work alongside parents, more lax regulations are in operation which suit not just parents dependent on family labour but also the owners of the enterprises in which the families are employed.

For those states that have work permits, interestingly, depending on the country, they must be signed by the employer, by the parent giving permission, by the school principal and by the family doctor, but, in most cases, not by the child worker. This locates the child as unable to make responsible decisions regarding their employment without the interference of well-meaning adults. Of course, many children work without proper permits. For example, in Leonard's (2004a) research in Northern Ireland, only 8% of the working children who took part in her research held work permits. Hobbs et al. (2007) argue that children have little to gain from having a work permit and therefore the legislation in place to protect children is ineffective. This means that adults can exploit the labour power of children and Hobbs et al. give a range of examples where children are employed in occupations and under conditions forbidden by the legislation. While acknowledging these abuses, the overall thrust of these legislative frameworks is to protect children rather than empower them in the labour market. Leonard (2004a: 49) argues that 'the key distinction between adults and children as workers appears to be that most adult employment legislation is concerned with promoting adult rights in employment, whereas most child employment legislation is concerned with protecting children'. For example, Hobbs et al. (2007) argue that there appears to be no concerted effort in most countries to recruit children into trade unions. Again, this is because they are often not considered as proper workers but as school pupils with money-making hobbies.

As a result, their bargaining power within the labour force is muted and indeed their overall position in the labour market reflects and reproduces wider imbalances in power between adults and children (Denniss, 2005). The next chapter will explore employment from children's points of view and illustrate some of the ways in which their attitudes and experiences differ from those expressed in local and national legislation and international conventions, and call into question their positioning by adults in this context.

Before leaving this section, it is important to recap on the significance of this period for childhood. In reviewing this era, Qvortrup (1999) argues that what is crucial is that these macro-structural changes produced changes in childhood rather than changes in childhood impacting on macro structures. Hence, the driving force lay in economic macro structures and, as the chapter will go on to illustrate, subsequently impacted on other areas of childhood within the family, the education system and children's play. This renders the unpacking of these macro structures as crucial for understanding modern children, because, as Qvortrup (1999: 5–6) emphasises, these changes took place without any significant input from children themselves:

> it is therefore of upmost importance for childhood research to deal with macro-societal forces … a sociology of childhood which ignores these forces to the advantage of primarily studying how we talk about childhood or how children react in a number of circumstances will have failed its task.

Family

The major changes outlined above had an enormous impact on family life. The family became more privatised. Prior to the Industrial Revolution, children lived in a diverse range of households where work and family life overlapped. Indeed, in charting the history of childhood from the 15th to the 17th centuries, Aries (1962) argues that in many European countries it was commonplace to send one's children away from the age of 7, to become apprentices in other households. There they would remain, performing a range of menial tasks or learning the trade of adult members of these households, and this was considered a more suitable preparation for adult life than living in the private domain of one's own family. Prior to the Industrial Revolution, children who remained within their families had to work to ensure the economic survival of the unit. During the cottage industry period which preceded the Industrial Revolution, families worked in the textile industry operating looms in their own homes to satisfy the demands of their merchant/manufacturing employers who provided raw materials (sometimes looms) and collected and subsequently sold finished products. While during this time, sometimes referred to as the proto-industrial period, families worked long hours in often terrible conditions, they nonetheless had some control over the production process. Parents, grandparents, children and other relatives worked as a team. Hence, there was no separation of home from work. Indeed, most of this work was performed by rural families who could meet the shortfall from living off the land by working in these cottage industries, particularly during times of the year when farming was less intense or not productive enough to meet family needs, such as during winter time. By the end of the 19th century, the factory system had become widespread in manufacturing industries, not only in Britain but also in other developed countries. The loss of control over the production process had a fundamental impact on family life. The family remained important but lost some of its crucial roles. It became weaker as an institution with many of its formal responsibilities being taken over by outside bodies.

Aries outlines how before the 18th century, wealthy families lived in large houses where space was shared between children and adults and indeed between servants and masters and a host of other individuals. The newly emerging middle classes in Western Europe initiated the notion of 'the self contained family led by a strong father with a central focus on the upbringing of children' (Clarke, 2004: 8). These ideas gradually spread to the working class. As outlined above, children and then women were increasingly excluded from the labour market. New roles emerged for women, with housework and childcare becoming their new exclusive, undervalued, productive activities. The nuclear, two-generation family became the norm, although other family forms continued to co-exist. As outlined in Chapter 2, the family became a major location for socialisation and parents were seen as core agents of socialisation. Children were located as dependents of adult family members and their needs were not defined independently of the family.

The nuclear family, as reflected in the work of Parsons (1954), depended on men and women undertaking what he saw as complementary roles, with the husband as the breadwinner and the wife taking primary responsibility for housework and childcare. This restrictive family type was short lived. The increased involvement of women in paid work outside the household from the 1970s onwards ushered in a whole host of other changes to this 'idealised' family type. In recent decades, families have become characterised by increasing diversity and children's experience of family life has become increasingly complex. Rising divorce rates and a dilution of the stigma attached to birth outside marriage results in more and more children likely to grow up in households without fathers. Indeed, Jensen (2011) argues that the absence of fathers in children's lives is one of the most prominent changes in contemporary family life, with their biological fathers likely to live with other children and with new step-fathers likely to enter their lives at some point during their childhood. Fathers' (and indeed mothers') biological link to children is diluted through fostering and adoption. Artificial insemination enables adults in a range of relationships (including same-sex families) to have children. Marriage, cohabitation, divorce and remarriage bring a range of adults into the households children grow up in. Increasing life expectancy brings a host of grandparents (biological and non-biological) into children's lives. These changes impact on roles and responsibilities and on relationships between both adults and children in these often unstable arrangements.

As the 20th century progressed, children increasingly became the responsibility of the state and a host of child 'experts' intervened in almost every aspect of children's lives from health to education, to upbringing and morals. Parents became bombarded with advice, which was often contradictory, on how to bring up children properly and 'responsible parenting' became increasingly regulated. As Hendrick (1990: 36) puts it, by the beginning of the 20th century 'a recognisably "modern" notion was in place ... childhood was legally, legislatively, socially, medically, psychologically, educationally and politically institutionalised'. Parents were subject to surveillance and if they did not meet societal expectations around protecting children, then the state had the legislative clout to remove children from their parents' care and place them in state institutions. Parents became accountable to the state to prove their ability to act responsibly, and, as Wyness (2014: 64) points out, 'the concept of the responsible parent has been used in child protection and care, education and criminal justice realms to "police" and sometimes punish poor disadvantaged parents'. Hence, new relationships between the state and the family emerged throughout the 20th century.

These changing relationships between parents, children and the state impacted on social welfare policies. Children were increasingly moved from the private world of families to the public world of policy makers. Despite the plurality of family units, child welfare policies reinforced the notion of an ideal family type and justified intrusion into family life on the basis of investing in the future of disadvantaged children, particularly those located in unstable or lone-parent households. This was partly motivated by an acknowledgement that child poverty remained a core problem in many countries, despite the increasing involvement of women in paid work outside the household. This was largely due to macro changes in the workforce with the loss of well-paid (male) manufacturing jobs and their replacement by low-paid service jobs, often monopolised by women workers who also tended to work part-time rather than full-time. This restructuring of the labour market was also accompanied by the spread of precarious and flexible types of employment, leading to poverty in employment. Hence, the movement of women into the formal labour market at times perpetuated, rather than lifted families out of, their poverty. As Jensen (1994) points out, the feminisation of poverty resulted in the pauperisation of childhood. Lewis (2006) argues that at the beginning of the 21st century, while child poverty rates have declined in some European countries, the overall trend has been for the child poverty rate to be greater than the overall poverty rate and this is particularly pronounced in the USA, Canada, the UK and Italy. Many governments view paid work as the most effective route out of poverty and have pursued policies to enhance the labour market participation of groups particularly vulnerable to unemployment, such as lone mothers and the disabled. Women (particularly lone mothers) who choose to remain at home to look after children are targeted through activation measures and are encouraged or indeed compelled to enter the labour force. Interestingly in countries such as the UK, women who look after their own children are labelled non-workers, whereas if they look after other people's children they are deemed respectable workers (childminders). Hence, childcare is being increasingly formalised and commodified. Paid work, regardless of quality and earnings, is seen as a panacea for the prevention of the intergenerational transfer of poverty and disadvantage.

At the level of the OECD and the European Union (EU), policies are being increasingly structured around social investment, a term coined by Anthony Giddens (1998a) in his influential book *The Third Way: The Renewal of Social Democracy*. Acting as policy advisor to UK Prime Minister Tony Blair, Giddens argued that in order to respond proactively to the social and economic risks associated with changing family types and the changing world of work, states needed to invest in the human capital of their populations and focus on long-term rather than short-term gains. This future-orientated approach was seen as the best chance of preventing the transmission of intergenerational poverty. Hence, children and their needs were seen in terms of investment in their future. While investing in children can be viewed as a laudable policy goal, it often locates the child in terms of 'becoming' rather than 'being' (Lewis, 2006), although Lister (2007) cautions against presenting what she views as a false dichotomy between future- and present-orientated child strategies, as she suggests that most countries are likely to embark on policies that embrace both. However, she also points out that some children, such as the disabled, gypsy and traveller children and children of asylum seekers, continue to exist on the margins of social policies. The extent to which this dual approach to social investment achieves a satisfactory balance between considering children as 'beings' and 'becomings', remains debatable.

These changes also have implications for childcare. While parents continue to assume primary responsibility for childrearing, the state, through a range of social policies, also provides varying degrees of support. However, this has developed differently across nation states. Lewis (2006) points out that in most Northern European and Western European countries, states have seen it as their duty to support parents financially in the care of their children. This is most pronounced in Scandinavian countries, where partnerships exist between the state and parents regarding the economic costs of caring for children. However, no universal system of state support exists in the USA, while, until recently, the UK saw childcare as primarily the private responsibility of parents. Recent policies to increase the labour market participation of women (particularly lone mothers) have been accompanied by a proliferation of formal childcare arrangements. The EU, for example, has expressed a commitment that 90% of children between the ages of 3 and the compulsory school leaving age in member states should have access to childcare (Lewis, 2006). However, apart from Scandinavia, the quality and cost of childcare remain problematic for many European countries. Moreover, the policy drivers have been less concerned with promoting the needs of children and more concerned with enabling adults to enter the labour market. Wider demographic changes around falling birth rates and ageing populations in the majority of developed countries position children against adults in an era of dwindling government revenue and growing welfare expenditure. Qvortrup (1987) argues that this is resulting in a battle between older adults and children over scarce resources. However, children are unlikely to win this struggle because, unlike pensioners, they have no voting rights and have little impact on election outcomes. He develops this argument further by pointing out (2011) that since elderly populations are growing more numerous while birth rates are declining, then the voting power of older people is likely to intensify and the implications for childhood in general remain unclear.

Childhood sociologists point to other underlying macro processes at work here. As children move from being 'economically useless to emotionally priceless' (Zelizer, 1985), adults, particularly middle-class adults, invest in fewer children. Children become parents' life projects. Unfulfilled dreams, hopes and ambitions can be realised through the child. The emphasis on the child becomes all the more intense due to changing adult relationships. Contemporary social life is characterised by individualism and intimacy (Beck and Beck, 1995; Giddens, 1991). The emphasis on intimacy results in less stable and more fragile relationships between adults. Adults want self-fulfilment from intimate relationships, and if after investing feelings in relationships there is insufficient return on their deposits, they may move their affections to new relationships, where the exchange rate may be higher and more satisfactory. As a result, adults are likely to move in and out of intimate relationships and this means that children are likely to experience a diversity of family arrangements during their childhood. The fluidity of modern family life may cause children practical and emotional difficulties. Children may have to commute across different households, managing their time with biological mothers and fathers and trying to appease both. This may take children away from routines, communities and day-to-day relationships, and some children complain that they 'are shared as if they are parental property' (Jensen, 2011: 151). Children may also have to adjust to new partners and experience divided loyalties towards separated parents and parents' new partners. These changes have been instigated by adults not children. They reflect wider structural processes and impact on how children experience family life and relationships with parents. How children deal with these macro changes in the micro setting of the family will be returned to in the next chapter.

Education

One of the first influential accounts of the potential of education to promote a specific notion of childhood was Rousseau's classic book *Emile* (2003 [1762]). Rousseau challenged the Puritan view of children as 'naturally' sinful and hence in need of correction by suggesting that children were 'naturally' innocent and pure and that with the right education, these 'natural' traits could flourish and develop. Of course, this romantic, idealised notion of childhood contrasted sharply with the reality of many children's lives throughout Western European societies, at the time of Rousseau's writings. Children from working-class backgrounds lived lives characterised by hard labour, poverty and exploitation. Nonetheless, from the end of the 19th century onwards, the mass exodus of children from the world of work into the realms of educational institutions had a major impact on the conceptualisation and experience of childhood. According to Cunningham (2012), by the turn of the 20th century, many countries had made schooling compulsory. His analysis charts significant increases in school attendance in England, the USA, Austria, the Netherlands, Norway and Italy. This facilitated the increasing surveillance of children and indeed their childhood.

While education had always been an option for the upper classes, particularly for the male children of the aristocracy, for Qvortrup (1994) it was the introduction of mass schooling that accompanied the Industrial Revolution that had a significant impact on childhood. There were a number of drivers at play here. For the bourgeoisie, educated workers were necessary to produce a more efficient future workforce that could compete with the emerging economies of Germany and the USA (Shilling, 1992). There were also moral and political concerns around children roaming the streets, and education was seen as having the potential not only to take children off the streets but also to transmit 'useful knowledge' (Cunningham, 1991). Children were placed in educational settings and school attendance became a legal obligation. Schooling served as a long-term, unpaid apprenticeship, preparing children for their eventual place in the labour market. The increased specialisation of the labour force demanded an educated workforce. In effect, Qvortrup argues that the state seized the labour power of children from parents, but in such a way that the economic value of children's school labour was unacknowledged. Hence, parents were not compensated financially for the loss of their offspring's economic potential. Instead, school was presented as 'an offer or a gift to families, the nature of which was such that one could not refuse to receive it' (Qvortrup, 1995: 64). Qvortrup goes on to discuss the enormous amount of time children spend in school. Focusing on secondary schooling in the USA, Rutter (1982) estimates that children spend on average around 15,000 hours in school. This leads Qvortup to question: 'given this tremendous quantity of time used by children on scholastic activities, does it make sense at all to indicate that children's long-lasting involvement in schooling should not have an economic value?' (1995: 66). Yet, the economic value of children's school work remains unrecognised because in the short term it is not marketable and indeed only becomes marketable once children leave school and enter the workforce. Elsewhere, Qvortrup (2001) develops this line of argument by suggesting that school should be considered a form of work. In an influential article, Oldman (1994) points out how these 'workless' children create 'childwork'. A whole host of adult experts work in a formal, paid capacity to teach and monitor children throughout their schooling. This ranges from teachers to dinner ladies to playground monitors to the educational departments of governments. Hence, children's location in school provides a range of adults with remunerative opportunities. These adult-specific activities are highly regarded, imposed on children and labelled as 'proper work', while children are considered workless pupils.

Leonard (2006) outlines how school straddles the boundaries between the private and public spaces of childhood. On the one hand, schools are public spaces where the education of the child is taken out of the home and away from parents and placed in the hands of teachers who are deemed other, additional adult experts on childhood. On the other hand, schools are private spaces of childhood. They are constructed specifically for the education of children and as the 20th century progressed, the majority of European countries and the USA introduced and consolidated policies which made school compulsory. Within school, children occupy a particular status. They are located as dependents in a highly formal institution which provides an ordered and controlled journey to adulthood. Wyness (1999: 356) argues that 'the school reflects, if not amplifies, the child's lack of social status'. He points out how schools are sites of segregation and regulation. School timetables establish rules and routines and structure the child's engagement with education. In the USA, buses transport children to school and children must turn up at designated places and at designated times to avail themselves of this service, with parents accountable for ensuring that bus schedules run smoothly. Throughout the school day, children are shuffled from one classroom to another. Even break times and lunchtime are carefully monitored and, at all times, children are subject to adult surveillance of where they should or should not be. Schools also sub-divide children into fixed positions in terms of age, class, gender and academic ability, reinforcing macro structures of inequality and power in micro settings. States are also increasingly involved in early years education. This is partly spurred by the need to provide childcare for children, while their parents, mainly mothers, go out to work, but it is also motivated by attempts to dilute the chances of school failure among those from disadvantaged backgrounds (Jensen, 2008). Dockett's (2004) research on Australian children's first experiences of school found that many defined school in terms of controlled spaces in which adults designated many areas as 'out of bounds'. What pupils wear, how they behave and indeed how they talk is subject to adult surveillance and control.

Schools also clearly locate children as in a process of 'becoming'. The core goal of educational systems is to prepare children for their future role in the economy. Hence, schools are sites where children are seen as investments in human capital. This often results in collusion between sets of adults such as teachers and parents. School choice is often made by parents. Schools often target parents rather than potential pupils during 'open days'. Wyness (1999) outlines how league tables are published in adult formats and in adult media such as newspapers. Home–school contracts are often established between parents and teachers, which include recommendations for how long children should spend doing homework in the evenings. Hence, the monitoring and surveillance of children's educational activity is not limited to the sphere of the school but extends to the home. Parents are accountable for sending their children to school and are made responsible if children engage in truancy. Drawing on a textual analysis of core documents regarding day-care centres in Belgium from 1845 to 2006, Vandenbroeck and Bouverne-De-Bie (2006: 138) argue that there is an entrenchment of relationships between families and the state to produce the 'governing' of children so that social problems tend to be 'educationalised and individualised'. Moreover, as states place more value on the need for a global, mobile, educated workforce, schools become more accountable to deliver mobile citizens. Drawing on the Scandinavian countries of Finland and Norway, Strandell (2010) and Kjorholt (2013) outline what they see as the gradual incorporation of instrumental social investment discourses into education so that, in the case of Finland, even after-school care arrangements structure children's time around future-orientated goals, ensuring that the child's leisure time is increasingly governed. This research reflects the ongoing intrusion of global, neo-liberal values into local and national educational systems, whereby children's education is increasingly evaluated through a narrow economic lens, with preparing children for their future role as workers in the global economy, accorded paramount importance. In this vein, schools seem to provide limited opportunities for children's agency. Global processes appear to be at play here and impact on local and national educational structures and reforms. As Wyness (1999: 363) puts it, 'Schools have become steadfastly more bureaucratic and more adult centred through the need to measure output and regulate the internal and external activities of school children'. Of course, pupils can resist these practices and this will be discussed in the next chapter but, for the most part, a range of adults, who often have a longer engagement with school structures and who are located in a hierarchal position, can impose adult conceptions of 'normal', regulated childhood on to pupils, who are after all temporary occupants.

Play and Leisure

Time and space are crucial for understanding the role of play and leisure in childhood. While childhood itself is a time-phased phenomenon which each current generation of children will eventually leave, the discussion thus far suggests that time is a fundamental component during childhood. The exclusion of children from the formal labour market, their collective location in schools, changes in family types and the increasing likelihood of parents being in employment all impact on children's use of time including free time. The separation of home from work and of adulthood from childhood has shaped the spaces where children spend their spare time and as the 20th century progressed, this became increasingly regulated. Play and leisure are associated with children's desire for and use of leisure products, hence their role as consumers needs to be articulated. The 20th century has been characterised by children's exclusion from the labour market and their economic dependence on adults. Alongside this development has been their inclusion in the marketplace as buyers of consumer goods, although in many cases this is through the mediating purchasing power of adults. While children consume a range of products from food to clothing, for the purpose of illustration, children's consumption of toys and other leisure products will be articulated in order to explore their role as consumers and how this feeds into changing conceptions of childhood.

Aries' (1962) seminal work outlined how in medieval society there was no conception of childhood as being different from adulthood, hence children played the same games and engaged in the same leisure pursuits as adults. During this period, there was no conception of a separate marketplace for children. However, during the Enlightenment, children emerged as separate entities in their own right.

Aries points out how childhood became a social construction and how a separate phase of life called childhood emerged. Part of this involved separating the child's world of leisure from the adult's world of leisure. Alongside this, a specific market in children's toys, games and other leisure pursuits came about. Hence, the emergence of childhood, as a separate stage of life, led to the increasing commercialisation of childhood.

The dual processes of 'becoming' and 'being' provide a useful lens for considering how children were first located by manufacturers. Children were positioned as belonging to both realms. Initially, they were seen as 'becomings' in that they had no independent purchasing power. Their withdrawal from the labour market and economic dependence on parents and other adults meant that they could not be considered as independent consumers in their own right. In the absence of their independent purchasing power, parents were targeted as buyers of children's goods. Cook (2000) traces the development of children as consumers from 1910 to 1990. He argues that up to the 1930s, manufacturers assumed that mothers were the primary market for children's goods, so advertising and marketing focused on mothers rather than on children. While Cook focuses mainly on the clothing industry, his analysis shows how even in the realm of sweets and toys, which retailers assumed were core products that mothers would purchase for their children, there were no separate sections of shops stocking these items. Instead, mothers were targeted to buy sweets and toys during shopping trips for adult products aimed at an adult market. Cunningham (1995: 25) cites children's transformations from producers to consumers as 'the most important transition in the history of childhood'. Some authors argue that the commercialisation of childhood even predates children's birth. For Schor (2004), children are 'born to buy'. Her book outlines the increasingly commercialised world of childhood and the increasing ubiquity of the marketplace in children's everyday lives.

As childhood became transformed, so too did advertisers' attitudes to children as a potential market, undergo significant changes. They moved from seeing children as customers in the making to customers in the present. Using the USA as a case study, Cook (2000) outlines how from about the 1930s onwards, retailers began to target children as potential customers. Childhood was seen as a set of stages towards adulthood and producers of toys and games could tap into these various stages to sell products to children. During any current trip to a toy store, one is likely to confront a shop layout organised around age (and gender). Most toys and games, for example, have recommended age groups clearly stated on the packaging. Child psychology was often applied to children's marketing behaviour. Psychologists were employed by marketing consultants to help them understand how preferences for certain products could be encouraged in children. Kline (1993), for example, outlines how Fisher-Price in the USA set up its own nursery school to observe children at play through one-way mirrors and feed the observations into the design of toy products. This strategy became more pronounced from the 1950s onwards with the spread of television, which Kline (1993) argues promoted a global consumer culture and played a specific role in defining children's culture. By constituting children as a separate audience, television drew more and more children into the marketplace. Television transformed children from passive viewers into an active market that could be nurtured and cajoled into buying certain products. Television exposed children directly to advertisements and encouraged a framework whereby their desires could be taken into consideration by parents and other adults when purchasing decisions were being made.

In its early stages, the toy market also drew upon and reinforced gender stereotypes. Part of this was to appeal to parents' nostalgia for their own childhood. Hence, Cross (2010) outlines how train sets from the 1910s to the 1960s were advertised as a way of enhancing cross-generational male bonding. Kline (1993) outlines how GI Joe and Action Man were targeted at boys while Barbie and Sindy were aimed at girls. All of these products were imbued with personalities and back stories and in some cases, acquired their own television shows. When sales of Barbie, for example, began to fall in the 1980s, Mattel, the toy manufacturer, was able to resurrect Barbie's place as the best-selling doll in the marketplace by giving Barbie her own television show. As attitudes to gender changed over the decades, these could be incorporated in how toys were portrayed. For example, to mark Barbie reaching her 55th birthday in 2014, Mattel produced a résumé of the 150 jobs held by Barbie over the decades. While her job choices during her launch and early years in 1959–1961 reflected gender-typical occupations of the period, such as flight attendant, registered nurse, ballerina, fashion editor and model, since then Barbie has acquired a range of occupations that were once the exclusive preserve of males, such as fire-fighter (1995), airline pilot (1999), baseball player (1999) racing driver (2000), soccer coach (2008), computer engineer (2010), architect (2011), and she was even a presidential candidate for a number of years between 1992 and 2012. Russell and Tyler (2002) outline the growing importance of tweenies (young people not quite old enough to be teenagers) as a growing sector of the child market and how companies respond to tweenies' purchasing power through manufacturing forms of femininity around the notion of Girl Power popularised by the Spice Girls in the 1990s. Their research shows how a chain of retail stores called 'Girl Heaven' sought to sell cosmetics to tweenies by exploiting children's enjoyment of sweets so that lipsticks were marketed in strawberry and cherry flavours.

To some extent, this can be considered as moving from seeing children as 'becomings' to viewing them as 'beings' with a right to childhood in the here and now and with notions of childhood as a period of innocence and play being dominant. Hence, manufacturers and retailers engaged with dominant discourses on changing attitudes to childhood in order to exploit the commercial potential of these changing conceptions. There was a growing realisation that children had an important influence on family purchases. Companies became more aware of changing parent and child relationships. Having fewer children led to parents valuing them more individually. While this approach could be seen as recognition of the child as an active agent (and this will be returned to in the next chapter), there were a number of processes at play here. First, manufacturers became increasingly aware of the commercial potential of tapping into changes in the family. More and more children were being brought up in families where both parents worked. This had two effects: (1) these families had increased purchasing power; and (2) they could be coaxed to compensate for their absence from the home or to ease their guilt by buying their children a range of consumer products. Other children were brought up in one-parent families and there is some evidence to suggest that lone mothers try to compensate for this by buying children consumer products. Part of this is concern around the child not 'fitting in' and 'standing out' or being bullied by peer groups because of the inability to display whatever is the latest brand-name product. Daly and Leonard (2002) show how this extends to lone parents on low incomes, who go without necessities to buy children brand-name products. Hence, children were targeted not just as individuals but as a collective, subject to peer pressure around 'fitting in'. Part of this strategy involves recruiting children to sell products to other children (Mayo and Nairn, 2009). Nairn (2010) gives an example of a US company called the Girls' Intelligence Agency which encourages girls aged 8–18 to become 'secret agents' by showering them with free products on condition that they show these off to their peers and encourage them to buy. Tufte and Rasmussen (2010) outline how children's activities on search engines can be monitored by manufacturers and retailers and then used to target them to buy products. They also outline how children playing online computer games are subject to 'advergaming', whereby pop-up advertisements, which will appeal to them and their peers as they show products that manufacturers and retailers glean from their online activity, are repeatedly displayed. In all these ways, manufacturers and retailers tap into the social pressure that children can place on one another in order to 'fit in' and which may in turn result in them placing pressure on parents to buy them the products necessary to forge collective identities with their peers.

Absent fathers are also brought into this process. Children of divorced parents often live with mothers and see absent fathers at weekends or during school holidays and there is some evidence to suggest that absent fathers try to compensate for their absence by showing their love and affection for their children through the purchase of consumer goods. This reflects Beck's notion of contemporary society where adult relationships take place within an ever-increasing risky environment. As he says:

> The child is the source of the last remaining, irrevocable, unexchangeable primary relationship. Partners come and go. The child stays. ... The excessive affection for children, the staging of childhood which is granted to them – the poor overloved creatures – and the nasty struggle for children during and after divorce are some symptoms of this. (Beck, 1992: 118)

In this environment, the child's needs and wants become sentimentalised. The child is compensated for the inability of parents to live together through the purchase of consumer products. Play also brings adults together who collude in defining and satisfying children's need for play. Hence, toy manufacturers appeal to parents and teachers, through highlighting the educational value of toys and games, as a mechanism for selling toys and associated merchandise. Toy manufacturers and retailers have been astute observers of these wider macro trends and of the changing importance of the child within the family and were able to transform the macro drivers of change into commercial opportunities. Marshall (2010) points out that by 2009, in the USA, the annual amount spent on child-related goods and activities amounted to approximately $921 billion, while the figure for the UK was around £117 billion.

Of course, children do not just watch television for advertisements. Rather, despite the emergence of the internet and other digital technologies, watching television remains a core pastime for children. In an influential publication in 1982, Postman provocatively argued that we are witnessing 'the disappearance of childhood'. For Postman, the core culprit was television. By bringing the outside adult world into family living rooms, television was challenging the sanctity and privacy of family life. It was obliterating necessary secrets between the world of adulthood and the world of childhood. In his view, by bringing knowledge of the adult world, particularly sexual knowledge, to children via television programmes, they were being thrust prematurely into the adult world. These debates have intensified in recent years with the increasing dominance of the internet. While children's technological competency is not questioned (and this gives rise to further concerns which will be discussed more fully in the next chapter), their moral competency and lack of savvy to process the vast range of information available is leading to new moral panics. Internet sites and social networking are creating new connections between advertisers and consumers and, increasingly, companies are turning to online sites to sell products to children.

The internet is seen as further dismantling the boundaries between adulthood and childhood and, in response, parents are increasingly encouraged to monitor their children's access, with companies helping in this process through the introduction of internet content filters which restrict what content can be viewed. Many countries have regulations in place to police the internet industry, with governments setting up helplines for parents and children. To take one example, Australia pursues a government-backed initiative called Stay Smart Online (www. staysmartonline.gov.au). The website informs parents: 'protecting your children from harm is just as important online as it is in the real world. As a parent or carer, you can play an important role in helping children have safe and positive experiences online'. The website goes on to outline core threats such as cyberbullying, the viewing of sexually explicit material and contact with strangers. Hence, the ability of the internet to dissolve boundaries between adulthood and childhood is restricted due to strategies to enhance and reassert the moral authority of parents and other adults to regulate and monitor children's everyday lives.

Before leaving this section, I want to turn to children's outdoor play. Leisure spaces have been transformed throughout the 20th century. Some commentators argue that children's outdoor games have almost disappeared and play has become much less spontaneous and highly organised. Children's games have moved indoors to formal environments that are often adult initiated and adult controlled. Conceptions of safety and risk saturate discourses on children's play and leisure time. While children experience multiple realities, the dominant notion of them as innocent, immature, naive and incompetent, and thus in need of protection by (and from) mature, worldly, savvy, competent adults, results in children spending their childhoods in highly structured environments. As a result, children's private and public space is increasingly controlled and monitored by adults. Children are presented with contradictory portrayals of adults as the natural protectors of children and as one of the biggest threats to the innocence of childhood. Hence, children are simultaneously encouraged to both trust and mistrust the adults who surround them. This dualism finds expression in adults' attempts to manage the everyday spaces of childhood in response to their conceptions of children being at risk from other adults. Katz, for example (cited in Valentine, 1997), uses terms such as 'terror talk' and 'stranger danger' to describe parents' heightened fears and insecurities around giving children autonomy in public spaces.

Moral panics about unruly children in public spaces increasingly characterise adults' attitudes to children's presence on the streets. Where once children non-problematically occupied street corners and other open spaces, 'hanging around' has been redefined as 'being up to no good' or anti-social behaviour. Hence, there is a growing hostility to children's use of public space. Children's use of public space is increasingly subject to adult surveillance, and the use of Mosquito devices outlined in Chapter 2 is an example of this. Valentine (1996, 1997) in the UK and Lareau in the USA (2003) bring a class dimension to their analysis and suggest that middle-class and working-class parents have different styles of childrearing, with middle-class parents more likely to be able to afford, organise and restrict their children's leisure pursuits to controlled, formal establishments, whereas working-class parents are more likely to allow their kids to 'roam the streets'.

The widespread macro changes in work, education and family life outlined thus far impact on children's leisure in additional ways. The widespread movement of women into the formal labour market, the rise in divorce and the heterogeneity of family types facilitate the emergence of increasingly regulated activities for children. Before and after school clubs, extra-curricular activities, leisure centres, play zones, children's and youth clubs all contribute to a notion of the over-scheduled child (Elkind, 2001). The child is hurried from one activity to another under the watchful gaze of a variety of adults. Parents' excessive expectations for their children's future, motivated in part by the increasing individualised nature of their own everyday lives, feed into their pursuit of countless hobbies that foster their children's individuality and give them (or at least middle-class children) the cultural capital they need to engage in an increasingly multi-tasked, complex adult world. In all these ways and reflecting wider macro-historical structural changes, children can be seen to be increasingly isolated, compartmentalised and restricted to places set up by adults, run by adults and reflecting adult assumptions of contemporary childhood.

Conclusion: Collective Impact of Macro Changes

The macro changes outlined thus far have had a major influence on children and childhood. From being an economic asset, children became economic burdens on their families. Their ability to earn a wage was restricted by the introduction of mass schooling as preparation for the world of work. This meant that families had to bear the costs of childhood while children served this long, unpaid apprenticeship in educational institutions. The separation of home from work and the accompanying introduction of compulsory schooling fundamentally separated children from many areas of adult life. Childhood became reconstructed as a 'walled garden' (Holt, 1975), whereby children should be protected from the concerns of the adult world. Biological immaturity was considered to account for children's incompetence and therefore justified their exclusion from the world of work. The economically inferior position of children was considered natural and underlined notions of children as immature beings. According to Qvortrup (1994), this transformation from pre-industrial to industrial society profoundly transformed children's role in society. It fundamentally altered relationships between adults and children within families. These changes had demographic effects, as families became smaller and poverty became associated with family size, with larger family units having significantly fewer material resources than smaller families. Moreover, notions of 'normal childhood' provided justification for the intervention of the state and other agencies into family life. As parents, particularly women, increasingly entered the labour market, children impacted on career opportunities and aspirations. Childhood became reconstructed as an age of innocence, with childhood becoming increasingly sentimentalised and, although this became increasingly contested particularly around cases of sexual abuse, notions of children not having a proper childhood or becoming adults too quickly continue to permeate dominant discourses, especially regarding the sexualisation of children. Education and even play and leisure further institutionalised childhood. Children's daily lives became increasingly compartmentalised. Schooling became a longer experience, extending downwards to younger and younger children and upwards through increases in compulsory school leaving age (and indeed the move towards mass higher education has extended schooling into adult life). Play and leisure began to take place in organised settings supervised by an array of adults.

Collectively, these processes demonstrate how childhood as a life stage has changed historically over time and space. It also suggests that childhood needs to be located within wider social, economic, political and cultural processes. As Qvortrup (2011: 23) puts it, 'To think in structural terms breaks with personal life plans; it asks you to think in terms not of child development but rather the development of childhood'. This means moving beyond the study of individual children and underscores the importance of considering childhood as a permanent structural category, which although constantly changing nonetheless exhibits ongoing continuity. This also necessitates adopting an intergenerational focus in order to illuminate the interactive processes and practices between members of different generations and their consequences for both children and adults. The scope for change is implicit within these constantly evolving intergenerational relationships and this will be fleshed out in Chapter 6 through the concept of generagency. Children, as well as adults, are central to understanding how macro-global processes are played out in local, regional, national and international contexts. This means moving beyond considering childhood as a biological entity and instead necessitates unpacking the universality of childhood along a range of social, cultural and historical dimensions. Such an approach illustrates the importance of childhood to central theoretical concerns within sociology. The messy, complex relationship between structure and agency remains a core concern in terms of understanding childhood as a structural form, alongside the agency of children to adapt to, contest, contradict and negotiate macro processes. How children respond to the wider macro-structural processes outlined in this chapter sets the scene for the next chapter, where children's everyday lives will be explored at the micro level.

QUESTIONS FOR DISCUSSION

1. To what extent is childhood a structural component of modern societies?
2. Outline the impact that the Industrial Revolution had on how childhood was conceptualised.
3. In what ways have wider structural changes impacted on children's experiences of family life?
4. Critically evaluate Qvortrup's claim that schooling should be considered as a form of work.
5. Describe and illustrate the ways in which children's consumption practices reflect wider changes in the conceptualisation of childhood.

Recommended Reading

Cunningham, H. and Viazzo, P. (eds) (1996) *Child Labour in Historical Perspective 1800–1985: Case Studies from Europe, Japan and Colombia*, Florence, Italy: UNICEF Child Development Centre.

Hendrick, H. (1994) *Child Welfare: England 1872–1989*, London: Routledge.

Jensen, A. (2011) 'Pluralisation of Family Forms', in Qvortrup, J., Corsaro, W. and Honig, M. (eds) *The Palgrave Handbook of Childhood Studies*, London: Palgrave Macmillan.

Kline, S. (1993) *Out of the Garden*, London: Verso.

4

MICRO CHILDHOODS: PRIORITISING AGENCY

Chapter Aims

1. To illustrate how children practise agency in their everyday lives.

2. To outline the significance of paid employment for children during their school years.

3. To demonstrate, with examples, how children practise agency in the family.

4. To explore how children interact with adults within educational settings.

5. To outline how children actively engage with consumer culture.

Learning Outcomes

By the end of this chapter you will:

1. Understand the significance of children's agency in their everyday lives.

2. Be able to acknowledge how paid employment challenges notions of childhood as a dependent status.

3. Be able to draw on specific examples to illustrate how children practise agency in their families.

4. Understand how children actively negotiate relationships with adults in educational settings.

5. Be able to critically assess the myriad ways in which children actively engage with a range of adults in their attempts to influence their play and leisure.

The macro changes outlined in Chapter 3 had a fundamental impact on children and childhood. Childhood as a structural stage of life became universalised. Qvortrup (1994: 56) argues that documenting the significance of these changes is less about comparing differences between children but 'rather to look at the changing power constellation, economically and politically during the transformation from preindustrial to industrial society'. Of course, Qvortrup goes on to outline how these changes impacted differently on the working class compared to the bourgeoisie, although his overall analysis remains concerned with broad generalisations. At the same time, Qvortrup's core point is to demonstrate how childhood is socially constructed. This means that rather than being limited to a biological and psychological state, childhood is fundamentally shaped by and in turn shapes wider social, cultural, political and economic processes. This, therefore, necessitates looking much more closely at children's everyday lives. It involves unpacking and illuminating the micro worlds of children and their childhoods and paying attention to the ways in which age, gender, class, ethnicity and other variables impact on their experiences. It has led some thinkers to suggest that it is more correct to focus on 'childhoods' rather than childhood. At the same time, structures are both constraining and enabling. Children, like adults, are unlikely to passively respond to wider structural processes and, like adults, are likely to impact on those structures and processes. In other words, children, like adults, are likely to practise agency. Agency is another key notion in contemporary sociological theory. Agency refers to the capacity of individuals to act independently. It is usually juxtaposed with structure and generally refers to the capacity for intentional action. Agency acknowledges that while the lives of individuals are shaped by social structures, nonetheless individuals have the capacity to impact on these structures; they have the ability to think and act in ways that accept, resist, challenge and transform existing social structures. Since the new sociology of childhood emerged in the latter quarter of the 20th century, a number of empirical accounts of children's agency have dominated books and journals on children and their childhoods.

In this chapter, children's agency will be discussed through the four spheres of work, family, education and play – the themes around which the chapter on the macro worlds of children and childhood was organised. These are not discrete spheres but overlapping locations where children spend a considerable part of their childhood. Moreover, while each of these areas has produced a vast amount of research, for the purposes of argument a selection of empirical research on each topic will be outlined. In one chapter, it is not possible to do justice to the vast volume of research in each of the four spheres and the intention is not to provide an overview of the literature in each domain. Rather, the core aim of this chapter is to demonstrate how some authors have focused on children's agency and in the process have outlined how it emerges within wider structural processes which nonetheless are enabling as well as disabling, giving children and young people various degrees of agency to act within and upon wider structures. This paves the way for Chapter 6 where agency as a theoretical tool is critically unpacked and articulated in terms of how it relates to children and childhood.

Work

It is worth recapping some of the core arguments around the transformations of work and childhood outlined in the previous chapter. As Chapter 3 demonstrated, the Industrial Revolution had an enormous impact on the relationship between childhood and work. Children were gradually banned from factories, mines and mills, and childhood became reconceptualised as a work-free period of life. The introduction of compulsory education was felt to effectively remove children from the labour market and the notion that work could be combined with schooling was rarely considered. However, a host of empirical studies from the USA, Australia and Europe show how education simply impacted on the time children were available for work, turning work into an activity children routinely engage in before and after school, during weekends and school holidays (Einarsdottir, 2014; Hanson and Vandaele, 2003; McKechnie and Hobbs, 2000; Mortimer, 2003; Samuelsson, 2007, 2008). It is worth mentioning here that the focus is on child employment rather than child work, the latter being a much broader category and incorporating school work (Qvortrup, 2001), housework (Brannen, 1995) and care work (Becker et al., 1998). Studies into child employment fall into two broad types. The first is concerned mainly with quantifying the numbers of children working while attending school in order to challenge the economic invisibility of working children. The research indicates that participation differs according to age, gender and class, confronting the need to dissect universal notions of children and childhood into sub-categories which more amply explain how childhood impacts on individual children. The second approach is to consider children's own accounts of their working lives, including why they seek jobs and their experiences of working. Both approaches will briefly be reviewed here.

If we turn first to the participation of school pupils in work outside school, a number of studies from the USA, the UK and the Nordic countries suggest that child employment is a routine feature of children's everyday lives, particularly during their early teenage years. Mortimer (2003: 117), for example, argues that almost 'all adolescents in the United States do paid work for considerable periods of time while attending high school'. In reviewing Nordic studies of child work, Einarsdottir (2014: 64) suggests that 'at the end of the 1990s the majority of young people aged 13–17 in all the Nordic countries – Denmark, Finland,

Norway, Sweden and Iceland – had experience of paid work'. Her research, carried out in 2007–2008, revealed that almost 50% of Icelandic pupils aged 13–17 undertook term-time work. In a similar vein, McKechnie et al. (2010) suggest that paid work is a majority experience for British school children. They go on to argue that gauging how many children work needs to take account of how children move into, out of and between jobs, hence previous jobs need to be taken into consideration. McDonald et al. (2012) produce similar findings, indicating that around one-third to one-half of Australian secondary-school children are engaged in paid work, while if previous jobs are taken into consideration this rises to around three-quarters.

Research findings from a number of countries – the USA (Mortimer, 2003), the UK (Howieson et al., 2006), the Nordic countries (Einarsdottir, 2014) and Germany (Ingenhorst, 2001) – indicate that the child labour market, like the adult one, is segregated by gender. This is prevalent in two of the most common types of child employment: delivery work, which is dominated by boys, and paid babysitting, which is dominated by girls. Some gender segregation is apparent even when boys and girls are involved in the same occupation. For example, Leonard (1998) found that children working in supermarkets in Northern Ireland performed different tasks, with boys more likely to be employed stacking shelves while girls were more likely to serve customers. Older children are also more likely to work than younger children, with the early teenage years being the most likely time period when children enter the labour market, with some exceptions. For example, Mansurov (2001: 153), drawing on Russia, comments that children as young as 7 years old are found in various forms of employment, but with these children 'demonstrating economic agency, as they actively search for work rather than being placed into employment'. Middle-class children are also more likely than working-class children to hold part-time jobs, although results here are contradictory (McKechnie and Hobbs, 2000; Middleton and Loumidis, 2001; Mortimer, 2003; Schoenhals et al., 1998), with some studies reporting the tendency for the child labour market to be dominated by middle-class workers, while other studies show an increased tendency for children from poorer households to seek jobs.

What kind of jobs do young people do? I have already mentioned that babysitting for money and delivery work, particularly newspaper delivery, are the two most common types of child work. However, alongside these two jobs, children work in a range of diverse occupations. Howieson et al. (2006) found that the 14–17-year-old Scottish pupils in their research were involved in 16 different types of jobs, while Mizen et al. (2001) found children working in sandwich shops, fish and chip shops, mobile burger bars, hot dog stands and tea and coffee shops. Mortimer (2003) classifies American high-school students' jobs into eight occupational sectors. A UK study by O'Donnell and White (1998) found that children were employed across a diverse range of occupations, including working in hotels, offices, factories, door-to-door sales, amusement arcades and on farms. Wider employment trends, such as the growth in casual jobs in the service sector and the increase in flexible types of labour with the associated growth in deregulated trading hours, enhance opportunities for school pupils to become involved in the labour market before leaving school.

Partly because of these trends, some childhood researchers dismiss children's work as unskilled. For example, Mizen et al. (2001: 40) argue that 'children can offer a ready source of cheap and flexible labour, one that is available at short notice, tolerates irregular hours and has low expectations of work'. While not denying that children are usually a cheaper source of labour than adults, when the work is examined from children's own accounts a different perspective emerges. Research from the USA and the UK indicates that children often consider their jobs as providing them with useful skills and enabling them to gain valuable work experience (Besen, 2006; McKechnie et al., 2010; Mortimer, 2003). In comparing children's experiences of work in the USA and Germany, Hansen et al. (2001) found that most children felt that their work provided them with skills that would be useful to them when they entered the full-time labour market. Leonard (2002) argues that the construction of childhood as a work-free stage of life renders invisible and undervalues the work that children do. She argues that the 'creation of specific types of employment for children allows adults to consider such work as less adult-like and hence less skilled than the unskilled jobs performed by adults' (Leonard, 2002: 201–2).

These studies have been useful in challenging the notion of childhood as a work-free period of life dominated by schooling. They have also been concerned with unpacking children's motivations for entering employment and the extent to which children practise agency in seeking work. The majority of studies consistently show that earning money is a primary motive for young people seeking employment (Howieson et al., 2006; Ingenhorst, 2001; McDonald et al., 2012; Mortimer, 2003). Earning money is rated positively by most young workers, particularly for the perceived independence it brings. Young workers discuss how they have autonomy over spending earnings, with some using earnings to buy things that their parents disapprove of (Hungerland et al., 2007; Mizen et al., 2001). While some young people use their earnings to contribute to family income or fund necessary items to remove the strain from households that are poor (see, for example, Middleton and Loumidis, 2001), others use money to buy mundane and/or luxury items. In Mizen et al.'s (2001) research, earnings were used to buy computers, designer-label clothes and entertainment, to fund leisure pursuits and holidays. Einarsdottir (2014) argues that children's motivations to seek employment need to be seen in the wider context of the increasing commodification of childhood, while drawing on the UK, Mizen et al. (2001) argue that young people have little option but to take part in the consumption practices that now characterise contemporary British childhood. To do otherwise is to risk exclusion. Modern-day leisure pursuits cost money, hence children use earnings to pay for admission to cinemas, bowling alleys, clubs and discos. White (1996) suggests that what differentiates the current involvement of children in employment, compared to previous eras, is that modern-day children work because they want to, not because they have to. The globalisation of childhood, with its concomitant focus on the child as a consumer, enables working children to participate in the consumer aspirations of their peers. Hence, while young people may be seen to spend money on 'discretionary' items, these could also be viewed as the necessary trappings of 'normal' consumer-driven childhood. At the same time, Einarsdottir (2014) argues that young people make choices over how to spend earnings and should not be seen narrowly as passively accepting the materialistic demands of consumer society. This issue will be returned to in a later section of the chapter.

Economic independence also leads to generational independence, with some young people reporting a loosening of parental bonds and authority once they become young workers (Einarsdottir, 2014; Hungerland et al., 2007). As children get older, they experience parent/child relationships as restricting but with work comes a new status that results in a dilution of parental authority over their everyday lives (Mizen et al., 2001). In Ingenhorst's (2001) research with young German workers, achieving a level of self-determination was positively rated. Young workers reported experiencing subtle shifts in generational relationships, with work giving them the opportunity to become more independent and make autonomous decisions. Some children also give opportunities for socialising and having fun as reasons for seeking employment. For example, Hungerland et al. (2007) suggest that German children rate fun highly in their experiences of working. Making friends is another reason rated positively by young workers. Besen (2006) found that young American teenagers saw work as providing them with the opportunity to make new friends, while Mizen et al. (2001) found that children emphasised the social dimensions of their work.

Seeing children as workers has implications for their capacity to practise agency. Collectively, the body of research reviewed here suggests that a work-free childhood is a fallacy. Many children have experience of the labour market prior to leaving school. They demonstrate agency in terms of working through choice rather than necessity (keeping in mind that poorer children may contribute to household income) and use their spending power to enhance their autonomy. Mizen et al. (2001), for example, argue that the independent income that young workers earn gives them an element of economic power which they can utilise to dilute traditional generational relationships within the family based on their economic dependence on parents. Hence, work gives children an opportunity to cross traditional boundaries that separate childhood from adulthood.

Family

This section turns to children's everyday experiences of family life. Of course, there is no one simple model of the family. Widespread changes in marriage, divorce, attitudes to same-sex couples and so on, have introduced a proliferation of family forms. Hence, children are increasingly likely to experience a plurality of family types, and their interaction with adults across a range of family structures and contexts is likely to impact on how their agency is experienced and practised. At one level, the family is seen as a hierarchal unit with parents placed in unequal power relationships over their children, reflecting wider intergenerational relationships that locate adults as more knowledgeable and experienced than children, and, thus, more intimately placed to protect children and further their interests. Chapter 2, for example, outlined how the family was traditionally viewed as a core site for the socialisation of children into adult society. This was seen as a unidirectional, top-down process. However, I outlined how Waksler (1991) articulated a number of problems with this model, calling for a re-conceptualisation of socialisation as reciprocal, messy and dynamic. This leads Brannen and O'Brien (1996) to suggest that sociology needs to move beyond adult-orientated interests and focus on 'children in families' rather than on 'families with children'. The literature on children's experiences of family life is huge and it is not possible to do justice to the vast volume of research on this topic, hence, as is the case for the other sections in this chapter, a selection of research on children's micro experiences of family life will be outlined and discussed in order to provide some examples of how they practise agency.

Some researchers, while acknowledging that agency is present in parent–child relationships and practised by both, nonetheless suggest that adults have the upper hand. For example, while Berger and Berger (1991: 32) locate socialisation as a messier process and give children some role in resisting or modifying socialisation, they cautiously add: 'the child can of course resist them (adults) but the probable outcome of any conflict is a victory on the part of the adults'. This suggests that those doing the socialisation have power over those who are being socialised, and indeed the winner, where there are differences in opinion, is in many cases predetermined. Adults can pull rank on children (Waksler, 1991: 66) and use argument stoppers such as 'because I say so'. At the same time, to suggest that adults' power over children is absolute or indeed that adults have the capacity for autonomous decision making within family structures ignores children's opportunities for negotiation and indeed the wider structural constraints that seemingly powerful adults may be subjected to. In other words, adults themselves are located in power networks which may impact on their scope for independent action.

For example, notions of a simplistic dichotomy between responsible adults and irresponsible children have been replaced by an acknowledgement that not all adults are competent nor all children incompetent. In relation to parenting, the increasing prevalence of investment welfare states with their onus on children as the future has placed considerable emphasis on 'responsible parenting' to ensure specific outcomes. Parents who appear ill-equipped to fulfil societal norms, in relation to their responsibility to bring up children in socially approved ways, are subject to state interference that shifts the balance of power between parents and children and brings in the state as a third party with legal powers to interfere in family life and parents' decisions, in order to ensure that they comply with wider societal expectations. In relation to the UK, Wyness (2014) argues that there has been a gradual shift in focus from parents to children within the family. He argues, for example, that the 'welfare of the child' has become the overriding concern of a host of professionals involved in family life, and indeed since the 1989 Children Act (England and Wales) professionals can remove a child from a family deemed unsuitable in the name of acting in the child's best interests. Hence, the agency of parents to impose their will on their children is far from straightforward.

When children are asked about their experiences of family life and their role as decision makers in the family, they outline myriad ways in which they impact on family decision making. Drawing on focus group interviews with children in two age groups – 8–9 years and 14–15 years – Bjerke (2011) reveals how age impacts on children's notions of fairness in relation to their contribution to family decision making. Younger children expect adults to make decisions on their behalf and accord adults with levels of maturity and life experience which in their view make them better able to make sound judgements. Children positioned themselves as having fewer responsibilities than adults and implied that their immaturity impacts on their ability to make rational choices so that dependency on adults is part and parcel of family life. As children get older, they expect a level of autonomy and increased input into decision making. But none of the children in the sample viewed themselves as passive recipients of adults' intentions. Even children in the younger age groups argued that there should be and was some element of discussion and negotiation around rules and expectations. Bjerke (2011) notes few gender differences in the sample, with both boys and girls indicating that they had input into a range of family decisions, from what to wear to how to spend their leisure time. Again, this challenges the notion of childhood as a universal or homogeneous stage of life, as clearly in this example age impacted differently on children's expectations and experiences of decision making within their families.

Issues of fairness also dominated children's accounts of participation in family life. For example, both age groups felt it was fair that they should be allowed to have a say about food choices. But children also accepted that autonomy over what to eat was rightly constrained by parents' responsibility to ensure that they had a healthy diet. In a UK study, O'Connell and Brannen (2014) found that children's eating habits exhibited the routine everyday practices of daily life in families and the relations of power and control between adults and children. They found that parents used a range of overt and covert measures to exercise power over children's food but that children in turn enacted a number of strategies to avert parental control. Some parents did not purchase certain food items, hence choice was determined at the outset by parents' food purchasing practices. Others bought less healthy food items on occasion, such as crisps or sweets, but either locked these away or used them selectively, sometimes to reward children for docile behaviour in terms of accepting other adult rules. However, O'Connell and Brannen also highlight a range of ways in which children attempted to avert parental control over food choice and practices by, for example, eating forbidden foods when out of the parental gaze. Hence, both children and parents employed strategies to enhance or reduce control over family food preferences and behaviour. In these mundane ways, adult–child relationships were subject to negotiation and renegotiation.

In a similar vein, Backett-Milburn and Harden (2004) discuss how parents and children construct and negotiate notions of risk. This reflects Brownlie's (2001: 519) observation that 'risk and its management are now central to how we in the West construct childhood' and indeed how we govern the real and imagined risks confronting contemporary children. In Backett-Milburn and Harden's research, everyday interaction in families provides a backdrop against which both children and parents attempt to reach shared understandings or at least compromise around the level of autonomy children are accorded outside the household. Parents and children were agentic in reaching settlements that veered between independence and surveillance. Parents' attempts to enforce boundaries were mediated by the gender, age and birth order of the child, hence children's capacities to negotiate terms of independence were not just dependent on their childhood status but also on other structural components of their childhood. For example, children expected that as they got older, they should be granted higher levels of personal freedom. Some children played one parent off against the other, negotiating independence with the parent deemed less strict. Others used older siblings as a bargaining tool in order to shift and dilute previously negotiated boundaries. In these ways, children sometimes accepted and sometimes challenged parents' intentions around their movements outside the household. Children and parents also made use of advances in technology, such as the widespread use of mobile phones, to negotiate spheres of autonomy. In Williams and Williams' (2005) research with teenagers, mobile phones were used as a tool by both parents and children to negotiate public space. Their presence enabled parents to enter previously uncharted places that their children occupied outside the home. While, on one level, this enhanced parental control over a wider range of public space, on another level, boundaries were negotiated so that children also saw mobile phones as giving them a level of empowerment over how they spent their free time outside the household. Both parents and children negotiated rules over space so that parental extension of spatial control and children's renewed ability to extend their spatial boundaries were simultaneous processes. These examples illustrate how parents and children attempt to negotiate mutually agreed boundaries around risk and its management, but Harden et al.'s findings (2000) remind us that while children often collude with parents in these strategies, at times they also challenge and undermine them.

Of course, the changing demography of the family has resulted in children being confronted with a plurality of increasingly complex living arrangements and indeed adjusting to more than one family type during their childhood. Some children may move from a two-parent family to a one-parent family as a result of divorce or move to a reconstituted family as a result of a parent remarrying. Indeed, Mason and Tipper's (2008: 443) research with young children in the North of England revealed a complex mix of kinship relationships:

> many had close relatives who were separated or divorced. Some had half siblings through a parent's previous relationship; most had half- and step-kind; many had relatives with cohabiting partners, or non-cohabiting parents, or ex-cohabiting partners and in some cases these partners and ex-partners had children together.

Some research has examined children's agency within these changing family structures in terms of how children negotiate these various transitions, particularly family breakdown. Neale and Flowerdew (2007), for example, illustrate how children demonstrate emotional competence in dealing with post-divorce relationships, which calls into question their common location as passive family dependents. They suggest that children try to balance conflict between parents by attempting to achieve an element of equality in terms of the amount of time they spend in each separated household. In an Irish study, Nixon et al. (2013) illustrate how children's agency was reflected in how they negotiated relationships between two households and how they weighed up the costs and benefits of potential new parental partnerships. Children felt that their opinions on new partners would be important to their mothers and that they would play an active role in mothers' choices. New partners had to win over children in order to be accepted by mothers into the family unit. In this way, children had an active influence on existing and new family relationships. Other research (Katz, 2013) found that children actively supported mothers who were abused by their partners, including actively contributing to mothers' decisions to leave the perpetrator. These studies challenge notions of children as passive victims of adult conflicts by emphasising not only their coping strategies but also their agency in dealing with difficult circumstances and their ability to manage and influence transitions. On the other hand, Kaltenborn's (2001) research suggests that children's agency in custody cases is often muted, not because of children's perceived lack of competency or willingness to participate, but because of the reluctance of many adult professionals to view the child as a competent decision maker. He argues (2001: 488): 'agentic children of parents disputing about custody or visiting access are acting in a matrix of social actors – such as custodial and non-custodial parents, stepparents, solicitors, social workers, judges, etc. – who support or counteract their agency'. This reminds us that agency may be respected and upheld by one group of adults but undermined by another. It also suggests that adult–child relationships are not fixed but dynamic, taking different forms in different contexts.

This snapshot of some aspects of family life suggests that traditional parent–child relationships within the family based on authoritianism are weakening and being replaced by more democratic relationships. This reflects the work of Giddens (1998b), who suggests that family life has become more democratic and based on trust, intimacy and mutual disclosure. In this 'pure relationship', family life and rules are less dictated by tradition and more the result of ongoing negotiations between parents and children. However, drawing on the wider structural imbalances in power between adults and children, Jamieson (1999: 488) questions the saliency of this 'pure relationship'. As she puts it, 'Parents cannot start as equals to their children, and no matter how democratic they try to be, it will necessarily remain a relationship between superordinate and subordinate for many years'. This is not to deny children's agency but to acknowledge that since adults and children start out from unequal power positions, then discussions of children's agency need to be located within and across their relationships with adults. This is why the notion of inter-generagency, which is discussed in Chapter 6, is conceptually useful.

Education

Chapter 3 outlined how transformations in education created new spaces where children were collectively brought together in adult-designed and regulated institutions. By placing children in special places, schools enhanced conceptions of childhood as a separate stage of life. Within schools, children could be nurtured and developed through their journey to adulthood by their contact with adult teachers. Schools created new relationships between adults and children, locating adults as holders of appropriate knowledge and children as receivers of this knowledge. To some extent, children were seen in terms of Locke's 'blank slates', i.e. devoid of knowledge, with the purpose of education being to transmit knowledge from the teacher to the child. However, a focus on interactions between teachers and pupils suggests that knowledge is not transmitted effortlessly, but that children process, accept, challenge and change the discourses on offer. As Hood-Williams (1990: 160) points out, within educational systems, children are actively engaged in 'reproducing themselves and reproducing society'. A range of research suggests that while children may be located as unequal members of educational institutions, they have the capacity to accept, resist and transform the knowledge they receive. By bringing children together in one setting, schools enable differences between children to emerge, take shape and assume (or not) wider significance. Children also play a role in these processes. Within classrooms, playgrounds and other spaces, children act out their relationships with each other, at times in ways not intended by adults. In other words, children practise agency and, in so doing, affirm, contest and bring new meanings to their engagement with adult culture and their relationships with each other.

Micro studies of children's experiences within school systems unveil a host of instances where they demonstrate agency in making choices regarding various aspects of the learning environment in which they are placed. According to Lanas and Corbett (2011: 417), 'Students constantly assume agency which challenges school structures. They talk loudly at inappropriate times, wear hats in class, challenge the teachers, argue and refuse to do homework.' Twiner et al. (2013) outline how children create meaning in classroom dialogue with teachers. Drawing on history lessons with 6–7-year-olds in the UK, the authors highlight how children unpack what they hear from teachers and ask unexpected questions which result in them contributing to collaboratively produced knowledge, rather than passively reproducing what they hear. Twiner et al. (2013) give a range of examples where teachers' planned lessons took unpredicted routes as children actively engaged with and, at times, disputed the knowledge on offer. Spyrou's (2000) research with school pupils in Cyprus produced similar findings. He argues that children do not enter classrooms as empty vessels. Rather, they bring the outside world into the classroom with them and this includes the attitudes and beliefs of their families and the communities in which they reside. In relation to the transmission of national identity, Spyrou outlines how teachers' attempts to articulate dominant discourses on Greek Cypriots' relationship to Greece as the mother country and their attempts to portray Turkish Cypriots as puppets of Turkey and long-term enemies of Greece, were often challenged by children in the classroom. While some children accepted the dominant discourses on offer, others rejected and modified the messages received so that meanings were constantly negotiated and reconstructed. In this way, children became 'co-constructors of classroom meaning rather than passive recipients of teachers' messages' (Spyrou, 2000: 70).

In a series of interactions between teachers and pupils in Italian schools, Baraldi (2008) outlines how children independently constructed and produced meanings. While teachers strived to support children's active learning, this was done selectively and only when they conformed to wider social norms around successful learning. Children, however, often refused to comply with the dominant discourses on offer. In a UK study on the transition of 11–13-year-olds from primary to secondary school, drawn from six local authorities, Croll et al. (2010) found that while many children defined themselves in terms of 'human becomings', seeing education as preparation for the future and acknowledging the importance that educational qualifications would have for their future lives, most also felt that they were accorded a high degree of personal agency in setting and realising their goals, and this finding emerged across different ability groups. Grytnes (2011) focused on 15-year-old Danish children's choices regarding the educational programme they would follow after ninth grade; he held that young people, for the most part, practised 'resourceful agency', reflecting on the choices available to them and playing an active role in providing reasons and justifications for their subsequent decisions. This entailed acknowledging wider opportunities and restrictions – these were not, however, passively accepted but actively negotiated by young people as they struggled to interpret and reinterpret the range of choices open to them and the likelihood of realising their intended choices.

While the classroom is the location par excellence where teachers can exert a level of control and regulation over pupils in their charge, some research outlines how this extends to other school spaces such as lunch rooms. Dotson et al. (2015) outline the strategies implemented by teachers in two pre-school settings in the USA. They suggest that pre-school is the first location where children encounter and negotiate power hierarchies outside the home, and draw on OECD data to indicate that pre-schools are an increasing feature of young children's educational experience. While half of all 3-year-olds are enrolled in pre-school programmes in the USA, this figure rises to over 95% for 3-year-olds in Belgium, France and Spain. Teachers used a range of tactics to control and regulate what children ate at lunchtime, but children implement a range of strategies to either dissent or feign assent to adult pressures over their lunchtime eating habits. Hence, in a variety of mundane ways, children demonstrate 'agentic responses' (2015: 10) to adult control.

The growing importance of the internet in shaping educational knowledge also needs to be briefly acknowledged. Through the internet, pupils can access information, rather than this being the preserve of the teacher as the traditional transmitter of knowledge. This dilutes the teacher's role as expert. The teacher also becomes a learner and, indeed, given children's increasing levels of competency in understanding and using technology, becomes the less competent user of the latest technological innovations. Thus, the increasing interpenetration of the internet into classroom teaching has the potential to undermine and reshape the usual hierarchies in knowledge production and dissemination which characterise traditional educational systems. For Slevin (2000), the internet provides exceptional opportunities for more equal forms of interaction to emerge between teachers and pupils within educational systems. Children's competent grasp of the internet vis-à-vis adults is a further example of the blurring of boundaries between adulthood and childhood (Lee, 2001), and in this instance is played out in the daily interactions between teachers and pupils in the classroom where the teacher's position as holder of appropriate knowledge is called into question by children's mature grasp of the latest technologies.

Of course, schools do not exist in a vacuum, separate from other domains of children's everyday lives. For example, adults in families and schools often collude in shaping and influencing children's acquisition of knowledge so that parents and teachers reinforce the engagement of each in influencing the child. However, drawing on research with 10–14-year-olds from six schools in the UK, Edwards and Alldred (2000) outline how children accept, reject and amend the level of their parents' engagement with school. They outline a range of ways in which schools encourage parental involvement through helping out in classrooms to extending the school reach into the home through homework and other out-of-school projects, including encouraging parents to adopt an educational component to children's leisure activities. Some children go along with their parents' wish to be involved in strengthening home–school relations. However, Edwards and Alldred (2000: 444) see this as an example of children being 'passively active', in that while adults in their role as teacher-parents may have initiated greater levels of home–school engagement, these initiatives cannot work without the child's active acquiescence. Hence, while their research also includes examples of children blocking, hindering or thwarting parental involvement in their everyday school lives, with children actively attempting to keep each sphere separate, they acknowledge that agency does not always imply resistance.

Children may make sense of and interpret schools very differently according to their class, gender and ethnicity. Thorne (1993) outlines how children do not reproduce mainstream gendered understandings of their roles but recreate gender roles based on their own child-centred gender experiences. Children socialise each other into gender roles. These roles do not emanate from teachers (or parents) but from children's own experiences in the playground, which enables them to develop their own gendered boundaries and the rules for crossing these boundaries. A number of authors (Renold and Allan, 2006; Skelton et al., 2010; Walkerdine et al., 2001) outline how girls actively try to negotiate being academically smart with traditional notions of femininity. This involves practising what Raby and Pomerantz (2013) call 'smart girlhood', which involves girls 'playing down' being smart. Hence, some girls in their Canadian study were concerned to balance being academically smart with being 'street smart' or 'socially smart'. For example, some girls, even though they knew the answers to questions posed in the classroom, chose to disguise their knowledge by not raising their hands to answer. This was not only to fit in with peers, both male and female, but also because teachers, at times, responded negatively to girls who appeared too smart. Girls also chose not to share their coursework marks with their peers, particularly where they were gaining high marks, to avoid accusations of boasting or being seen as nerdy or geeky. They also engaged in partying outside school and flirted with boys to enhance their popularity with their peers. In all these ways, for Raby and Pomerantz (2013: 16), girls 'can be conceptualised as agentically "doing smart girlhood" as they consciously negotiate the complex challenges and promises of their academic success both within their immediate school and peer environments'.

Masculinity also plays a role in how boys experience schooling. Connolly (2004), for example, focused on the interplay between class and gender by illustrating how working-class and middle-class boys display masculinity. Through their peer relationships, these boys accepted some dominant versions of masculinity and rejected others, but through their interaction with male and female peers actively reworked masculinity in ways that were peer centred. Connolly (1998: 5) also illustrates how ethnicity as a marker of identity is subtly reworked and transformed by children. His analysis illustrates the myriad ways in which 'children are able to appropriate, rework and reproduce racist discourses in relation to a variety of situations and contexts'. Ethnicity may also play out in how children practise agency in school. In an Irish study, Devine (2009) outlined how migrant children accomplish fitting into mainstream society and how they practise agency in cultivating and activating certain types of cultural capital within primary school, so that they can maximise the exchange value from their education. Older siblings actively helped younger siblings, and in some cases parents, to overcome language difficulties. They acted as active intermediaries between their parents and the school and wider Irish society, and their strategies enabled them to actively cope with and manage their positioning as 'ethic other' within and outside school.

Corsaro's (1985) classic ethnography of peer interaction among 3–4-year-olds in a pre-school in Italy and the extension of this empirical work to the USA (2015) is worth examining here, as his concept of 'interpretative reproduction' has been extremely influential in the sociology of childhood. Corsaro sought to demonstrate how child culture is different from adult culture. His analysis shows the multiple ways in which children selectively accept and reject adult rules and interpretations. Hence, children are not a product of adult culture, rather they actively create their own culture. He demonstrates this by illustrating how individual children try to subvert school rules but how this also becomes a collective practice. For example, one school rule forbade children from bringing toys from home into the classroom. Children averted the rule by hiding small toys in their schoolbags and then shared these toys with each other. Hence, the breaking of the rule was transformed into a collective activity that often reinforced peer group culture. Through resisting the rules, children developed a collective identity. Often, teachers were aware of these rule-breaking actions but chose to ignore them as these minor breaches enabled the rule to continue to exist without effective challenge. Corsaro draws on Giddens' articulation of structures being constraining and enabling to explain this action. His core point is that how childhood is defined, experienced and practised is the outcome of children's interactions with each other and the choices they make concerning what bits of adult culture they adopt or reshape in the process. His notion of 'interpretative reproduction' has three main elements. First, through collective behaviour demonstrated in their peer networks, children appropriate information and language from the adult world. Second, they do not merely reproduce this adult world but produce and participate in their own peer culture. Third, the outcome of these twin processes is the reproduction of adult culture. In this way, children engage both in cultural production and reproduction.

What this very brief overview demonstrates is that school is likely to be experienced differently on the basis of gender, class and ethnicity, and children and young people's active responses to their location as school pupils and how they interact with parents, teachers and peers are also likely to be dynamic rather than fixed. Drawing on a longitudinal ethnography of children's experiences of primary and secondary schooling in the UK, Pollard and Filer (2007) outline four core patterns of strategic action practised by school pupils: conformity, anti-conformity, non-conformity and redefining conformity. In the study, pupils practising conformity generally acquiesced with teachers' expectations. This extended to gender identities where children tended to gravitate towards same-sex peer groups, so that even when a choice of where to sit during classroom lessons was available, there was a tendency for boys and girls in this category to sit separately. For those school pupils in the anti-conformity group, boys and girls practised overt forms of masculinity and femininity and both engaged in behaviour typically seen as deviant such as smoking, drinking and implying that they were sexually active. Boys and girls who fitted into the non-conformity group tried to adopt more idiosyncratic ways of behaving and interacting with peers, both within and outside classrooms, including choosing to reject traditional peer gender norms. Finally, some children chose to redefine mainstream norms by 'pushing at the boundaries of teachers' and peers' expectations, negotiating, challenging and leading their peers' (2007: 451). Collectively, this research reminds us that children and young people are likely to respond in varying ways to school structures and teachers' practices, and engage in different patterns of action in relation to other identities such as gender, class and ethnicity.

Play and Leisure

Chapter 3 outlined the growing importance of children as consumers and presented a range of research which tended to portray children as passive recipients of manufacturers' and retail advertisers' attempts to persuade them to purchase, either directly or indirectly, through their parents and carers, a range of play and leisure goods. This section moves the focus to consider children as active agents who positively engage in the marketplace as buyers and users of consumer products. Cody (2012) outlines how the 'dichotomous child' dominates debates on children and consumer culture, veering between seeing children in terms of structure, whereby they are seen as passively internalising the advertising and selling strategies of consumption providers, and seeing children as active agents who process, evaluate and impact on the messages received. Langer (2005: 261–3) argues for a middle ground, stating, 'I am not suggesting that children are mere "subjects" of capital with no capacity for agency or creative play', while warning that 'children's capacity for spontaneity and creativity is exercised within a commercially constituted life world'. Her solution is to locate children's consumption within 'the social and cultural structures in which their active choices are made'.

While Chapter 3 outlined how children's everyday lives are increasingly managed and regulated by adults, giving them less and less autonomy and independence in relation to play time, King and Howard (2014) argue that these positions are not fixed but dynamic. They looked at children's degree of choice around play in three settings: the home, the school playground and out-of-school play groups. Children's interactions with adults and their capacity to practise agency differed across the three settings. While children were subject to a number of adult-imposed rules, nonetheless they recounted various incidents where they were able to engage in play without adults present, and the levels of autonomy granted to them impacted actively on how they participated in play activities. Perceived choice differed according to location, with children believing that they had greater levels of choice over play in out-of-school clubs and the least level of choice in school playgrounds. This suggests that when looking at adult–child relationships, context needs to be taken into consideration. Recent studies have focused on the 'pester power' of children and how children adopt a range of strategies, including bargaining, persuasion, begging and tantrums, to encourage and cajole parents into buying them consumer products. Again, this demonstrates that adult–child relationships are not fixed and static but open to a range of negotiations.

The notion of children as active agents who process information from adult advertisers has emerged in a number of studies which demonstrate children's ability to understand the persuasive nature of advertising. John (1999), for example, explores how children come to view and react to advertisements on television. She argues that by age 5, most children can distinguish between television commercials and other programmes. However, while they view adverts as entertaining and informative, in that they tell you about things you can buy, they tend to view content as a form of unbiased information. According to John, an understanding of advertising intent emerges when children are around 7–8 years of age. They begin to see adverts as attempts to coax them to buy something. By the time children reach the age of 11–12, they can see that adverts may not always be truthful and that marketing techniques are deliberately employed to encourage them to buy certain products and brands. In other words, children do not passively accept the messages transmitted to them by advertisers but actively process the information received and subsequently make judgements on the accuracy of the claims being made. Kline (1993) points out, for example, how children acknowledge that toys are sold in fantasy fashion, in that while toys can do magical things in adverts, in real life they depend on children's imaginations to enable them to move beyond being motionless products. Hence, children are able to process and evaluate adverts and decide for themselves whether or not to accept the partial view of reality encouraged by toy manufacturers. In this vein, Kline (2010) evaluates the extent to which children can be considered as 'competent' consumers. He reviews a range of studies which indicate that by the time children reach their 8th birthday, they are able to identify the persuasive techniques employed by advertisers. Drawing on McNeal (cited in Kline, 2010), he outlines how children are 'active' shoppers. They peruse catalogues searching for products to buy, they go window shopping, they engage sales personnel in conversation and make choices on how to spend their pocket money.

Russell and Tyler (2005) examine how young girls respond to their positioning by manufacturers and retailers as collective shoppers and the gender dimensions of this perception. Their research focuses on how a chain store called 'Girl Heaven' markets a hegemonic form of femininity to young girls on the brink of entering their teenage years. The first phase of their research involved accompanying eight girls aged 10–11 years to one of the stores. They found that the girls were critical of their looks and evaluated their body shape in relation to each other and consistent with dominant messages portrayed by the media in relation to young girls' ideal shape. They accompanied six of the original sample of girls on a return shopping trip when they were 13–14 years old. They use the term 'bricolage' to denote the ways in which the girls tried to reclaim and rework some of the dominant messages relating to femininity held by the marketing consultants. They argue that the girls should be seen as a perceptive and sophisticated audience, rather than a passive one, and that they respond through a series of contradictory measures veering between wanting to 'fit in' and wanting to 'stand out'.

Children may also use toy products in ways not intended by manufacturers and retailers. Drawing on research with 7–11-year-old girls, Nairn (2010), for example, points to the girls trying to show how they have outgrown Barbie by subjecting the dolls to various forms of barbarism. The practices ranged from 'decapitation and microwaving to burning and dismembering' (Nairn, 2010: 105). In a similar vein, Chin (2001) outlines how African-Caribbean girls in the USA reshaped the hair on white Barbie dolls to make it look more like their own. These examples suggest that children may use products in ways not initially intended by their makers. Alternatively, children may seemingly tap into expected ways to play with toys but in practice negotiate space and autonomy to play in ways not foreseen by adults. In a study of pre-schoolers in Finland, Ruckenstein (2010) focuses on their usage of a Japanese-designed virtual pet game called Tamagotchi. The game allows users to attend to the pet's needs through playing with three basic buttons which can be utilised to feed, play with and discipline their pets. Ruckenstein argues that the cultural contexts within which children live their daily lives need to be taken into consideration in order to fully understand and appreciate how children may appropriate games in ways that seemingly appease wider adult cultural discourses. She draws on the work of Allison (2006), who looks at how Japanese children are encouraged to bond with their virtual pets. While Allison does not explore how cultural differences may impact on Japanese children's use of this virtual game, Ruckenstein argues that wider cultural factors mean that children are drawn into toy markets in culturally specific ways. In Japan, the tendency to have fewer children, the noted pressures of the educational system with its high value on success, and children's reported loneliness and withdrawal from wider society encourage their compliance with the manufacturer's aim of bonding with virtual pets. However, in Finland, as in other Nordic countries, there is a heightened emphasis on the outside environment as children's natural playground and a suspicion that digital toys, particularly those aimed at younger children, encourage 'unnatural' play. Ruckenstein explores how this feeds into teachers' perceptions of acceptable and unacceptable toys in pre-school settings. In her study, the pre-schools had formal toy days where children were encouraged to bring in their own toys to play with and interact with other children. Teachers tended to negatively view digital toys and games as 'unnatural' so that, for example, boys were not allowed to bring handheld game devices into school. However, girls were able to bring in their virtual pets because of the pets' perceived value in encouraging care-giving qualities in girls. Ruckenstein outlines how children were aware of these adult dispositions and used these discourses creatively to seemingly adhere to adult values by over-emphasising how they were bonding with their pets and under-playing their game-playing skills and pleasure. In this way, Ruckenstein (2010: 500) argues, 'children are not simply mimicking the adult world ... they also make it distinctively theirs'.

Ruckenstein (2013: 476) extends her focus to a study of Habbo's virtual world where

> children and young people meet with their friends from school ... and they also talk to complete strangers. Children operate via modifiable cartoon-like avatars, perform make-overs with them, joke at other children's expense, visit each other's rooms, swap items, and try to find themselves a girlfriend or boyfriend.

Children play a role in managing and negotiating their online identities, pretending to be older or younger or taking on professional roles such as doctors and teach-ers. In Habbo's virtual world, children express individuality through furnishing and decorating private rooms, and class differences emerge in relation to richer children having the means to buy additional products from Habbo that lead to lavishly furnished rooms. In this way, children reinforce existing hierarchies between each other. Children also trade goods and build up relationships with each other through the technology and, at times, independently of adults, such as parents and teachers. Ruckenstein highlights the importance of Habbo as an example of the encroachment of technology into children's everyday lives. She argues that around a quarter of all children in Finland, aged 10–15, are active users of Habbo. She outlines how designers and manufacturers seek to understand children's social networks, as using children to attract other children to the site is a core marketing strategy. In practice, this means bypassing parents' and educa-tors' views of children and childhood and seeking children's own conceptions of what childhood means to them. For Ruckenstein, this leads to new kinds of adult–child relationships which locate the child as a knowledgeable holder of informa-tion. While on one level, manufacturers and designers appropriate and exploit children's perceived social behaviour in relation to their peers, Ruckenstein's core point is that ultimately the viability and success of Habbo depend fundamentally on the child users of the virtual world. Habbo has to engage in an ongoing strug-gle to outdo competitors and keep child users online. They achieve this through locating children as agentic in using Habbo and also as sophisticated consumers. Hence, Ruckenstein (2013: 487) concludes: 'commercial companies construct and define children's everyday spaces, but so do children; children are acted on as much as they act'. This reinforces the need to see children's agency in generational terms and this issue will be returned to in Chapter 6.

It is also important to emphasise here that many children have access to an independent income. This may be in the form of pocket money, earnings from part-time jobs, as the section on work demonstrated, or monetary birthday and Christmas gifts. Hence, to see children as 'becoming' consumers ignores their purchasing power as 'beings' in the present. For example, children can influence and shape what their parents and other adults consume through their knowledge of the latest consumer goods (especially the latest digital technologies). Children can therefore be agentive in terms of impacting on families' knowledge of consumer products and their subsequent purchasing decisions. This view is put forward by Ekstrom (2010), who highlights how children and parents are likely to interact in different social and technological realms, and as a result children are often more aware than their adult carers of the latest trends, particularly in technology. Hence, their knowledge may exceed that of adults and may subsequently impact on adults' decisions around consumption goods. In this vein, Ekstrom challenges unidirectional models of socialisation which assume that adults are the ultimate decisions makers of children's purchases, indicating that the processes at work are more likely to be reciprocal.

However, Cross (2010: 82) warns:

> It is very difficult to know when children became agents or how and when the age of children's consumer decision making changed. This is not only a matter of lack of data, but also a problem of sorting out the relative roles of parents and offspring in consumer choice.

His analysis distinguishes two types of child consumer – the 'cute' and the 'cool' (Cross, 2004). The former is dominated by parents wanting to relive their own childhoods through their choice of 'cute' toys for their offspring. These toys reflect adult conceptions of childhood as a period of innocence and cuteness and parents' toy and leisure purchases reflect these adult-based, taken-for-granted assumptions about contemporary childhood which often bear little relevance to reality. Through the concept of 'coolness', Cross outlines how children rebel against this positioning through their attempts to reclaim the toy and leisure market in ways which more effectively reflect the realities of their everyday lives in the present. Older children are to the forefront of these processes and being 'cool' is embraced as a sign of growing up. Manufacturers and retailers are able to tap into but not control this newly emerging market; to stay in business they quickly realised that they had to appeal to a much more active child market (Cross, 2004).

The internet and other digital technology enable children to communicate with each other across space. Children can develop online identities and communicate with their peers through Facebook and other sites. Children and young people use social networking to evaluate consumer products and to give ratings to consumer goods. According to Seiter (2004), the internet has become a virtual playground where children circulate and exchange information about toys, games and other consumer products. Hence, producers and advertisers of children's consumption goods have to pay attention to their evaluations of their products. In relation to branded goods, Nairn's (2010) research with 7–11-year-olds shows how they continually negotiate with their peers which brands are 'cool' and which are 'minging'. This means brands have to adapt to children's evaluations of their brands as 'cool'. Children also continually remind manufacturers and retailers that they are not a homogeneous group. While 'fitting in' with one's peers may be important in some contexts, expressing individuality through consumer products is also important to young people, particularly as they move towards adolescence. This is most often achieved through clothing and fashion whereby many young people strive to develop an independent identity. But there is some evidence to suggest that these processes are at work across the child consumer market.

Conclusion

Through a range of micro studies of children's everyday lives in the family, at work, in educational systems and during leisure time, this chapter has sought to illustrate how children can be seen as agents who make an active contribution to their everyday lives. However, how agency is defined within and across these various studies is far from clear. Is agency a possession of the self and contained within the self, so that in micro encounters the self actively engages with others to produce intentional outcomes that disrupt the intended outcomes of others? Or is it a collective possession so that groups and categories of agents have the ability to disrupt wider structural forces? Given the enormous significance of the 'new' sociology of childhood's claim that children are active agents and the widespread adoption of this concept by the varying disciplines located within the field of childhood studies, it remains surprising that there has been so little attempt to articulate what children's agency actually means. Rather, the field is dominated by accounts of the manifestations of children's agency often accompanied by vague terms such as 'children are active actors'. This is why a book focusing on sociology's contribution to theorising and understanding children and childhood needs to engage with defining and critically unpacking competing accounts of how children's agency is defined and expressed. The core theme of agency and how it relates to structure is central to Chapter 6.

QUESTIONS FOR DISCUSSION ?

1. To what extent does working alongside adults doing similar things enable children to negotiate a more individualised conception of themselves as co-workers rather than as children?
2. Giving examples, demonstrate how children are active and competent participants in family life.
3. Does children's knowledge of the internet call into question the traditional location of teachers as holders of knowledge?
4. Are children passive recipients of consumer culture?

Recommended Reading

Besen, Y. (2006) 'Exploitation or Fun? The Lived Experience of Teenage Employment in Suburban America', *Journal of Contemporary Ethnography*, 35, 3, 319–40.

Bjerke, H. (2011) '"It's the Way They Do it": Expressions of Agency in Child–Adult Relations at Home and School', *Children and Society*, 25, 93–103.

Cook, D. (2000) 'The Other "Child Study": Figuring Children as Consumers in Market Research, 1910s–1990s', *The Sociological Quarterly*, 41, 3, 487–507.

Corsaro, W. A. (2015) *The Sociology of Childhood*, 4th edition, London: Sage.

Leonard, M. (2003) 'Children's Attitudes to Parents', Teachers' and Employers' Perceptions of Term-Time Employment', *Children and Society*, 17, 349–60.

Ruckenstein, M. (2013) 'Spatial Extensions of Childhood: From Toy Worlds to Online Communities', *Children's Geographies*, 11, 4, 476–89.

Thorne, B. (1993) *Gender Play: Girls and Boys in School*, New Brunswick, NJ: Rutgers University Press.

5

FROM RIGHTS TO CITIZENSHIP: TRANSFORMATIONS AND CONSTRAINTS

Chapter Aims

1. To understand the importance of the CRC in promoting children's rights.

2. To outline and critically evaluate the significance of Article 3 and Article 12.

3. To consider the extent to which children's rights and adult rights are complementary or contradictory.

4. To explore how the CRC encouraged new thinking around the relationship between rights and citizenship.

5. To illustrate, with examples, children's problematic status as citizens.

Learning Outcomes

By the end of this chapter you will:

1. Have a general understanding of why the CRC is considered a watershed in promoting children's rights.

2. Appreciate the significance of Article 3 and Article 12 and their contribution to children's participation and children's voice.

3. Be able to evaluate and interpret the problematic relationship between children's rights and adult rights.

4. Be aware of the complexity around children's status as citizens.

5. Be able to draw on specific examples to illustrate the differing ways in which children's citizenship is articulated and practised.

The 'new' sociology of childhood did not emerge in a vacuum. Wider, global, macro changes were taking place in relation to children being considered as holders of rights. A number of themes thus far discussed are relevant here. The acceptance that children should be seen as 'beings' rather than 'becomings' involved acknowledging the importance of children's lives in the here and now and the need to become informed about children's everyday lives. It seemed logical that children themselves should be providers of information. The child's standpoint was seen as bringing new thinking to everyday issues that had traditionally relied on the partial views of adults. This involved reflections on the best way to give the child a voice and listen to and act on their attitudes and experiences. Once children were viewed as fully social beings, capable of acting in and on the social world, it became increasingly apparent that to understand children's worlds we needed to ask children themselves about their everyday lives and draw on their understandings, attitudes and experiences. Enabling the child to participate in society became viewed as a basic right and the recognition that many societies did not formally accord children this basic right led to renewed thinking on a global level around the meaning of rights and the extent to which rights were or were not extended to children. As theorising about children focused on demonstrating their competency, King (2007) argues, it became more difficult to revert to paternalistic conceptions of children as needing protection, and this further fuelled debates around locating children as holders of basic rights. Moreover, seeing children as agents made it more difficult to deny children rights, particularly the right to participate in decisions affecting them. These debates are central to the CRC, which is the core theme of this chapter.

Since generation is a key theme thus far, the impact of the CRC on adult–child relationships will be a core focus of this chapter. The chapter will discuss the relationship between rights and citizenship. Moreover, the child as an active agent is a further underlying theme of the book, hence the impact of the CRC on conceptualising children as active actors will be explored. As the chapter will highlight, the dichotomies around which the core arguments of the book are structured abound throughout this chapter – some worth mentioning are rights versus responsibilities, exclusion versus inclusion, citizen versus non-citizen and, of course, underpinning these sub-dichotomies is the adult–child relationship which forms the lynchpin of the chapter.

United Nations Convention on the Rights of the Child

The CRC reflected a widespread global commitment to advance children's rights. The Convention was adopted by the UN General Assembly in 1989 and was ratified more quickly and by more countries than any human rights treaty in history.

As is now commonly known, only two countries – the USA and Somalia – did not ratify the Convention. Because of the ongoing civil war in Somalia, the appropriate structures were not in place at the time of the ratification of the Convention by other UN member states. While Somalia has expressed repeated commitment to upholding children's rights and indeed Somalia's Ambassador to the UN signed the Convention in 2002, the ongoing unstable political situation hampered ratification until January 2015 when Somalia became the 195th State Party to ratify the Convention. In the USA, support for the CRC remains lukewarm. Hence, while the USA subsequently signed the CRC in 1995, it has yet to ratify it. Signing the CRC and ratifying it entail two different processes. Signing it is an endorsement of the main principles of the CRC but ratifying it entails being legally bound to uphold and implement these principles. While US laws are broadly consistent with the pact, the relationship between adults' and children's rights continues to provoke heated debate. Current US law places emphasis on the right of parents to make decisions on their children's behalf. The strong rights that parents hold also limit individual US states from interfering in family affairs. There are concerns that equalising children's rights with parents' rights could lead to more state involvement in family life, with parents' role as promoters of their children's best interests being undermined. Of course, such a view is based on the premise that parents always act in the best interests of their children, despite widespread evidence that many parents do not always act in this way (Bartholet, 2011). Pitting parents' rights against those of children is an unhelpful way of promoting children's rights but it remains a powerfully held view and upholds the notion that parents are entitled to make decisions on behalf of their children. This notion of parents' rights versus children's rights continues to provoke concern, even among states that have ratified the CRC. This issue will be returned to later in the chapter.

The CRC has become a core mechanism for improving conditions for children around the world. Along with the USA, South Sudan is the only country that has yet to ratify the landmark treaty (the country did not exist when the Convention was adopted by the UN General Assembly). Freeman (1997: 68) argues that, overall, the CRC represents 'an impressive manifesto on behalf of children', although he also points out that no children were consulted or involved in the drafting process. The Convention defines 'children' as those below the age of 18. While it is considered a 'soft law' (Freeman, 1997: 403), national governments are expected to set up legal procedures to bring the CRC's main principles into domestic law. Governments who ratify the CRC are required to submit regular reports on the status of children's rights in their countries and outline the progress made towards implementation. Hence, ratifying countries have to show how they have incorporated the ethos of the Convention into their national programmes and plans. Additional information may be sought from NGOs and other children's organisations, who have the right to respond to individual country reports. The Committee on the Rights of the Child, which is made up of an internationally elected body of experts, reviews the reports and provides commentaries and evaluations on the extent to which individual countries are making satisfactory progress in implementation. Their Concluding Observations are generally structured around identifying progress made, highlighting shortcomings and providing recommendations to further support the principles of the CRC.

The CRC's overall aim is to 'change the way children are viewed and treated, i.e. as human beings with a distinct set of rights instead of as passive objects of care and charity' (www.unicef.org/crc). At the same time, one could argue that the CRC sets up distinctions between adults and children in that, rather than overall human rights, these are divided into human rights for adults under the Universal Declaration of Human Rights and children's rights, specifically promoted under the CRC. However, the CRC could be seen as an example of where the agency of children has impacted on wider structures. Children's rights are now firmly embedded in national and international agendas. The CRC has made children and their interests and needs more visible within the policy-making process. Many countries have developed comprehensive national agendas to monitor and promote children's rights. The amount of public spending allocated to children has increased in many countries. Many formal bodies have been set up, including children's commissions and ombudspersons, to ensure that appropriate data are collected to raise awareness of children's positioning in wider society and to respond to issues raised. State parties have also undertaken measures to raise awareness of children's rights among children themselves, as well as those charged with their care. While all these developments have had differing impacts at national level, overall one could argue that the rhetoric still does not match the reality and many problems remain. For example, all these advances have been made by well-meaning adults acting on behalf of children, rather than by children themselves, and the thorny issue of what happens when adults' and children's interests collide continues to give cause for concern.

The Convention comprises 54 Articles grouped under what are known as the three Ps – Protection, Provision and Participation. Articles are broadly grouped under these three headings. Those which specify Protection include protection from sexual exploitation, physical and mental abuse and engagement in warfare. Those which specify Provision include the right to education, healthcare and play. Participation Articles have proven to be the most contentious and include the child's right to have a say and be listened to, along with states ensuring that the child's best interests permeate their approach to policy. The four areas of children's everyday lives that were the focus of Chapters 3 and 4 – family, education, work and play – are all addressed by specific Articles in the Convention. However, Davey and Lundy (2011) argue that it is difficult to view rights in piecemeal terms. They point out that if the focus is on the child's right to play, this is formally enshrined in Article 31, which specifies: 'States Parties recognise the right of the child to rest and leisure, to engage in play and recreational activities appropriate to the age of the child and to participate freely in cultural life and the arts'.

However, they argue that to disengage Article 31 from the rest of the CRC would result in a limited approach to children's right to play. Instead, they suggest that this right is fundamentally linked to other rights such as Article 2 (the right to non-discrimination), Article 3 (ensuring that the best interests of the child are a primary consideration), Article 6 (the child's right to life, survival and development), Article 12 (the child's right to express their views), Article 15 (freedom of association) and Article 19 (protection from harm). Hence, it is more appropriate to approach the CRC in a holistic way, and Davey and Lundy (2011: 11) see the 'UNCRC as the hub of a wheel, with each of the substantive rights (e.g. development, health, freedom of association, safety and play) as a core spoke in the wheel. If any of the spokes were to break, the wheel would buckle.' In other words, the CRC by its very nature is complex and multidimensional.

Rather than focus on specific children's rights in relation to specific Articles, the remainder of the chapter will focus on participation rights, as these continue to provoke the most contention. Moving children's participation rights centre stage has been narrowly defined as limiting the participation of adults or pitting adults against children. This remains a significant hurdle, preventing US ratification of the CRC, and brings sharply to the fore the importance of generation as a structural framework for understanding how agency and structure play out in relation to children's rights.

Article 3 and Article 12: Complementary and Contradictory Aspects

Children's participation in public decision making is central to the CRC. The two most relevant Articles in relation to participation are Articles 3 and 12 and it is important to discuss these two articles in detail along with their implications. Articles 3 and 12 are fundamental to all the other Articles in the CRC. They are, to use Davey and Lundy's (2011) analogy, the wheel to which all the spokes are connected. Freeman (2007: 1) argues that 'recognition of the child's best interests underpins all the other provisions in the Convention'. Before discussing the nature of Article 3, it is useful to set out the text. In many publications, Article 3.1 is outlined while Articles 3.2 and 3.3 are rarely mentioned, but it is important to consider Article 3 in full:

Article 3.1: In all actions concerning children, whether undertaken by public or private social welfare institutions, courts of law, administrative authorities or legislative bodies, the best interests of the child shall be a primary consideration.

Article 3.2: State Parties undertake to ensure the child such protection and care as is necessary for his or her well-being, taking into account the rights and duties of his or her parents, legal guardians or other individuals legally responsible for him or her, and, to this end, shall take all appropriate legislative and administrative measures.

Article 3.3: State Parties shall ensure that the institutions, services and facilities responsible for the care and protection of children shall conform with the standards established by competent authorities, particularly in the areas of safety, health, in the number and suitability of their staff, as well as competent supervision.

While declaring that 'the best interests of the child shall be a primary consideration' is a laudable sentiment, careful reading of the Article suggests that defining what are the child's best interests may be far from clear cut. For example, note the wording, *'shall be a'* not *'shall be the'* primary consideration. This suggests that other considerations may need to be taken into account. Freeman (2007) gives an extreme example of where the best interests of one child may collide with the best interests of another. He relates a case of conjoined twins in the UK, where the English courts had to decide whether they could be lawfully separated. Medical opinion indicated that since one twin was stronger than the other, the most likely outcome would be the survival of one twin and the death of the other. The court decided that separation was necessary to give at least one twin the chance of a normal life but acknowledged that its ruling was not in the best interests of the second twin. Freeman gives additional examples of some problematic cases. For example, what if a young person is anorexic and would rather die than eat food? Surely, the best interests principle would necessitate intervention to save the life of the young person, and, while this may result in force feeding an unwilling recipient, it would be difficult to consider supporting the young person in their wishes to abstain from eating food as serving their best interests. Freeman also outlines possible situations where those defined as children by their chronological age take on what is often seen as an adult role by becoming parents. For example, a 15-year-old becomes pregnant and gives birth to a child. Both are covered under the Convention but the best interests of one 'child' may conflict with those of the other. Say that the 15-year-old is from a disadvantaged background, is addicted to drugs and wants to keep the child, but it may be in the baby's best interests to be adopted by parents who can provide a more nurturing environment. Who makes decisions here? Who decides what is and what is not a nurturing environment? Who decides what 'best interests' are, and, if there are conflicting 'best interests', whose best interests should prevail? The newborn baby may be rendered more passive than the 15-year-old mother, who in turn may be rendered more passive than her parents or adult professionals who become involved in her antenatal and postnatal care.

Clearly, there are no easy solutions to cases like these where additional moral judgements are being made. But the example suggests that adults may have to be persuaded about what is in the child's best interests. Indeed, Article 3.2 goes on 'to take into account the rights and duties' of parents, but, as Freeman (2007) points out, these rights and duties are not defined. Freeman suggests that, in practice, these rights and duties are likely to vary from one legal system to another. But are these rights compatible? What happens in cases where parents and children disagree about what is in the child's best interests? Article 3.3 brings the notion of competency to the fore – 'competent authorities' and 'competent supervision'. Again, how is competency being defined here and by whom? Articles 3.2 and 3.3 also invoke a paternalistic conception of the state and this may throw up difficulties where adults' and children's rights collide; indeed, adults as parents may be deemed incompetent by state professionals, so their autonomy to act in the child's best interests is far from guaranteed. Before looking at this in more detail, let us now turn to Article 12.

Here, the CRC underlines the importance of obtaining, listening to and responding to the views of the child. This is enshrined in Article 12 which states:

> Article 12.1: State Parties shall assure to the child who is capable of forming his or her own views the right to express those views freely in all matters affecting the child, the views of the child being given due weight in accordance with the age and maturity of the child.

> Article 12.2: For this purpose the child shall in particular be provided the opportunity to be heard in any judicial and administrative proceedings affecting the child, either directly, or through a representative or appropriate body, in a manner consistent with the procedural rules of national law.

Freeman (1997) argues that Article 12 is one of the most important and radical Articles in the whole Convention. Article 12 involves more than just listening to the child. Rather, the child's views should be taken into account, particularly in decisions affecting the child. However, while children's opinions about issues which directly or indirectly affect their lives should be sought, does this mean that their views should be prioritised over other views or sources of evidence?

Indeed, is there a specific child viewpoint or is it more probable that different children will express different views and, if this is the case, then how do we evaluate one set of views over others? Lavalette (1999: 28), for example, argues that 'obtaining children's views on issues directly affecting them should be a central part of research agendas but the information obtained needs to be treated, like all research findings, as potentially partial and one-sided, requiring verification from other sources'.

Lansdown (2001) argues that Article 12 gives children the right to be informed, the right to express an informed view and the right to have that view taken into account. But again, subjecting the wording to detailed scrutiny throws up additional problems. The child's view is to be considered and given 'due weight in accordance with the age and maturity of the child'. Again, does this mean that, in practice, younger children will have less entitlement to have their views heard than older children? How do we define maturity? Is it simplistically equated with age? To suggest this is to imply that childhood is a homogeneous category and this clearly is problematic. Moreover, there is no stipulation that children will be core decision makers. The Article simply suggests that matters relating to the child should be informed and influenced by the views of the child, while it tends to locate adults as holding the main responsibility for outcomes.

Archard and Skivenes (2009) point to a fundamental dilemma in relation to the sentiments expressed in Articles 3 and 12 and their work is worth reflecting on in detail here, as their observations and research throw up all sorts of dilemmas where adults' and children's rights clash. As they state:

> The problem arises because the two commitments seem to pull in different directions: promotion of a child's welfare is essentially paternalistic since it asks us to do what we, but not necessarily the child, think is best for the child; whereas, listening to the child's own views asks us to consider doing what the child, but not necessarily we, think is best for the child. (2009: 2)

The authors draw on a range of legal cases from Norway and the UK to illustrate some problems in practice. They point to some fundamental differences in how each jurisdiction deals with the child's best interests. In Norway, children over the age of 7 have a legal entitlement to be heard in court cases, while by age 12 the voice of the child is to be accorded significant weight. Here, the courts are making judgments on the basis of age, with 7-year-old children only needing to be heard while 12-year-olds have to be listened to seriously. In determining the weight to be given to the child's views, Archard and Skivenes (2009: 13–14) outline five ways in which the courts in Norway take account of children's views: (1) the consistency with which the child's opinion is expressed; (2) the child's understanding of the consequences of their opinions (should they get their way); (3) a general adherence to respect for the child's view; (4) the age of the child expressing the view; and (5) the circumstances in which the child formed an opinion, including the available information, and the capacity of the child to have enough experience to form an opinion on whatever issue is at stake. However, putting these principles into practice is far from clear cut. Of the eight cases considered in their research, Archard and Skivenes indicate that in four the Court's opinion of what was in the best interests of the child concurred with the view of the child, making it difficult to judge the extent to which the child's opinion was given due weight. In the remaining four cases, the Court and the child had different opinions, and in three of these four cases the Court decided that its judgment was in the child's best interests, although the Court did explain and justify its rulings.

I will take one of the examples where the Court and child disagreed and the Court decided that it should be the proper decision maker of the child's best interests, in order to illustrate the complexities involved. Archard and Skivenes outline case 2006-1308, where a 14-year-old girl had been abused and neglected by her mother and had been placed in care. The girl wanted to return to live with her biological mother despite how she had been formerly treated. The Court accepted and understood why the girl should express this desire and acknowledged that she would have a strong sense of attachment to her biological mother. However, she was doing well in her care placement and this had enhanced her social skills. Hence, while her wish to return to her mother was considered understandable, nonetheless the Court ruled that in its view it was in her best interests to remain in care. The example illustrates the complexities involved when the state intervenes in family situations where the care provided by biological parents is deemed inadequate and unacceptable, reminding us that not all parents have the autonomy to be the final decision makers. In these situations, the Court has to manage conflicting goals such as listening to the voice of the child and respecting his or her wishes but ultimately being the judge of what are the child's best interests. In achieving a balance between the two, the child's wishes may be overruled; indeed, in this case, the 'deficient' parent was also rendered passive.

Turning to the UK, Archard and Skivenes point out that under the English Children's Act courts should seek out the views of the child and take these into account in accordance with the child's age and understanding. They draw on medical cases where the Gillick principle is applied to decide whether a child under 16 is able to consent to his or her own medical treatment without the need for parental consent or knowledge. This principle, also known as 'Gillick competence', draws on a case that occurred in 1985 where a health department circular was distributed to doctors in the UK, advising them that they could apply discretion in prescribing contraceptives to under 16-year-olds without parental consent or knowledge. This was challenged by a UK parent, Mrs Victoria Gillick, a mother of 10 children including five girls, who argued that her daughters should not have the right to receive confidential contraceptive advice without her knowledge. In his judgment on the case, Lord Scarman argued that in certain cases, children should be able to make decisions independent of their parents, provided 'the child achieves sufficient understanding and intelligence to understand fully what is proposed'. The issue brought to the fore parental rights versus child rights and Lord Scarman's ruling brought into question the right and authority of parents to make judgements on behalf of their children. This ruling has since been applied to a wide range of medical situations and adapted with some variations in a variety of countries. However, again, putting this ruling into practice is far from clear cut. Archard and Skivenes outline one case where a 15-year-old girl refused a life-saving heart transplant because she did not want someone else's heart in her body and she did not want to have to take tablets for the rest of her life. While the girl indicated that she was aware of the consequences of her wishes, in that she could die, she stated that she would prefer this to treatment. However, the Court judged that she was 'overtaken' and 'overwhelmed' by events so that 'she has not been able to come to terms with her situation' (Re M, 1999: 1100–1101, cited in Archard and Skivenes, 2009: 11). Hence, to save her life, it was deemed to be in her best interests for the transplant to go ahead. Of course, one may sympathise with the Court's judgment but Archard and Skivenes' core point is that if the girl had been an adult, her decision not to have a transplant would have been upheld. This is supported by Alderson's and Goodwin's (1993) research, where they found that any life-extending treatment is viewed as better than none and that if a child refuses such treatment then the child must be acting incompetently. Yet, they state that while adults reaching this decision may be deeply unsettling, nonetheless their right to make this decision is respected in law. Archard and Skivenes conclude that judging best interests, hearing the child's views and balancing best interests and the child's views are not easily resolved. All involve judgements on the child's maturity and competence and these judgements are often made by adults. All these cases are located in and emerge from intergenerational relationships and the agency of the child to act clearly takes place within these relationships. Such cases bring to the fore adult rights versus children's rights and this becomes particularly messy when the adults in question are also parents, though, as the above indicates, parents' autonomy to make decisions on behalf of their children is far from absolute. Bearing this in mind, the next section turns specifically to questioning how the best interests of the child can, in principle, be equated with the rights of parents to make decisions on their behalf. Are these rights complementary or contradictory?

Parents and Children: Complementary or Contradictory Rights?

In its Preamble, the CRC articulates how children and adults should have equal human rights but then goes on to state that the 'child by reason of his physical and mental immaturity needs special safeguards and care'. Article 5 states:

> State Parties shall respect the responsibilities, rights and duties of parents or, where applicable, the members of the extended family or community as provided for by local custom, legal guardians or other persons legally responsible for the child, to provide, in a manner consistent with the evolving capacities of the child, appropriate direction and guidance in the exercise by the child of the rights recognised in the present Convention.

Hence, the Convention accords rights to parents and other adults over children, and indeed since parents and other adults should provide children with 'appropriate direction and guidance', one could argue that the Convention seeks to strengthen adults' obligations towards children. Thus, while the Convention is often viewed as creating a situation where granting rights to children undermines the rights of parents, Article 5 tries to achieve a balance between the right of children to some level of autonomy and self-determination, and the right of parents to raise their children in ways they see fit. Indeed, as the above section illustrates, the Convention supports state intervention where parents and other adults fail to meet their perceived duties towards children. Lansdown (2005) argues that the 'evolving capacities' concept tries to achieve a balance between autonomy and protection. She argues (2005: 3) that 'it provides the framework for ensuring an appropriate respect for children's agency without exposing them prematurely to the full responsibilities normally associated with adulthood'. On the other hand, Burman (2008) suggests that the notion of protection is premised on a notion of the child as innocent. In her view, this not only takes agency away from children, but also pathologizes children deemed not innocent, such as children who have sex. While Article 5 does not stipulate an appropriate age range for assessing the capacities or competences of a child, there is a clear indication that the term 'evolving' implies that capacities develop as children grow older. Lansdown (2005: 34) notes that when children are very young, parents will make decisions on numerous aspects of their daily lives from diet to choice of clothes, to where to live and where to be schooled, whereas as the child grows up, there will be a gradual relaxation in the parents' decision-making role. To some extent, this can be viewed from a developmental psychology perspective on childhood. As children age, they should become more competent and therefore they should have more autonomy to exercise their rights, with parents taking more of a back-seat role. However, where parents and children disagree, an evaluation of the child's competency to make informed decisions and indeed who decides this become crucial.

There appears to be an assumption that parents will always act in the best interests of the child. Article 18 states: 'Parents or, as the case may be, legal guardians, have the primary responsibility for the upbringing and development of the child. The best interests of the child will be their basic concern.' The Preamble to the CRC suggests a very rosy view of family life, 'recognising that the child for the full and harmonious development of his or her personality, should grow up in a family environment, in an atmosphere of happiness, love and understanding'. The burgeoning number of cases of parental and other adult carers' physical and mental abuse of children in their care calls into question the assumption that parents and other adults always act in the child's best interests. Cohen (2005) argues that even if we start at parents' decision to have children in the first place, their reasons may not always be altruistic. Among possible reasons, Cohen (2005: 226) lists: 'to fulfil personal needs, to create an heir, to knit together a broken relationship, to discharge a sense of responsibility to a religious community, to have someone to love and so on'. She also notes that adults are rarely prevented from bringing children into the world. Hence, parents who cannot materially provide for existing or future children continue to procreate. Drug addicts or adults with hereditary diseases are able to procreate without restriction. With advances in technology, older women are able to have children despite this carrying potential risks for the unborn child or the possibility that the child may end up caring for an ageing parent. Cohen (2005: 232) is not arguing that these adults should be prevented from having children, her point is that 'the adult right to reproduction under almost any circumstances far outweighs any possible right a child might have to be born into circumstances of physical and emotional safety and health'. At the same time, there may be cultural differences at play. For example, in the Republic of Ireland, abortion laws continue to prioritise the right of the foetus over the right of the parent. This was brought forcefully to the fore in a case in 2012 where an Indian woman residing in Ireland was denied an abortion. The woman was admitted to hospital with a bacterial infection at 17 weeks pregnant which could have resulted in a later miscarriage. The couple requested an abortion, with the husband stating that as Hindus they were not morally opposed to a termination. However, their request was denied and the woman subsequently died later during the pregnancy. Abortions are available in the Republic of Ireland, since a Supreme Court Ruling in 1992, but only where a woman's life as distinct from her health is at risk from the continuing pregnancy. In this case, doctors judged that at the time the abortion was first requested, the woman's life was not significantly at risk. The husband stated that he was told: 'This is a Catholic country, we cannot terminate because the foetus is still alive' (McDonald, 2013: 3). The example further illustrates the often messy relationship between the best interests of the child and the best interests of the parent and how the state, at times, becomes the ultimate judge.

Acknowledging children as having equal status with adults yet at the same time recognising that children often experience specific vulnerabilities and hence are in need of protection, is far from straightforward. Where adults' and children's rights collide, all sorts of assumptions concerning the nature of childhood are brought into play. Some anti-rights holders view children's participation in rights frameworks as problematic. Lansdown (2001) suggests that opponents of children's rights often make four objections to children's participation. First, children are often perceived to lack the competence or experience to participate. Of course, what is crucial here is how competence is defined and who does the defining. Is competency a thing that one possesses or does not possess? Traditionally, adults have been seen as competent and children as incompetent, but competency is likely to vary across different spheres and contexts, so that both adults and children may demonstrate competency in one sphere but not in another.

Second, Lansdown notes that some commentators feel the balance between rights and responsibilities has become skewed and children need to learn to take responsibility before they can be granted rights. The relationship between rights and responsibilities has produced a range of academic reflections, some of which are worth examining briefly here. Purdy (1994: 227), for example, argues that there are 'sufficiently large differences in instrumental reasoning between most children and most adults to justify different treatment'. She argues that children need maturity and experience in order to 'develop the kind of responsibility essential for exercising adult freedoms relatively harmlessly' (1994: 231). She cautions against giving children the freedom to make their own choices in case they make the wrong ones. For example, she outlines how this could impact on compulsory schooling. If children could freely choose whether or not to attend school, then some may decide to opt out. She suggests that this would more likely appeal to working-class children who may be already disaffected by educational systems, or because of poverty may find working at an early age more appealing than attending school. As a result, poor children may make the wrong choices and in the process reproduce existing class inequalities. This throws up the 'dark side' of agency in that children may practise 'bad' agency by engaging in 'forms of agency which are destructive towards the self' (Hoggett, 2001: 38). In a reply to Purdy, McGillivray (1994) argues that to conflate rights with the freedom to do whatever you want is to misinterpret the nature of rights. Rights holders do not exercise rights in a vacuum. They have a duty to other rights holders. Giving children rights does not mean that rights are then denied to adults. Adults and children have responsibilities towards each other. As rights holders, children have to learn to respect the views and experiences of other rights holders, and to gain responsibility one needs opportunities to act responsibly. As McGillivray (1994: 257) concludes, 'rights like childhood are premised on relationship and interdependence'. This also entails the possibility of making the wrong decisions, as adults often do, but with the capacity to learn from one's mistakes. Indeed, challenging the nature of the child as incompetent is one of the core strengths of Article 12. As Krappmann (2010: 502) argues:

> In fact the inclusion in processes of decision making clearly demonstrates that the idea of the child enshrined in the Convention differs from long-standing views, which stressed that the child is incompetent, lacking responsibility, in need of protection and therefore, still in a phase of preparation for life – in short: The child is an incomplete human being. Article 12 of the Convention definitely contradicts this conception.

Returning to Lansdown's articulation of core objections, her third consideration is the argument that giving children rights is seen to interfere with childhood, which is often simplistically portrayed as a time when children should be protected from the realities of the adult world and when rights are positioned as requiring adult knowledge. For example, in cases of parental divorce, children have a right to be consulted about their post-divorce living arrangements. However, this right can place children in the uncomfortable position of having to decide between two adults whom they love, although, as demonstrated in Chapter 4, some children are skilful managers of these difficult decisions. Fourth, opponents argue that giving children rights will lead to a lack of respect for parents. Purdy (1994: 234), for example, argues that 'children, especially teenagers, would be even less willing than now to take their parents' advice seriously. Parents in their turn would be less able to steer their children away from trouble.'

These issues throw up a fundamental problem in trying to reconcile Article 3 with Article 12. What if adults and children have different views on what the best interests of the child should be? What if we grant the child the right to be heard but then the child expresses a view that goes against what others might define as the child's best interests? In other words, what if children are simply listened to but their views and wishes are not taken into account because of their perceived immaturity or because their wishes seem to go against what is in their best interests? The literature is abound with examples where the best interests of the child principle is far from clear cut and the above section drew on Archard and Skivenes' research outlining how courts often intervene to decide what is in the child's best interests.

In focusing specifically on parent–child relationships, Cohen (2005) argues that in some cases the child's views are left out of the equation altogether. She cites two cases from the USA involving education where parents were deemed appropriate judges of the child's best interests. In the first, Pierce *v.* Society of Sisters, parents were accorded the right to choose a religious over a public school for their children. This might seem reasonable but Cohen argues that such a decision could go against the child's best interests if the child was homosexual or became pregnant and had to face the consequences of being located in an environment where these issues were deemed sinful, with the child involved either coerced into denying their sexual identity or having to give up their unplanned baby. In the second case, Wisconsin *v.* Yoder, an Amish couple were given the right to withdraw their child from the public education system and teach the child at home. Cohen argues that while on one level this could be seen as the parents' legitimate right to raise their child as they see fit, on another level the child concerned is without access to wider ideologies or belief systems and thus denied exposure to a world outside their home. These examples reflect the problematic nature of parents' versus children's rights, which permeates dominant discourses in the USA and elsewhere.

These issues do not just relate to children and young people. Adults may find themselves facing similar dilemmas, but where the subjects are children, notions of not being capable of making 'mature' choices are more likely to come into play. Moreover, children and young people may be surrounded by more powerful adults whose views hold considerable weight. Indeed, Cohen (2005) argues that because children have no independent voice in politics, adult views are prioritised at children's expense. Acting in the best interests of the child is far from straightforward and if this is decided on by adults, there is a possibility that even with the best of intentions adults may conflate their views with those of their offspring. Some countries try to resolve this tension by providing an avenue for airing both the child's and the adult's views. James (2011), for example, illustrates how in divorce proceedings in Norway, children from the age of 7 have the right to be heard in court, whereas in the UK, children have no such right. She argues that Norway and other Scandinavian countries have a much more sophisticated notion of children as competent beings, facilitated to act in the present rather than the future. However, as indicated earlier and illustrated through the work of Archard and Skivenes, balancing the interests of parents and children is fraught with difficulties.

Rights and Citizenship

I now want to turn attention to citizenship as the CRC, with its focus on participation rights for children, encouraged new thinking on the relationship between childhood and citizenship. By locating children as independent holders of rights, the CRC encouraged a focus on children as citizens in their own right. Moreover, if childhood is to be understood as a state of being rather than becoming, then children's status as citizens deserves attention. Citizenship is often seen as an ambiguous, elusive concept and within this chapter it is not possible to do justice to the huge range of literature devoted to unpacking its multiple definitions and dimensions. Rather, the aim here is to suggest that children's relationship to citizenship remains ambiguous, conditional and partial, and as participation is fundamentally linked to citizenship and as this is central to the CRC, then the capacity of the CRC to promote children's citizenship rights needs to be acknowledged. The remainder of the chapter will focus on three core issues. The first section will briefly discuss attempts to transmit citizenship values to children by focusing on school councils as one example of initiatives in this area. Children's lack of voting rights remains the most visible aspect of their non-citizenship status so the chapter then turns to exploring this issue and its implications for children's citizenship status. This is followed by an examination of how citizenship also needs to be considered as 'lived citizenship' (Lister, 2007), and this involves understanding and illuminating how it is practised through a range of interdependent relationships, rather than being seen as an autonomous status or reduced to its formal legal dimensions.

Fostering Citizenship Skills: Preparation for Future Citizenship

While many states' legal dimensions of citizenship position children as 'citizens-in-waiting', this future-orientated practice has been accompanied by initiatives which acknowledge that children need knowledge and practice of democratic, decision-making processes prior to reaching the official voting age of 18. Lansdown (2000: 7, cited in Davies, 2007: 125) argues that 'without access to these processes which are integral to the exercise of democratic rights, children and their experience remain hidden from view and they are, in consequence, denied effective recognition as citizens'. Attempts to equip children with the abilities and skills deemed necessary for effective citizenship have been made through citizenship education and the setting up of school councils. These initiatives aim to transform schools into democratic arenas where pupils have a say in day-to-day rules and procedures and make decisions regarding school rules and classroom practices. Torney-Purta and Amadeo (2011: 197) refer to such schemes as providing effective niches for children's 'emerging participatory citizenship'. Hence, while children may be denied voting rights, their capacity for deliberation and social action may be promoted through these schemes. To assess the effectiveness of these initiatives, this section will focus on school councils. It is suggested that through these school councils, children can learn the democratic values necessary for participation in wider society. In most instances, children are formally elected by their peers and represent them in school affairs. School councils bring teachers and pupils together in periodic meetings to discuss and make decisions about school policy. Their core aim is to encourage active citizenship through getting young people to 'do democracy' through building trust, taking part in negotiations and sharing responsibility for decision making. However, a range of research has suggested that, in practice, many are little more than talking shops, and children and young people gain little experience in active decision making. Research from the UK, Ireland and Sweden calls into question the extent to which pupils' engagement in 'democratic' structures within school results in any meaningful change (Davies, 2000; Devine, 2002; Raby, 2008; Thornberg and Elvstrand, 2012). Collectively, these studies suggest that compliance with school rules and subordination to teachers' authority remain a structurally resilient aspect of pupils' school experience, despite some blurring at the edges through democratic councils where pupils at best input into mundane decisions such as 'non-uniform day', whereas core decisions around what is taught and how it is taught remain firmly in teachers' hands.

While, throughout the 20th century, changes in teaching encouraged pupil-centred pedagogical approaches and collaborative learning, some research suggests that the circumstances of such learning remain largely under adult control, with children subject to varying levels of adult surveillance. Wyness (1999), for example, looks at the relationship between childhood and agency within the context of education reform in the UK. He argues that the increasing need to produce 'schooled' citizens dilutes children's potential to practise agency within school settings. Research on teachers' views of school councils suggests that many are less than enthused about their existence and purpose. Alderson's research in the UK (2000: 123) found that teachers' views ranged from 'seeing councils as central to positive activities and relationships in the school, or as merely a formality, or an unnecessary burden for over-stressed staff, or even as a danger to be avoided'. Devine's (2002: 318) research in primary schools in Ireland found that 'the involvement of children in decisions which may directly affect them was discounted by most teachers for practical and ideological reasons, relating to large class sizes and time constraints, as well as the perceived immaturity of children and the need to learn self control'. From a slightly different angle, Thornberg (2009) found that teachers in Sweden use a variety of strategies such as reasoning and persuasion to coax pupils to follow rules. Quoting Denscombe (1985: 111), Thornberg argues that democracy within schools may be little more than illusory, with its core purpose being to ensure that pupils support the existing social order by taking part in the construction of that social order.

Other research suggests that once children are elected onto research councils, they are treated more favourably by teachers, causing resentment among non-council pupils or a perception that only favoured students are approached for consultation (Raby, 2008). Drawing on her research in Canada, Raby (2008) found that most students felt that they had never been consulted about school rules, which, in their view, were often very inconsistently applied. Some children in Raby's research suggested that they had little knowledge about whether or not their input made any difference. One girl suggested that she was 'randomly chosen to participate in a dress code discussion group', while another two girls indicated that they had 'been allowed to vote on the potential introduction of school uniforms, although they did not know if their vote counted' (Raby, 2008: 83). Similar findings emerge in Alderson's (2000) survey of schools in Great Britain and Northern Ireland. Half of the 2272 pupils aged 7–17 from the 250 schools who took part in the research indicated that their school had a school council but less than a fifth considered the council to be effective. Alderson (2000: 121) concludes that 'simply introducing a token council can increase students' scepticism'.

However, despite the perceived impotency of many student councils, research shows that rather than passively following rules, young people negotiate their way around rules, suggesting a more active engagement with school structures. In Raby's (2008) research, for example, pupils broke dress codes by wearing clothes not endorsed by the school, ate food in areas where consumption was forbidden and brought ipods and mobile phones to classrooms, even though these were banned by the school. Often though, these infringements were little more than temporary deviations and often resulted in an increase in rules, surveillance and enforcement. Thornberg (2009: 230) argues that, in the process, good citizenship becomes defined as 'compliance to authority and competence in following their rules'.

While there are various examples in the literature of children and young people actively engaging in school councils and making their voices heard, Percy-Smith (2006: 142) notes 'a growing realisation that young people's voices alone may not be sufficient to bring about effective and meaningful outcomes'. While his research provides examples of how young people can introduce new thinking and create opportunities which can lead to change, overall young people's participation remains a top-down rather than bottom-up process. Agendas are often set by adults and the structures themselves can encourage children to behave like mini-adults, with only the most resourceful children becoming participants (Cairns, 2006). As Tisdall (2008: 427) points out, 'there is an irony that if children's rights can be described as a "new social movement" or a "civil rights" movement, it is currently still predominantly led by adults'. She argues that children's participatory projects often rely on funding opportunities, with successfully financed initiatives reflecting adult discourses and adult indicators around targets, outcomes and performance. Moreover, media connections to policy makers often reflect links between well-meaning adults acting on behalf of children.

Children and Young People's Ongoing Lack of Voting Rights

Children's absence from adult decision-making processes is also evident in their lack of voting rights. While the initiatives outlined above have had varying levels of success, Wall and Dar (2011) argue that children's rights and citizenship should include their direct political representation. As they put it (2011: 596): 'Children's political rights should be exercised not only indirectly through voice, organisation, protest and participation, but also directly through using power, influencing policies and voting.' One of the most important attempts to define citizenship is T. H. Marshall's (1950) seminal account on the evolution of citizenship rights through his focus on civil, political and social rights. According to Marshall's conception of citizenship, children have some social and civil rights, but they have no voting rights and therefore do not participate fully in the political life of society. Hence, they are 'citizens-in-waiting' rather than child citizens. The lack of voting rights for young people under 18 is seen as one of the most important shortcomings in children's rights to citizenship by a number of commentators. For example, Earls (2011: 8) asks: 'How can children be citizens if they are thought to be too immature to vote?' Similarly, as Wall and Dar (2011: 595) point out: 'it remains the case that the third of humanity around the world who are under eighteen exercise relatively little political power, whether in electing representatives, influencing laws, or shaping policies'. Cohen (2005: 230) states: 'As things stand, children form the largest group of unrepresented people in every liberal democracy in the world,' while Bohman (2011: 129) argues that children's lack of full citizenship rights results in 'the domination of non-citizens by citizens'. Collectively, this body of work suggests that children's lack of voting rights impedes on other rights. In recent years, there has been a renewed commitment to revisit the age at which children and young people should be allowed to vote. Wall and Dar (2011) outline how a number of countries have in recent years lowered the voting age to 16 on the basis that this would encourage politicians to pay more attention to children and young people's issues. Children's lack of voting power leads to a disregard for their immediate interests, whereas electoral clout through direct voting power would provide a strong motivation for making politicians accountable to a younger electorate.

Wall and Dar (2011) also highlight the growth of children's and youth parliaments as a potentially positive development and outline how around 30 countries, including Norway, Finland, Germany, Slovenia, New Zealand and the UK, have some form of youth parliament. However, they acknowledge the limited powers of these structures and shortfalls in the selection of children and young people to take part in these initiatives, highlighting, as indicated above, the tendency for older, middle-class children to be involved. They also suggest caution in the extent to which the setting up of youth parliaments can be seen as a positive development. As they put it (2011: 607):

> separate parliaments are not typical of how marginalized groups have historically gained power. There are no separate women's parliaments, minorities' parliaments, poor parliaments, or the like. This is because operating apart from a general parliament is on some level inherently tokenistic, placing a distance – however wide or narrow – between the electoral process and the actual exercise of power.

In their view, real political power lies in the ability to influence policy. However, as with school councils, separate parliaments could end up as talking shops where children and young people can air their views on a range of issues but remain excluded from exercising direct political influence.

Drawing on the USA as a case study, Rehfeld (2011) outlines a number of creative proposals for encouraging the gradual involvement of children in politics. He believes, as has been argued elsewhere, that children are denied access to politics because of their perceived political immaturity, yet they are given few or no opportunities to gain experience in achieving political maturity through practice. He suggests three ways in which political systems could adopt incremental approaches to involving the younger generation in politics.

First, he suggests allocating fractional voting shares to children. He takes age 12 as the starting point, although this could be lower, and suggests that at age 12 a child could receive a seventh of a vote, at age 13 two-sevenths, and so on, until they reach age 18 and acquire the full vote. This method would address the common concern that giving children voting power gives power to those who do not know how to use it. Factional voting, by default, only gives factional power. Rehfeld argues that this would have a powerful citizenship effect on young people, encouraging them to become members of the polity at a young age. Factional voting would give children a 'learner's permit' (2011: 158) to practise politics. This, in turn, would make political representatives more accountable to young people and more attuned to their needs and interests since votes could be at stake.

Rehfeld's second proposal is to establish electoral constituencies by age. While currently most political systems define constituencies by territory, basing some constituencies on age would encourage politicians to pay more attention to children's issues. Again, he supports an incremental approach, so that, for example, all 12-year-olds could nationally elect a single representative, 13-year-olds could elect two representatives, and so on, up to age 16 or 18 when children would be assimilated into the political system.

His third proposal involves the state giving a small political allowance to all children in their jurisdiction to be used to fund non-profit or political organisations. Using the USA as an example, he argues that there are between three and four million children in each cohort between the ages of 13 and 17. If each child cohort was given, for example $10, this would create a potential revenue of $30 to $40 million for political and interest groups. In his view, the monetary incentive involved would encourage adult political systems to become highly interested in promoting children's issues. Rehfeld's core point is that the most effective way to promote the political power of children and their active citizenship is through their direct involvement in voting systems. His proposals provide interesting ways of thinking through the need to respond to children's current exclusion from the political arena. While he is aware that his proposals are not by themselves a panacea for addressing the various forms of exclusion that children and young people face in most modern societies, and indeed could potentially be open to abuse, nonetheless they reinforce the need to address in imaginative and innovative ways how societies can flexibly adapt to children's citizenship in the here and now, rather than relying on the transfer of full voting power once they reach a certain age.

Another core way in which children can practise active citizenship is through involvement in children's movements. While most of these movements are located in majority world countries and are formed mainly in relation to children's right to work (Liebel, 2004), Stasiulis (2002) outlines the emergence of the 'Free the Children' movement initiated by a 12-year-old Canadian boy. While the organisation focuses on child poverty in majority world countries and the necessity of child employment, its remit also extends to child poverty issues in 'western developed' countries. Stasiulis notes that since its formation in 1995, the Free the Children's movement has become one of the largest networks of children in the world, with a membership of over 100,000 children in more than 35 countries. The organisation fosters a form of global citizenship for children, advocates children's competence in understanding matters affecting children and facilitates their agency in voicing children's issues, needs and interests. Stasiulis argues that these organisations may have a more direct influence on policy making than initiatives based on lowering the voting age or having politicians represent marginal interest groups (such as children), as the impact of the latter on the wider world of politics is likely to be minimal. Rather, these social movements composed of children may have greater clout in embarrassing politicians to move beyond platitudes around the best interests of children and to live up to their claims and obligations around protecting children and promoting their needs by having to demonstrate specific ways in which the rhetoric matches the reality. For Stasiulis, such social movements have the potential to move children from the realm of pre-citizens to citizens in the here and now.

'Lived' Citizenship

While the previous section suggested that children are to some extent non-citizens or pre-citizens, this approach relies on a very narrow definition of citizenship. This section focuses on the body of work which attempts to unpack what citizenship might mean for children. Some commentators, for example, suggest that at a basic level, children are citizens in terms of their entitlement to a passport and to nationality of the country in which they are born (with some exceptions). Moreover, their status as non-citizens, in terms of more formal rights such as the right to vote, is temporary, as once they reach adulthood they will acquire full citizenship status. However, a number of authors have recognised that during childhood, children's citizenship status is restricted and, in many respects, they are treated as non-citizens. Full citizenship status is equated with adulthood and draws on what are seen as adult traits such as competency and responsibility, with children located as possessing lesser forms of these traits.

Commentators such as Roche (1999) argue that children should have some form of partial citizenship during childhood, and as their level of maturity increases so too should their entitlement to citizenship. Cockburn (1998) also advocates an incremental approach to citizenship, arguing that children's entitlement to rights and participation should increase as they get older. Cohen (2005) uses the term 'semi-citizenship' to account for the middle ground that children occupy in which they are both accorded and denied certain citizenship rights, while Cockburn's (2012) more recent work argues that the concept of citizenship should be flexible enough to account for how children are both similar to and different from adults. All of these authors advocate the critical unpacking of adults' and children's supposed traits around competency and rationality, and propose subjecting discourses of citizenship to scrutiny so that more imaginative usages of the concept are envisioned.

This notion of sameness and difference is a core aspect of Moosa-Mitha's (2005) work in which she critiques child protectionist and liberal paternalistic notions of citizenship. In her view, both are premised on a number of faulty assumptions. Both tend to view children in essentialist terms, locating all children together under the monolithic label of childhood and placed in opposition to adulthood.

This results in children being judged in terms of their perceived non-possession of adult characteristics such as rationality and independence. Lister (2007) suggests that similar sentiments were initially applied to women. However, if we return to children, notions of them having different traits to adults continue to influence theorisations of children's citizenship. Moosa-Mitha argues that child protectionists view children as clearly unequal to adults, therefore attempts to treat children as equal citizens could end in disaster. According to this approach, children are clearly more vulnerable than adults and indeed are dependent on adults, thus treating them as equal would result in children shouldering responsibilities beyond their capabilities. This leads to suggestions that what children really need from adults is not equality but structures which promote adult duties to protect the interests of children, either in the family or, where this breaks down, through the state intervening. According to Moosa-Mitha, this view was put forward by liberal paternal advocates of citizenship such as Freeman (1996, 1997). In her view, Freeman's liberal paternal argument emphasises that parents, and where necessary the state, should adopt a paternalistic approach and intervene, where appropriate, to ensure that adults fulfil their responsibilities and commitments to the younger generation. Elsewhere, Freeman (1983) acknowledges that children should be considered as persons of equal worth but he argues that they should be protected from 'irrational acts' (cited in Moosa-Mitha, 2005: 379). He justifies this through the principle of 'future-orientated consent', whereby the decisions made by adults on behalf of and in the best interests of children are ones which children would understand, appreciate and agree were right and appropriate once they became adults.

These approaches clearly locate children as not-yet-citizens by emphasising how children differ from the adult norm. Moosa-Mitha argues that what is needed is a more nuanced model of difference and she proposes a 'differently equal' model of citizenship as an alternative theorisation of children's citizenship rights. This argument is also put forward by Lister (2007), who advocates a 'differentiated citizenship' for children. Both authors suggest that once children are taken into the equation, then a different model of citizenship might need to be applied, one that acknowledges children's differences compared to adults in terms of needing protection and so on, but one which also fully accepts that children can and do participate in society, perhaps in ways that are not fully acknowledged by dominant discourses. This also involves delinking citizenship from a legal status to explore how it is also a socio-political and lived practice accomplished within the realm of everyday life. This model defines the 'self' as relational rather than autonomous (similar arguments will be put forward in Chapter 6 where agency is subject to detailed scrutiny). Rather than the rational, autonomous, independent (male) adult being seen as the norm, this approach takes difference as the starting point.

Difference is celebrated rather than being seen as a deviation from the norm. Citizenship then becomes a dynamic, multi-layered concept that is practised in a multitude of relational settings.

Broadening the meaning of citizenship and moving beyond using adulthood as a yardstick means that children's participation becomes redefined as a struggle for recognition. As James (2011: 172) argues, it involves 'how adults are actively interpreting the competences and capacities that children have. And what is more, it would also involve discovering how children themselves are experiencing and responding to these adult conceptualizations of childhood.' Concepts such as participation, rights and responsibilities may mean different things to children than they do to adults – in other words, they may take different forms. Children may locate these concepts within the realm of their everyday experiences, rather than consider them through the lens of formal processes. Thus, this entails taking into account children's own lived reality. The notion of 'lived citizenship' (Lister, 2007: 695) moves citizenship from beyond a legal status to a practised phenomenon and draws attention to children's own understandings of citizenship and their agency in terms of their ability to exercise participation rights in everyday life.

Davies (2007) presents an interesting overview of the relationship between discourses of participation and discourses of social exclusion. As with adults, social exclusion results in children experiencing a sense of non-belonging and disconnection from their communities and indeed from many aspects of the wider adult society. Social exclusion, for both children and adults, is the result of wider structural inequalities, but children experience additional forms of exclusion by not being listened to or treated seriously or with respect by adults. Hence, to enhance children's sense of belonging is to encourage value systems whereby they are treated with respect by adults and their views are taken seriously. This entails demonstrating the impact that children have on daily life through their contribution to interdependent relationships. Participation in daily relationships, under the right conditions, is seen as promoting children's independence, sense of responsibility, confidence and self-esteem. Davies' empirical work, which focused on children and young people's own views on participation, belonging and exclusion in Liverpool in the UK, suggests that not only do young people already hold the skills which formal participation processes are expected to develop, they also subscribe to discourses of exclusion that fundamentally relate this to issues of connectedness within their families and communities. Davies' research, which he suggests is applicable elsewhere in Europe, prioritises children's notions of interdependent relationships and their desire and need to foster and develop what they see as mutually reciprocal relationships among themselves and with adults within the home, community and educational systems. Above all, they want respect and recognition from adults, suggesting that children's perceptions of their sense of belonging go beyond their lack of formal participation rights. Social exclusion should not just be reduced to material resources but to generational relationships between adults and children which, at times, place them as outsiders or lesser members of society. This means that formal participation processes by themselves will not automatically enhance children's feelings of inclusion and belonging, if, in myriad ways in their daily lives, there is insufficient acknowledgement of their existing contribution to society and recognition of their ongoing daily attempts to realise mutually reciprocal relationships with adults. This approach necessitates fundamentally challenging discourses that continue to see these activities as mundane and unimportant.

Thomas (2012) applies Honneth's theory of the 'struggle for recognition' as a useful way of thinking about children's participation. He argues that Honneth may provide a framework for understanding the social position of children and what participation may mean in practice. Applying Honneth, Thomas argues that identities are socially formed through processes of mutual recognition but that the possibility of misrecognition is always present. Recognition plays a fundamental role in human interaction. Recognition is inter-subjective and draws on three concepts – love, rights and solidarity. Love can refer to children's friendships and to their relationships with significant adults based on affection and trust and a 'mutual recognition of independence' (2012: 456). Rights refer to respect for others, with individuals accepting each other as morally and reciprocally responsible beings. Social respect leads to self-respect. Solidarity refers to 'social relations of symmetrical esteem' (2012: 457). Values are not narrowly linked to one's place in society but emerge from a recognition of shared goals, although Thomas acknowledges that it may be challenging to transfer reciprocally shared values to the wider sphere. Thomas argues that although children did not feature much in Honneth's framework, other than in the restrictive context of primary relationships based on love and care, his framework of love, respect and esteem is useful in understanding how children are already morally responsible persons who contribute in multiple ways to society and so are deserving of respect and esteem. Being morally responsible, children are therefore rights bearers. Thomas argues that this model enables us to see children not just as recipients of care but as givers of care. This issue will be returned to in Chapter 6 and illustrated through the concept of generagency and its offshoots inter-generagency and intra-generagency. Agency also needs to be seen as a moral accomplishment, with children embedded in relationships with each other and with adults, and with agency practised as the outcome of reciprocal interactions.

It may seem that this focus is misplaced here but the core point to make is that if children are not recognised or respected in intimate relationships, then it is difficult to envisage how they can gain mutual respect through less intimate, more formal processes of participation. Indeed, Taylor et al.'s (2008) research on what the core values of citizenship, in terms of rights and responsibilities, mean to children in New Zealand, found that most did not define these in relation to formal representation processes but rather drew on discourses around being listened to, respected and treated fairly. Children wanted opportunities to express opinions and to be involved in making decisions but located these within the realms of family, school and the local community. Taylor et al. (2008: 195–6) argue that

> without the opportunity for meaningful participation in their everyday lives, children are unlikely to have a good understanding of citizenship concepts … whether they feel they belong in society is likely to influence whether they are confident and motivated enough to believe that they can bring about change.

This involves acknowledging children as persons who have a role to play in constructing and reconstructing the shared values on which their everyday, interdependent relationships depend and which are formed and reformed through daily life practices. This also involves unpacking the 'moral' dimensions of citizenship and how children demonstrate moral competence and moral agency in their dealings with others (Bacon and Frankel, 2014).

At the same time, issues of power have been underplayed here. Indeed, returning to Thomas' application of Honneth, Thomas acknowledges that the power dimensions of interdependent relationships need to be teased out in greater detail. Being different and making a difference are not the same and it is when we turn to more formal attempts to encourage children's participation in making changes to their everyday lives that, as suggested above, their reliance on supportive adult structures becomes increasingly apparent.

Rights and Agency

The final issue I want to discuss in this chapter is the relationship between rights and agency. According to Freeman (2006: 90), 'rights are important because those who have them can exercise agency'. The CRC considers children as active agents who have an element of autonomy in constructing their own lives and acting in their own best interests. However, recognising children as agents who are also still in need of protection is an ongoing dilemma. Cohen (2005) notes that this often results in parents being located as the primary judges of the child's best interests and in effect this excludes children from public life, with their everyday lives being regulated to the private world of the family. While the state may intervene when the family fails to perform its normative duties, the state further renders children passive, viewing them as victims of problem families. These factors privatise children's citizenship and often preclude children from practising active citizenship. Participation rights, however, acknowledge that children are not just vulnerable and dependent but have the capacity to practise agency. As Roche (1999) points out, the participation component of the CRC, specifically Article 12, rejects normative and passive conceptions of children as future citizens and facilitates their active agency.

The 'right to be heard' has led to a mushrooming of initiatives aimed at obtaining the voice of the child in a variety of different contexts. It has facilitated a rise in children's organisations (which are usually staffed by adults), children's commissioners and other representatives. Being heard is fundamentally linked to Article 3, which relates to the child's best interests. Determining what are the child's best interests necessitates giving them the opportunity to be heard. However, in practice, Articles 3 and 12 have facilitated a significant rise in employment opportunities for adults, as states demonstrate to the CRC Monitoring Committee their ongoing commitment to the ethos of the Convention. Indeed, Reynaert et al. (2009: 520) argue that the CRC has fuelled the development of a huge 'human rights machinery', creating a global, adult-led children's rights industry around articulating and implementing children's rights. This raises questions about the meaning of participation and the extent to which adults facilitate children's participation and enable them to practise agency. For example, what does the right to be heard mean in practice? Does it apply to the right to influence a decision or the right to make a decision? Reynaert et al. (2009) argue that there remain unresolved power issues – at times, children are involved in a tokenistic way or some children are selected as child spokespersons, while others are excluded and, in practice, often only trivial matters are debated.

To what extent are children viewed as actors and to what extent is their agency promoted through participation? Some research suggests that children's engagement with the policy-making process has been less than meaningful. Lansdown (2001) argues that, at times, children are consulted in a tokenistic way to promote adult agendas. They are involved in dissemination events without any real understanding of the issues or the impact they had on the decision-making process. At times, they are not presented with appropriate information. In reviewing a range of government strategies in Northern Ireland involving consultation with children and young people, Byrne and Lundy (2015) found that the majority of policies surveyed had not produced child-friendly versions of consultations or final-version documents, and indeed 'it was not always clear what impact children's views had on the final strategy and there was little evidence of particular examples where views had informed a final policy' (2015: 272). Hence, in this case, the balance of power between adults and children remained intact and there appeared to be little structural change in the organisations consulting children. Indeed, Byrne and Lundy (2015) point out that while civil servants in Northern Ireland are required to attend mandatory training on human rights, training in relation to the CRC is not compulsory nor is it consistently provided, leading to a general lack of understanding of what consultation with children and participation actually mean. In relation to Canada, Mitchell and McCusker (2008) note that in its Concluding Observations in 2003, the monitoring committee of the CRC requested that the CRC should be a fundamental part of the training curricula for professional groups dealing with children. Yet, their research revealed only piecemeal attempts to apply this recommendation. Indeed, their research of students enrolled in post-secondary human rights education courses in Canada found that the majority of students interviewed had never heard of the CRC and had not been taught anything at all about the Convention during their entire public school years. Limiting knowledge of the CRC to professional groups clearly does not meet the CRC's stipulation that nationwide education should be adopted to inform both adults and children of the principles of the Convention, and participation at the outset requires appropriate information. Other research which focuses on children's knowledge of the Convention has revealed further concerns around the extent to which children are aware of the Convention. In Alderson's (2000) survey of young people aged 7–17 in Great Britain and Northern Ireland, over 75% indicated that they had never heard of the CRC. Moreover, to reiterate an earlier point, sometimes certain types of children are consulted who may not be representative of local childhood populations (Tisdall and Davis, 2004). Indeed, Lansdown (2001) argues that there is an ongoing concern that articulate, middle-class children may become 'professionalised' child speakers.

At the same time, there are success stories. Lansdown's (2001: 18) report to UNICEF contains a number of positive examples of children's effective participation in democratic structures where they exercised agency in the decision-making process. One of her examples is worth outlining here. It refers to a Euronet consultation with children in five countries on whether they felt discriminated against as children and whether they wanted more opportunities to participate in political decisions both at national and European levels. While the consultation was initiated by adults, once the children were brought on board they played a significant role in further developing the project, so that the final recommendations were prepared and produced by the children with the adults playing a secondary role. In this case, adults exhibited a willingness to give children a voice, listen to what they had to say and provide opportunities for them to have their voices heard.

However, a core dilemma remains. Children's capacity for political agency is highly dependent on supportive adult contexts and this exposes the fundamental differing levels of power between adults and children and also reiterates the need to see children's agency in generational terms. James and James (2001) warn that creating opportunities for children to participate in policy making may have unintended consequences, in that the space where children can be relatively free from adult control or influence may be even more severely restricted. Indeed, Smith (2011) argues that, paradoxically, by weakening the boundaries between adulthood and childhood, participation strategies based on acknowledging the child's agency could lead to new forms of regulation by using agency in an instrumental way to create the 'responsibilised' child. Hence, by creating opportunities for participation, the child may take an active part in his or her self-regulation.

Conclusion

The CRC celebrated its 20th anniversary in 2009 and this led to a plethora of reflections on its achievements and limitations. However, Freeman (2000: 282) warns: 'we must not assume that a Convention formulated in the last third of the twentieth century will fit the needs of children of the new millennium. There is a need for revision, reform and innovation.' Quennerstedt (2010) argues that perhaps the way forward is to consider children's rights as human rights and to replace the terminology relating to provision, protection and participation with a more general discourse on universal human civil, political and social rights. She suggests that the existing vocabulary detaches children's rights from human rights. This view is supported by Besson (2005), who argues that adopting a special Convention for children ghettoises children's rights. At the same time, glossing over differences between adults and children risks rendering invisible the specific positioning of children in modern society and, while immaturity and competence may be socially defined, to deny any biological input is a fallacy. Veerman (2010) argues that perhaps the CRC has run its course and needs urgent unpacking to fit in with how childhood has changed from the time the CRC was initiated. As has been highlighted in this chapter, one of the core advances put forward by the CRC is the focus on participation and the importance of obtaining the child's voice. But how should this voice be expressed? Veerman (2010: 593) points out that in the modern world, children communicate as much with 'their thumbs as with their tongues'. He argues that the growing omnipresence of the internet and all its offshoots means that the CRC is no longer up to date in relation to children's competency and ways of communicating, where, rather than not having access to information, the problem might be information overload. The impact of these changes lies outside the scope of this book but it is worth remembering that as childhood changes, the structures and institutions purporting to represent children and their interests, such as the CRC, may need changing as well.

The purpose of this chapter has been more modest and has outlined the basic elements of the CRC, particularly in relation to Articles 3 and 12, which underpin all the other Articles in the CRC. The messy relationship between achieving a satisfactory balance between acting in the child's best interests and hearing the child's voice was debated. This throws up unresolved tensions between the positions of adults and children, and continues to invoke dichotomous thinking around allocating different traits to each grouping. Many adults remain suspicious of the ability of children to act competently. The rights of the child and the rights of parents continue to be seen as mutually incompatible and still stand as a fundamental barrier to the USA ratifying the Convention. The Convention accords rights to parents and promotes other adults' rights over children but attempts to do this in ways which respect the voice of the child. However, Stasiulis (2002: 516) argues that 'the participation of children will always occur in dialogue that is fundamentally asymmetrical given the dependency of children, the duties and responsibilities of adults, etc.'. This remains an unresolved dilemma and it points to one of the core arguments underpinning the book and that is the need to see rights, duties, citizenship and agency as all embedded in networks of intergenerational relationships. While the CRC remains a landmark achievement in the history of childhood and many gains have been made, James (2011: 177) argues: 'Irrespective of their rights as enshrined in the CRC, a continued reliance on the determinism of the development paradigm will work to legitimize adults' power over children. It is this that enables adults to ignore the interdependency that necessarily characterises all social relations.' It is within this context that children's agency needs to be contextualised and problematised. Again, it underscores the importance of generation as an ongoing, overarching framework impacting on many aspects of children's everyday lives. The next chapter fleshes out the messy interplay between children's agency and their generational positioning.

QUESTIONS FOR DISCUSSION

1. Why are Article 3 and Article 12 considered as the two most important Articles of the CRC?
2. Are children's rights compatible with adults' rights?
3. How does the notion of 'lived' citizenship enhance understandings of children's citizenship?
4. Critically evaluate Rehfeld's recommendations for promoting children's political citizenship. Do you find his claims regarding the impact of these recommendations convincing?

Recommended Reading

Archard, D. and Skivenes, M. (2009) 'Balancing a Child's Best Interests and a Child's Views', *The International Journal of Children's Rights*, 17, 1–21.

Freeman, M. (2000) 'The Future of Children's Rights', *Children and Society*, 14, 277–93.

Lansdown, G. (2001) *Promoting Children's Participation in Democratic Decision Making*, Florence, Italy: Innocenti Research Centre, Innocenti Insight 6.

Lister, R. (2007) 'Why Citizenship: Where, When and How Children?', *Theoretical Inquiries in Law*, 8, 2, 693–718.

Moosa-Mitha, M. (2005) 'A Difference-Centred Alternative to Theorization of Children's Citizenship Rights', *Citizenship Studies*, 9, 4, 369–88.

Rehfeld, A. (2011) 'The Child as Democratic Citizen', *The Annals of American Academy of Political and Social Science*, 633, 141–66.

6

BRIDGING STRUCTURE AND AGENCY: BRINGING IN INTER- AND INTRA-GENERAGENCY

Chapter Aims

1. To develop an understanding of why some childhood theorists view generation as an essential component of contemporary childhood.

2. To unpack and critically consider the claim that children are active agents.

3. To introduce and illuminate the concept of generagency and its two components: inter-generagency and intra-generagency.

4. To demonstrate the usefulness of generagency as a framework for understanding how children practise agency.

Learning Objectives

By the end of this chapter you should:

1. Be aware of the complexity behind the claim that children are active agents.

2. Clearly understand the importance of generation in understanding childhood.

3. Have a general understanding of the concept of generagency and be able to distinguish between inter-generagency and intra-generagency.

4. Be able to apply generagency as a framework for exploring and illuminating children's relationships with adults and with each other.

The concepts of structure and agency have underpinned some of the core arguments of the book thus far. While these twin concepts could be regarded as outdated, they continue to exert a considerable influence on sociological theory and serve as a useful framework for bringing together the themes outlined in previous chapters. The relationship between structure and agency is by no means straightforward but it lies at the heart of much theorising about children and their childhood. In Chapter 3, I outlined childhood as a structural component of 'western' societies, while Chapter 4 focused on children as active actors who through their micro everyday lives exhibit various forms of agency. Chapter 5 introduced additional complexities in adults' structural positioning in terms of their overarching presence in the burgeoning industry around children's rights, bringing to the fore potential limits to children's agency and highlighting ongoing difficulties surrounding balancing children's rights with their need for protection. The chapter also gave examples to suggest that balancing children's rights with adult rights is fraught with challenges. In this chapter, the focus is on bringing to the fore, in much more detail, the ongoing messy relationship between structure and agency and how sociology contributes an understanding to these concepts and their relevance to children and childhood. According to Qvortrup (2011), the balance between structure and agency is one of the most significant issues for childhood studies. This reflects Giddens' (1979: 69) often cited statement: 'Every act which contributes to the production of a structure is also an act of production, and as such may initiate change by altering the structure at the same time as it reproduces it.'

Valentine (2011) argues that Giddens' notion of structuration has been especially influential in childhood studies. This is because Giddens tries to move beyond the structure–agency dichotomy by suggesting that the two concepts are interrelated. Hence, rather than asking whether structures influence people or people influence structures, Giddens articulates how structures are both constraining and enabling. Individuals continually, routinely, habitually make choices (Bourdieu, 1977) within the constraints that they face, and in doing so create and recreate the social institutions that surround their daily lives. While Valentine goes on to articulate some problems with the application of structuration theory in understanding children and childhood, and this will be returned to later, the interplay between structure and agency sets the scene for the core themes that will be explored in this chapter. The chapter commences by suggesting that generation is a fundamental structuring device for understanding children and childhood, and the work of core theorists who take this approach will be outlined. This will pave the way for a discussion of agency and its various meanings. Attempts to fuse the two concepts together and their implications for understanding the interlocking processes of structure and agency, as played out in children's lives, will be articulated through the concept of generagency, which is further sub-divided into inter-generagency and intra-generagency. The meaning of these terms and their potential to serve as a useful framework for bridging the gap between childhood as a structural entity and children as active agents will be outlined.

Generation

In Chapter 3, I drew on the work of Qvortrup, who is one of the most influential exponents of the view that generation is crucial for understanding childhood. Qvortrup argues that childhood must be understood at the aggregate level. It is children's collective location in childhood which should be of interest to childhood theorists rather than individual differences among children. As Saporiti (1994: 193) puts it, 'whereas children are the unit of observation, childhood should be the unit of analysis'. As outlined in Chapter 3, Qvortrup charts how children's exclusion from the labour market and the subsequent introduction of compulsory education set in motion new conceptions of childhood as a distinct phase of life separate from adulthood. This separation became entrenched through a host of state institutions which used generation as a structuring device to regulate the everyday lives of children and firmly establish childhood as a generational phase of life largely distinct from adulthood. While Qvortrup divides the adult generation into two groups, separating out the elderly who are also excluded from the labour market, he sees the latter as holding political power and clout as voters, in opposition to children, who have no such power. He articulates this as an opposition between generations for dwindling resources in which the older generation holds the upper hand. Qvortrup (2009) argues that while childhood is simultaneously characterised by continuity and change as children move in and out of childhood, nonetheless the structuring of generational relationships continues, although the form and content of these relationships may vary over time and place.

Alanen (2001) also takes the view that generation is essential to understanding childhood and the relationship between childhood and adulthood. She argues that generation as a structural feature of society can be considered as similar to other macro-structural components such as gender, class and ethnicity. She draws on Mannheim's (1952) work on generations as a useful tool for understanding children and childhood as a generational category. While Mannheim (1952) did not specifically focus on children, other than to suggest that awareness of generation may begin in adolescence, his thesis on generation has been appropriated by childhood theorists such as Alanen, as a useful filter for understanding the positioning of children within the category of childhood. Mannheim argued that generational cohorts based on age may share and experience a common history and this may lead them to develop a sense of solidarity. Through living through the same historical, political and cultural period, cohorts develop similar attitudes, which can turn into a shared consciousness that could facilitate social transformation.

According to Mayall (2013), the concept of generation is crucial in enabling us to draw out interconnections and interdependencies between adulthood and childhood. In adopting a generational approach, Alanen (1994) draws on feminism as a theoretical model to justify an understanding of childhood from the standpoint of children. She argues that just as the gender system was structured to promote patriarchy, generations are structured to promote 'adult-archy'. Society is not only gendered but also 'generationed'. Alanen suggests (1994: 38) that 'a sociology of childhood would need to take into account the origins and development of the generational system, of childhood and adulthood as both ideological and practical social constructions'. She turns to the lessons learned from the rise of academic feminism in the 1970s, whereby feminists documented the systematic male bias in social science research and argued for the need to introduce new topics based on women's standpoints in order to address their former exclusion. She argues that initially the response to the challenges posed by feminists was to 'add women and stir' so that gender became a variable that was increasingly applied to research designs, which then sought to uncover differences in the social conditions and experiences of men and women. However, the perspective also elevated issues that were once considered 'trivial' or marginal to mainstream sociological analysis, such as housework (Oakley, 1974).

Alanen draws a parallel between women's studies and childhood studies, and argues that just as women's studies moved women to a more visible and important location within mainstream sociology, so too has childhood studies moved children centre stage. Moreover, just as feminism highlighted the relational aspects of social life between men and women, childhood studies need to illuminate the relational aspects of everyday life between adults and children. They also need to articulate the myriad ways in which power impacts on these relationships. Social life is organised around other powerful systems, such as class and ethnicity, and Alanen argues that her account could be extended to these other systems, but for manageability she uses gender as a core framework through which to highlight the existence of these systems and their implications for children and childhood. However, she cautions against taking her analysis too far in terms of focusing on similarities between women and children as 'muted groups' (Hardman, 2001: 502), as women, as part of the adult generation, exert power over children and their childhoods. At the same time, she argues that this power may have different manifestations for the generational relationships between adult women and children and adult men and children.

To be effective, Alanen (2011) argues that the sociology of childhood needs to move beyond simply making children visible. It necessitates unpacking and challenging social theory which has, for the most part, been written on the presumption that the social world is an adult world (one that children fit into through socialisation). It also needs to illuminate how children's relationships with the social world are systematically and repeatedly structured around generation, which impacts fundamentally on how children practise agency. Generational relationships locate children and adults in particular relational positions and it is from within and between these positions that both act and impact on the world around them.

Narvanen and Nasman (2004) are very critical of Qvortrup and Alanen's usage of generation and their criticisms are worth outlining in some detail here. They suggest that the work of both has had a significant impact on childhood studies but that their views have not been subject to 'critical discussion and are, thus, uncontested' (2004: 71). In relation to Qvortrup, Narvanen and Nasman argue that his usage of the term generation is conceptually vague. They suggest that his usage could be more adequately captured under the notion of life phase – a term they prefer. Life phase concerns the social construction of life stages (including but not limited to childhood) and how they remain stable or change over time. For example, in the book *Growing Up and Growing Old*, Hockey and James (1993) examine the various stages an individual experiences throughout the life course and the meaning, stability, divisions and changes that occur over time. Drawing on insights from life course or life phase research, Narvanen and Nasman argue that understanding life processes means that analysis cannot be limited to the macro level – a methodological approach advocated by Qvortrup.

They draw on Mannheim's notion of generation to provide further criticisms of the work of both Qvortrup and Alanen. Mannheim argued that a person's affiliation with generation, while subject to modification, remains throughout the life course. However, Qvortrup's usage of generation is based firmly on age, thus once young people reach a certain age they leave one generation and enter another. Narvanen and Nasman argue that simply being born during a particular time period is not by itself enough to typify a generation in the Mannheim usage of the concept. Mannheim's conceptualisation of generation has three components: generation as a location (the sense in which, according to Narvanen and Nasman, Qvortrup uses the term), generation as an actuality and generation as a unit. For the second and third aspects of generation, individual members of a generation must actively reflect on their shared experiences and use their common location to implement change, or at the very least draw on their common experiences 'consciously to penetrate, question and problematize, for example, the knowledge and ideas created and passed on by previous generations' (2004: 80).

This obviously has implications for agency, particularly the ability of very young children to critically reflect on their positioning and shared experiences, and brings to the fore questions around the ontology of the child. Narvanen and Nasman further question whether children can be considered as a generation. They argue that the life span from birth until 18 years of age seems very long for a generation. How could collective experiences emerge from within such a vast age range? How could 3-year-olds share common experiences with 17-year-olds? How could each engage in shared intellectual reflections? These questions are important but they do not detract from the positioning of children within a generational order. Instead, they draw attention to the fallacy of considering children as a homogenous group within this generational order. Hence, rather than abandoning the concept altogether, their criticisms highlight the need for a framework that would tease out age differences within the broad positioning of childhood as a generational location.

While noting these criticisms, my argument here is that generation remains useful for understanding children and childhood. Qvortrup (2011) acknowledges that there is 100% mobility from childhood to adulthood. However, he argues that his dual conception of childhood as a temporary period for individual cohorts of children and its status as a permanent form with constantly evolving membership can and do co-exist. Hence, childhood is both dynamic and enduring. As he puts it (2011: 26): 'When this child grows up and becomes an adult, his or her childhood comes to an end, but childhood as a form does not go away and will stay there to receive new generations of children.' The notion of generation underscores the relational aspects of childhood, therefore understanding childhood also necessitates understanding adulthood. Agency also has to be understood within this relational context. How children and adults relate to one another is essential for understanding the opportunities and constraints under which children practise agency and can be considered as agentic. Qvortrup and Alanen both argue that power permeates relationships between adults and children. This is not to simplistically imply that adults have power while children are powerless, but rather that children's ability to act emanates from within these power relationships. Within these relationships, children adopt, resist, challenge and negotiate their positioning and the positioning of the adult generation. Alanen (2011: 170) argues that empirical research drawing on generation as a conceptual lens could reveal:

> (1) those structures that can be identified as specifically generational, (2) the interdependent positions that these generational structures define for generational groups to take and to act from, and (3) the social and cultural practices of positioning – both self- and other positioning – through which the current generational structures, and the generational order as their composite structure, are generated, maintained and (occasionally) transformed.

I will illustrate this below in relation to the notion of generagency, but before turning to this it is necessary to unpack in more detail what is meant by agency.

Children's Agency

While children may be viewed as occupying a distinct social category based on generation and similar to other categories such as class or gender, they are also viewed as social actors who influence the world and the worlds of those around them. Chapter 4 presented a range of research which illuminates the multiple ways in which children exercise agency at work, in the family, in education and through their play. However, for the most part, children's agency is an abstract concept, taken as an established fact rather than the meanings of agency being articulated and critically unpacked. As Wyness (2015: 7) comments: 'there is some conceptual ambiguity over the nature of children's agency. In part, this is due to agency's taken-for-granted status, a largely assumed conceptual starting point.' Hence, childhood researchers adopting a micro analysis often make quite bland statements regarding the ability of children to make decisions and then relate this decision making to agency. In the process, agency remains something of a 'black box'. Kieser (1999: 162) remarks that 'the use of agency theory in sociology is in its infancy', while Alexander (1993) suggests that sociology tends to have an over-romantic (western) notion of agentic individuals.

Valentine (2011), for example, argues that a minimal meaning of agency employed by some childhood sociologists is to view agency as acting purposively so that almost every conceivable action becomes defined as expressing agency. She quotes from Alderson et al. (2005: 79) who accord young babies with demonstrating agency and resistance through their reactions to adult care:

> The babies' share in promoting and sustaining their basic health care, such as, with difficulty, breathing and feeding, could be taken as evidence of their incipient responsibilities. … Their agency as rights holders was interpreted during our interviews with parents and staff in the babies' positive responses and possible resistances; babies' crying out for care, wriggling into a comfortable position.

I recently examined a PhD where the student defined agency as 'any act which produces a different outcome'. The student was focusing on children's attitudes and experiences of childrearing practices in middle- and working-class families. One example of agency given by the student, which she defined as an exemplary illustration of her conception of agency, was the refusal of some children to go to bed at the specific time designated by their parents. This was defined as expressing resistance and producing a different outcome as bedtime was extended for a brief period of time. However, there are a number of problems with this kind of analysis. First of all, agency does not necessarily imply resistance. Children who go to bed at the time specified by parents choose to do so. So, could following parental rules be seen as practising agency? Foucault (1982) reminds us that power is present even in the most restrictive of locations and among groups seen as powerless, while Giddens (1984) and Bourdieu (1977) remind us that habitual and routine forms of behaviour are by no means devoid of agency. Were relationships between parents and children transformed by those children whose actions 'produced a different outcome'? The example could be related to Alexander's (1992) notion of 'moments of freedom'. The student was unable to demonstrate any wider significance to this act. The parents who took part in her study still had control over bedtime, subject to some minor adjustments. The act of going to bed later did not mean that all other parental rules were open to negotiation. The example suggests that relationships between parents and children are likely to be messy and multifaceted. But it reminds us that agency needs to engage with actors' responses to situated circumstances. It also suggests that individual action takes place in a world of social structures. How, then, can we understand such actions? Viewing children as social actors is the most significant aspect of the 'new paradigm' for the study of children and childhood. To think through children's agency, we need to consider other elements such as intentionality, reflectivity, intended (and unintended) consequences. These notions bring to the fore questions around children's competency. Time is another important notion. Children's temporary location in the time period of childhood influences their capacity for independent action yet most studies of agency do not incorporate a time dimension (Hitlin and Elder, 2007). Each of these elements is linked so theories of agency need to explore and illuminate the dynamic interplay within and between these elements.

One of the most influential accounts of the relationship between time and agency is provided by Emirbayer and Mische (1998). They argue that agency involves a temporally embedded process of interaction that draws on the past and projected future to impact on action in the present. The past represents the habitual aspect of agency. Actors draw on past action and routinely repeat this action, giving stability and order to the present. Emirbayer and Mische argue that in imagining alternative possibilities, actors turn towards projected futures. Habits and routines may be reconfigured in light of their hopes, fears and desires for the future and their anticipation of future interactional relationships. In other words, actors act in the present but their action is shaped by the past, which is not stable but constantly reinterpreted in the present and may involve an anticipated future (Hitlin and Elder, 2007). These processes impact on the agency practised in the present. Actors make choices based on their perceptions of the past and future and reflect on possible alternative strategies for action. These orientations operate simultaneously, although in certain contexts and during certain time periods one may gain precedence over the other two. Their core point is that contexts are both temporal and relational and 'are themselves ever changing and thus always subject to re-evaluation and reconstruction on the part of the reflective actor' (2007: 175). Hence, actors are located in multiple, overlapping and temporally evolving relational contexts. Thus, the relationships within which action takes place are dynamic rather than fixed and unchanging.

Drawing on the notion of 'bidirectionality', which implies an interactive process of socialisation and accords the child a central role, Kuczynski (2003) and Lollis (2003), working from the perspective of psychology, outline the crucial impact of time on interactional relationships. Their work demonstrates the blurred boundaries between psychology and sociology in relation to the child as active agent. Kuczynski and Lollis both make the obvious point that adult–child relationships develop through interaction. However, they make a distinction between one-off interactions and repeated interactions that bring individuals together over time. They focus specifically on parent–child relationships, which Kuczynski suggests are based on recurrent, reciprocal exchanges during which each influence the other's behaviour, but they suggest that their conceptions are extendable to other enduring adult–child relationships. Their purpose is to explore the interconnections between past, present and future as played out in repetitive relationships. As parents and children interact over time, each subsequent interaction draws on past interactions. Parents and children bring into each present interaction some knowledge and a perception of previous interactions. Their past history may impact on their perceptions of future interactions and both the past and the future may impact on their current interaction. Lollis (2003) argues that perceptions of the past do not necessarily depend on accurate memories but go through processes of deconstruction and reconstruction, whereby each party to the current interaction reinterprets the past, and while the future has yet to be realised, recreated pasts produce anticipated futures. Where relationships are durable, past experiences may create mutual expectancies about current and future behaviour. Both parents and children contribute to the formulation of the past, present and future. Each may have expectations of how the other will respond in the current interaction based on past experiences. Whether or not these expectations are realised will impact on future interaction and, if unanticipated responses are forthcoming, then adjustments may be made for future interactions. The overarching point being made here is that adult–child relationships are far from static and are likely to be dynamic and transformative.

In relation to the sociology of childhood, this underscores the 'new' sociology of childhood claim that childhood needs to be considered as a social construction open to historic and cultural variation. How agency is practised needs to incorporate this time dimension. Childhood itself is also a temporal stage. Children may accept their 'limited' agency in the present because they can project to a future where their agency becomes more pronounced or where their resources for practising agency become less problematic. Hence, they may acknowledge that their present location within childhood is subject to continual re-evaluation, is likely to be challenged and reformulated and, even if durable, is applicable to constantly evolving new groups of children, rather than being a static condition. Moreover, James and James (2004) argue that children's actions over time might lead to structural change so it is difficult to limit agency to the immediate act. Hence, considering children as agents may necessitate an extended temporal focus.

I now turn to intentionality and reflectivity. At a basic level, the agentic child should act with intention or purpose. Agency implies intentionality which is generally achieved through goal-orientated action. The child should be able to attach meanings to his or her action and to reflexively ponder on the action and anticipate its consequences. Since children and adults may have different goals, the child may engage in action which goes against the adult's wishes or intentions. Chapter 4 gave a range of examples where children at work, at school, in their families and during leisure periods acted in purposeful ways to achieve goals not condoned or intended by adults. However, Moran-Ellis (2013) accuses childhood sociologists of not making clear enough the distinctions between meaning making, action and agency so that action is seen as tantamount to agency. But do they differ and, if so, in what ways? Quoting Giddens (1984: 22), Moran-Ellis argues that a simple solution is to ask the 'purposive' actor who 'has reasons for his or her activities and is able, if asked, to elaborate discursively upon those reasons'. But Moran-Ellis notes a number of problems with the application of Giddens' notion of discursive abilities of actors to account for their actions, when applied to children, particularly young children. This relates to the inability of very young children to communicate in meaningful ways with adults, partly because of adults' constructions of child talk and partly because of children's cognitive abilities or inexperience in imagining and articulating their actions as purposeful and with the capacity to act otherwise. Drawing on Willmott (1999), Moran-Ellis brings another problematic aspect of intention to the fore. She argues that the capacity to be agentic depends on the power and resources available to agents to implement or achieve their intentions, and since these are differentially distributed then children may have much greater difficulty than adults in realising their intentions. Nonetheless, Moran-Ellis argues that it is still possible to empirically observe even very young children acting purposively and effectively, and indeed some examples were given in Chapter 4. But questions around intentionality remain, as it may be adult childhood researchers who through their 'child friendly' methods determine whether or not children act intentionally and with purpose.

How power is defined is also important. Childhood sociologists point to the asymmetrical power relationships that exist between adults and children and see this as an enduring feature of all adult–child relationships. In this conception, adults have ultimate power over children. However, for Lollis (2003) power should not just be seen vertically but also horizontally. In a similar vein, Kuczynski (2003) argues that just to see power in vertical terms leads to a static, mechanised conception of power which locates it fundamentally in adults' capacity to coerce children into doing what they want. This one-dimensional conception of power pays too little attention to what adults and children actually do in daily interactions and ignores the give-and-take reality of most adult–child relationships. Lollis (2003) notes that if we turn to parent–child relationships as an example, we see power played out within these interdependent relationships. This leads Kuczynski (2003: 15) to suggest that power in parent–child relationships should be conceptualised as 'interdependent asymmetrical power'. In this view, both children and parents have resources to draw on in their interactions with each other and this applies even to very young children. In other words, children are never powerless in adult–child interactions. For example, coercion often does not produce the desired outcomes, with negotiation emerging as a better tool for reconciling conflicts between parents and children. Parents may use reasoning and persuasion to get children to engage in what they perceive as desired actions. Lollis (2003: 72), for example, suggests that 'parents attempt to influence the children's behaviour by means of requests, commands, prohibitions, threats, punishment, with the objective of securing children's compliance or cooperation with the parent's agenda'. This implies that there are limitations on parental power to shape what children do. Children may also engage in acts of non-compliance. They may undermine and evade parents' attempts to influence their behaviour, actions and movements. They may question parents' authority, negotiate compromises or respond in such a mechanical way that the power of the adult to enforce coercion is severely comprised. Moreover, children may adopt strategies to achieve future- rather than present-orientated goals. In all these ways, children interpret, evaluate, accept and resist the power of adults and the manner and context in which it is transmitted.

How does this impact on agency? For Kuczynski (2003: 9), 'agency means considering individuals as actors with the ability to make sense of the environment, initiate change, and make choices'. Using this definition, he considers adults and children as possessing equal agency. Both adults and children can make sense of each interaction, and within each interaction there are choices available, which may subsequently bring about change. However, most childhood sociologists would call into question Kuczynski's notion of equal agency. In relation to children and the structural location of childhood as an inferior status to adulthood with adulthood backed formally and informally by myriad resources, the structural forces facing children may be greater than their ability, individually or collectively, to mobilise their agency. Hence, their resulting actions may only be manifested in multiple and, in many cases, individual incidents of resistance, while the dominant framework remains largely intact, calling into question children's ability to implement change on a structural level. Moreover, while the structural conditions under which all actors, whether adults or children, act may impact on the ability to be agentic, Moran-Ellis (2013: 325) argues that young children will face specific hurdles due to three factors:

> one is the nature of the institutionalisation of their lives; the second is the dominance of intergenerational relationships which positions them as development actors and hence repositions their actions as material for learning and correcting; the third is their limited access to resources they can mobilise in support of their own intentions.

What this suggests is that adults and children have differing access to resources, which renders problematic any possibility of agency being seen as an equal process. It also fundamentally depends on how agency is defined. Is it a possession of the individual? Or is it located in the hierarchal structures that continue to influence how childhood is experienced in relation to adulthood?

These questions reflect some of King's (2007) criticisms of the theoretical aspects of the 'new' sociology of childhood, which were outlined briefly in Chapter 2. Here, I want to return to his work and focus in more detail on his critique of the 'new' sociology of childhood's conception of children's agency. Using Luhmann's (1995) theory of social systems, King argues that the 'new' sociology of childhood presents a very selective account of the social construction of childhood. For Luhmann, society is made up of a set of social systems all communicating about the social world. Each social system has its own distinctive way of understanding and processing the social world and each system exists within the environment of other systems, with each claiming scientific status for its version of reality. But each system constructs in advance the lens through which its claims are made and analysed. It is within this framework that the 'new' sociology of childhood communicates 'facts' about children. This involves making ontological claims about children and emphasising the false gap between children and adults in terms of one being seen as incompetent while the other is rendered competent. Hence, the 'first-order observations' of the social system of the 'new' sociology of childhood is based on these assertions. The 'second-order observations' refer to the 'new' sociology of childhood's goal to prove its claims through empirical research, but it does this from within the perspective it has already set up for itself as part of its 'first-order observations'. Part of this involves demonstrating that children, like adults, possess agency. It does this through a host of small-scale micro studies, illustrating how what children do makes a difference to micro relationships, and then communicates findings to other childhood sociologists who share its pre-existing ideological beliefs. This leads King to suggest that the sociology of childhood produces 'information' rather than 'facts' about children. The ultimate irony for King (2007: 200) is that the 'new' sociology of childhood 'minimises differences between them [children] and adults while at the same time retaining the children/adults distinction as the binary code of the system'.

What is particularly problematic for King is the sociology of childhood's usage of the concept of agent. He asks 'is it the same "social agent" as exists in social theory, that is an agent capable of bringing about changes in social structures or has the concept mutated in entering the pedagogical programme of children's autonomy?' (2007: 207). This brings to the fore the tendency of some childhood researchers to see agency as the property of the self. This has led to a plethora of small-scale micro studies based on illustrating children's subjective, active, mean-ing-making everyday activities. However, most childhood sociologists acknowledge that agency is an interactional accomplishment rather than a property of indi-viduals (Moran-Ellis, 2013). But empirical demonstrations of this are often restricted to examples of children making a difference to a micro relationship or a set of micro relationships, with much less attention given to their impact on the wider macro-generational order. Hence, while agency is practised in interactions with others and these interactions are variable, they are often imbued with power. This leads King to question whether, singly or collectively, all these incidents of children affecting the behaviour of others in micro settings have facilitated wider change at the macro level. Drawing on Giddens' conception of agency, King argues that the theory of agency necessitates actions contributing to social change or actions having the ability to resist social change. It is in this vein that King notes that the 'new' sociology of childhood's claims about the agency of the child fall short. As he puts it:

> the account of the child as 'social agent' owes much more to the new sociologists of childhood's preferred image of rational, competent, self-controlled children than to any evidence that the social institutions on which society depends actually change themselves as the direct result of children's concerted actions and that these changes reflect what the children wanted or intended. (King, 2007: 208)

I am not suggesting here that because of all these problems, children should not be considered as agents. To make such a claim would clearly be tantamount to labelling children as sub-human. Part of the human condition and what separates humans from matter is the ability of humans to reflect on what they are going to do, to think over possible alternatives and to ponder likely outcomes. Whatever choices are made, humans could always have acted otherwise. There are a number of path-breaking, small-scale studies of children, particularly in relation to children making decisions about their medical treatment or responding actively and competently in dealing with terminal illness (Alderson and Montgomery, 1996; Bluebond-Langner, 1978), which richly illustrate the myriad ways in which children strategically interact with the world around them and impact on the lives of others. Moran-Ellis (2013), for example, argues that children may act in strategic ways and be seen as competent actors and agents, even if they are not able to change their situation. But to illustrate agency solely through a range of small-scale social settings does not fully engage with the thorny issue that while actors act, they usually do so under circumstances not of their own choosing (Marx, 1974).

My point is that childhood sociologists should make more explicit the way in which they are conceptualising agency. Fuchs (2001: 30), for example, suggests that the interesting question for sociologists should be 'why some observers use "individual" or "intention" to make sense of an event or a result and why different observers use, say, social structure instead' (sometimes to explain the same event). Fuchs argues that rather than treat structure and agency as dual processes, they should be considered as variations along a continuum. Hence, 'instead of persons and agency, sociology might start with variations in social structures' (Fuchs, 2001: 30). Emirbayer and Mische (1998) argue that structure and agency are mutable processes. Empirical social action is never completely structured (or determined) but neither is agency ever completely free of structure. The empirical challenge then becomes one of 'locating, comparing and predicting the relationship between different kinds of agentic processes and particularly structuring contexts of action' (1998: 1005). This involves the recognition that actors' engaged responses to situational circumstances may initiate different forms of agency. The way forward, according to Hitlin and Elder (2007), is to map out how different types of agency emerge in different situated contexts.

Unresolved Tensions

In a recent book, *The Agency of Children*, Oswell (2013) outlines what he sees as five unresolved myths in sociological accounts of children and childhood and their implications for the structure–agency debate. Some of these myths have been articulated above but they are worth revisiting here. The first mistakenly focuses on 'the myth of the individual child'. In so doing, the notion of children as fundamentally social beings becomes undermined and capability becomes defined as an individual trait rather than emerging from within situated contexts. Traits are not possessions of individuals but emerge from and are interpreted through children's relationships with other children and with adults. This paves the way for the second myth around seeing children and adults as occupying separate worlds. This presupposes that children and adults have separate identities emanating from this division. Oswell suggests that the notion of a structurally universal 'generative binary' between adults and children is false and does not allow for social and cultural differences. As he puts it, 'it nevertheless is repeated as a constant structure such that the child is not adult and the adult is not child' (2013: 265). This is perhaps overstating the case. There are numerous accounts of social, cultural, economic and political diversity in manifestations of both childhood and adulthood which nevertheless keep the binary intact. Moreover, age as a device for locating the child in a specific structural setting is open to varying interpretation within and between different local, regional, national and global settings. For example, the age of criminal responsibility is particularly revealing in terms of specific instances where the child is labelled as an adult and where decisions around the ontology of the child are clearly problematic and political. This suggests that there is no overarching universal binary separation, yet this example also brings to the fore surviving adult notions of children as inherently evil and in need of punitive action to nip their wickedness in the bud.

In the third myth, Oswell extends his critique of binary divisions between adulthood and childhood to the 'myth of divided, separated and homogeneous space'. Here, Oswell makes a valid point – that so-called child-specific spaces, such as playgrounds, facilitating peer interaction also involve interactions with other people, and one presumes here that he is referring to adults. These adults do not necessarily need to be present. Playground designers may have conceptualised play space either with or without consultation with the subsequent users of such spaces, but nonetheless, in their deliberations, they are likely to have been motivated by adult attempts to capture what they may have defined, through adult eyes or interpretations, as child space. Of course, children's actual use of such spaces may challenge these pre-existing adult conceptualisations and promote all sorts of unintended usage. Oswell accepts that many childhood sociologists recognise the blurred boundaries between adulthood and childhood, but suggests that this acknowledgement does not go far enough as notions of neat, fixed, homogeneous spatial divisions continue to dominate thinking. This leads to his fourth myth and that is the overwhelming location of children's agency within small-scale, local, micro interactions. How agency is being defined here is crucial. As outlined in Chapter 4, there are numerous studies of children's small-scale interactions across a range of micro settings, all purporting to demonstrate children's agency. This leads to Oswell's final and core myth and that is the 'myth of the social agent'. Here, reflecting the discussion above, Oswell challenges the notion of agency as an individual possession and suggests that 'agency neither starts nor finishes with any individual agent' (2013: 269). He also challenges binary constructions of agency as being active or passive, competent or incompetent and powerful or powerless. While I do not want to uncritically uphold these binary divisions, nonetheless the core argument pursued throughout this book is that agency, whether practised by adults or children, is always relational and this necessitates illuminating the binaries from within which agency is practised.

Generagency

I am introducing the concept of generagency as a potentially useful model for understanding these relational processes and the links between macro childhood and children's everyday lives. The 'gener' aspect of the concept involves acknowledging the ongoing relevance of generation for understanding the location of childhood and adulthood and the implications of this positioning for both parties. Both children and adults are part of a wider social order based on generation that permeates and demarcates everyday life. The 'agency' aspect of the concept recognises children as agents who actively construct their own everyday lives and the everyday lives of those around them, while emphasising the importance of locating children's agency within the positioning of childhood relative to adulthood. Hence, the term encapsulates the structural positioning of childhood while simultaneously acknowledging children's active agency in generational relationships. These relationships occur across and within two core dimensions, hence the concept is further articulated through the notions of inter-generagency and intra-generagency. The former focuses on relationships between children and adults, while the latter looks at relationships between children, from within their location in childhood. This acknowledges the need to move beyond the simplistic adult–child binary and suggests that continuity and change occur across and within these relationships.

Inter-generagency

I am using the term inter-generagency to refer to the myriad ways in which childhood and adulthood have to be performed and enacted across the various locations that make up the everyday lives of adults and children. The term underlines the fact that adults and children do not live in separate worlds, rather they share the same world but from different locations, based largely on generation. Hence, childhood, like adulthood, is a relational status. As a number of sociologists have pointed out, childhood is only meaningful in relation to adulthood. Each status only makes sense because of the existence of the other. This does not mean that these categories are in opposition to one another or can be reduced to a simplistic binary division. It is to suggest that boundaries exist between adulthood and childhood but, like all boundaries, these positions are not fixed and immutable but porous, fluid and constantly shifting and changing. Indeed, childhood is ultimately a temporary status as all children will one day become adults. It is also temporarily a universal status in that all adults were at one stage children. However, it would be inaccurate to imply that the category of childhood or indeed adulthood is homogeneous. Complex relationships are likely to exist within both childhood and adulthood and other factors, such as gender, ethnicity and class, are likely to impact on how each is experienced. Hence, while childhood and adulthood are distinct social categories, they are also dynamic and multidimensional categories. Locally, national and globally (at least in minority world countries), a host of formal and informal institutions and practices are premised on making relational distinctions between adults and children. If adults' and children's macro and micro lives are experienced relationally, then it makes sense to argue that agency may also be experienced and practised relationally.

Following Alanen (2011: 161), this approach emphasises that 'childhood and adulthood are produced and reproduced in the interactions taking place between members of existing generational categories – in other words, in intergenerational practices'. Alanen argues that through these everyday micro practices, the generational social structure simultaneously re-emerges. She takes the family as an example and here she stresses the need to think about the family in terms of the internal relationships between members. The position and nature of any one individual within the family is related to the holders of other positions such as the relationship between parent and child. These relationships are, for the most part, asymmetrical. However, this does not mean that agency is unidirectional. Within this broad asymmetrical relationship, children accept, resist, challenge and transform action in myriad ways, so that while relationships may be largely unequal, they are also interdependent and reciprocal and may also be impacted on by other structures such as gender. Hence, any focus on children's agency needs to acknowledge its variability.

Intra-generagency

Up to now, I have illustrated how societies are structured and organised in multiple ways around age. While the previous section underlined relationships between adults and children, the purpose of this section is to highlight through the concept of intra-generagency the heterogeneity of children's everyday lives within the structural location of childhood. It involves the recognition that children do not experience the structural boundaries between adulthood and childhood in uniform ways. Since children (like adults) are positioned differently in the social order around other structural variables such as gender, class and ethnicity, then clearly how these variables intersect with childhood needs to be taken into consideration. These other variables, like childhood, are social constructions and operate differently across varying time and space dimensions. But the core point to make here is that these variables interact socially and practically with generation. As Alanen (2011: 162) points out:

> the social world is not only simultaneously gendered, classed, 'raced' and so on; it is also organised in terms of generational ordering – it is also 'generationed' – and it is this insight that calls for structural and relational thinking in the sociology of childhood.

In some cases, children are confined to age-based institutions such as schools, while, in other instances, age locates childhood as a specific category and brings children together, enhancing their opportunities to develop a peer group identity. By spending a considerable part of their everyday lives in age-related contexts, children not only interact with adults but with each other, and in the process develop knowledge and understanding of how the social world is structured by age and how power relationships underpin age categorisations. At the same time, they do not simplistically reproduce prevailing norms. In practising agency, children appropriate, use and transform adult understandings of the social world. Working within the context of anthropology, Hardman (2001) was one of the first researchers to put forward the view that children are located in an 'autonomous world', in which they rework adult culture, thus demonstrating their capacity as social actors. In Chapter 4, in relation to education, I outlined three influential sociological studies that highlight the processes at work. These were Corsaro's (1985, 1997, 2015) work on peer cultures, Thorne's (1993) work on 'gender play' and Connolly's (1998) work on ethnicity. Each can be considered through the filter of generation because each draws on school as the location for the performance and rejection of adult rules and norms. Hence, the generational location of children in school settings based on age brings children together as a generation and provides a backdrop for enabling them to negotiate and renegotiate adult structures, often in ways not intended by adults.

While the above discussion focuses on how children appropriate and transform adult rules and expectations, agency needs also to be sensitive to differences between children and not just differences between adults and children. Hence, agency needs to accommodate not just what is shared between children but also what accounts for differences between children and how these differences are produced, reproduced, challenged and transformed. I have already outlined how age may impact on agency so that the opportunities and constraints experienced by 3-year-olds may be very different from those experienced by 13-year-olds, and the resources at their disposal and their ability to make independent choices are likely to vary widely. But even if we limit our focus to the same age group of children, gender, ethnicity and class will all impact on how children of the same age experience childhood. If we take economic resources as an example, a wealth of research suggests that privileged and disadvantaged adults will have differential access to power. Hence, power is not simply an adult attribute but is fundamentally connected to other structural factors such as class. The differing economic resources generated by class will impact on children's relationships with adults in the family, school experiences and access to work and play opportunities.

Figure 6.1 represents a tree of life showing how inter-generagency and intra-generagency are interrelated.

Figure 6.1 Generagentree: Bridging Structure and Agency

The figure presents a model of a tree of life, with the trunk of the tree representing the one world that both children and adults occupy. This is to underline the fact that children and adults do not occupy separate worlds but rather they stem from and exist in the same world. All action and agency emanate from membership of this one world. The tree branches in two broad directions, illustrating how children and adults are divided by generation, but the arrows showing 'inter-generagency' show the inter-linkages across this division, producing connections that operate in both directions from children to adults and vice versa. Hence, the branches indicate that generation plays a core role in structuring the world that both children and adults occupy, while simultaneously demonstrating how children and adults are concurrently linked and separated by generation. Moreover, the leaves of the branches suggest that generation is not simplistically equated with age. Figure 6.1 indicates that age is not a fixed state, hence it appears and reappears on various leaves. This is to illustrate that age is a dynamic rather than a static variable. Hence, age appears as a recurring feature of both children's and adults' lives. This is also to challenge notions of 'becoming' relating to children and 'being' relating to adults. Rather, through the repetition of the variable, age, the intention is to suggest that age impacts on all individuals as they journey through life. Age impacts in an active rather than a motionless way on how children experience their childhood, and their interactions with adults and with each other will differ along this continuum. Furthermore, age also impacts on adults and their engagement with children and with each other. For example, grandparents are likely to have different relationships with grandchildren compared to the relationships that exist between parents and children. Adult children will have different relationships with their parents as co-adults, rather than as children. However, the trunk of the tree highlights the ongoing importance of generation as an overall structuring framework.

Each branch of the tree has additional offshoots so that while age is a fundamental variable, in recognition that identities are likely to be multiple, age interacts with gender, class and ethnicity. These variables are also repeated on various branches throughout the tree to indicate the fluidity of each of these variables and to suggest that, individually and collectively, these variables may have varying impact on and consequences for individuals across the life course, and, of course, their engagement with these variables is likely to differ. The inclusion of these additional variables is to further challenge notions of universal, homogenous childhood and universal, homogenous adulthood. Rather, each is experienced within overlapping, additional, structural categories of class, gender and ethnicity, and agency is practised within and across these varying categories. Hence, these offshoots extend the notion of inter-generagency to its intra-generagency dimensions. Other offshoots could be added to the branches such as ability–disability, rural–urban, and so on. Some of the branches interconnect, showing how childhood and adulthood are intertwined in messy ways reflecting manifold processes at work. The crossing of the branches illustrates how inter-generagency and intra-generagency are simultaneously occurring practices. Moreover, they are not top-down processes, whereby the agency of adults supersedes that of children. Rather, the actions of adults impact on children but the actions of children also impact on adults. The tree could also be considered as a deciduous one rather than an evergreen tree. The leaves on deciduous trees drop away after their purpose is finished or when they are no longer needed. This also means that new leaves form every year at the top and bottom of the tree. The outworking of these complex, messy relationships could take multiple forms and the figure could be adapted to show additional connections. The variables outlined here are social constructions and emerge historically, culturally, socially and economically within specific societies and therefore may play out differently, but the figure could be adapted to reflect different local, national and international contexts. The core aim of Figure 6.1 is to present a general framework that illustrates the interplay between inter-generagency and intra-generagency, underlining the need to view agency as a relational process simultaneously occurring within and across generational relationships.

Applying Inter-generagency and Intra-generagency

I now draw on and revisit some of my earlier work to illustrate how these concepts work in practice. This work is limited to children's participation in housework and paid work. The research focuses on children aged 14–16, hence application of the processes at work may be more problematic for very young children. Indeed, Moran-Ellis (2013) argues that childhood sociologists have, for the most part, neglected the extent to which very young children can be considered as social actors. However, for the purposes of manageability and to illustrate my arguments through a re-examination of my own empirical work, the focus will be on older children. My intention here is to apply the dual concepts of inter-generagency and intra-generagency in order to articulate how the concepts bring added value to understanding and illuminating the interplay between the macro and micro aspects of children's everyday lives.

I am going to discuss three of my former research projects. Project A involves my PhD research into the formal and informal work strategies of adults and children from 150 households on a working-class Catholic estate in Belfast characterised by very high levels of unemployment (Leonard, 1994, 2005); 120 children aged 14–16 were interviewed as part of this research. This is the only one of the three projects to involve both adults and children. Project B involves survey data and classroom discussions with 446 young people aged 14–15 from

11 schools located in both the North and South of Ireland; six schools were located in Northern Ireland and five in the Republic of Ireland. The research was funded by the Royal Irish Academy and was concerned with examining young people's perceptions of and participation in housework (Leonard, 2004b, 2009). Project C was funded by Save the Children in Belfast and comprises questionnaire data from 545 young people aged 15–16 on their attitudes to and experiences of term-time employment. The questionnaire data was supplemented by focus group discussions with 94 young people (Leonard, 2002, 2003, 2004a).

All three projects were concerned with examining the everyday lives of children within their families, communities and among their peers through the lens of formal and informal work. Wider macro processes and their impact on families, and changing relationships between parents and children, were articulated in order to contextualise young people's everyday lives and experiences. For example, Project A was set within the specificity of Northern Irish society where decades of employment discrimination had resulted in high levels of working-class Catholic unemployment. In the working-class estate where the research was carried out, the majority of adults were unemployed or located at the lower end of the labour market and poverty was an endemic feature of daily life. The research focused on how households managed their poverty and the various informal work strategies they utilised to cope with or alleviate their situation. Households actively responded to their wider structural disadvantaged position by actively recreating social structures based on norms of reciprocity and ties of obligation. These networks were actively established as a way of challenging the state's inability to provide employment and were seen as political strategies rather than simply ways of coping with individual or community disadvantage.

I use the concept of social capital, defined by Putnam (1995: 67) as 'features of social organisation such as networks, norms and social trust that facilitate coordination and cooperation for mutual benefit', to understand these household and community networks. However, I point to the adult theorisation of social capital evident in the core accounts of Coleman (1988), Putnam (1995) and Bourdieu (1986), who, at the time, were leading commentators on the concept. There were two components to this thinking. First, there was a tendency to focus solely on strong or weak ties between adults, with social capital in the lives of children being considered as a by-product of their parents' relationships with others. The possibility of children creating their own social networks with adults or with their peers was unacknowledged in this literature. Second, there was a focus on the future convertibility of social capital into other forms such as human or economic capital. In relation to children, social capital was regarded as an asset they could draw on in the future, rather than in the present. In my research (Project A), I demonstrated how both conceptions were flawed by exploring how children perceive and make use of existing networks and, at times, create and manage new networks.

These networks occurred across adult and peer relationships. They emerged from the positioning of childhood within the wider community though children transcend this positioning. Children acted within but also across this positioning. In terms of inter-generagency, children's relationships with other adults outside the family drew on ties developed and sustained by adults' relationships with other adults within the neighbourhood. However, children forged relationships with a range of other adults outside their parents' networks and these networks facilitated their access to scarce resources. For example, many children ran errands for other adults and received small amounts of money which they used to buy mundane luxuries such as sweets, which their families could ill afford. Adults with no children, particularly older adults with grown-up children long departed from the family home, relied on children who provided these often daily services by making frequent visits to local shops for daily necessities such as bread and milk. Children actively developed networks with adults needing babysitting services. While within their families there was an expectation that older children would babysit younger siblings as part and parcel of family obligations and this often extended to the wider kinship network, children formed economic relationships with adults outside these networks and often independently of adults' connections. For this age group, babysitting emerged as either an unpaid family expectation or an autonomous paid choice, depending on the relationship between the child and the adult. Age and gender characterised how intra-generagency played out in this context. Older children, for example, had a greater level of autonomy from parents to form and sustain their own networks with other adults. Girls had more opportunities to babysit than boys because of wide gendered assumptions and expectations around caring roles and traits. In all these ways, social capital had use value in children's lives in the present rather than having perceived future exchange value.

Moreover, social capital was not limited to economic forms. The independent networks initiated by children provided them with a source of emotional capital. Many children derived emotional satisfaction from family, community and peer relationships. They embedded themselves in tight, collective social networks. One in three children stated that they did favours for other children and for adults. For example, some children ran errands for no payment for adults they perceived as particularly economically vulnerable. They used these favours as currency to embed themselves into reciprocal relationships with their peers and adults. These favours could be called in when needed. Of course, life for many of these children was characterised by poverty, but these strategies enabled some of them to play an active role in diluting family and wider community disadvantages and, at times, these networks were independent of those that existed for the adult members of households.

Notions of reciprocity and interdependence permeated Project B with its focus on teenagers' participation in housework. Widespread changes in Irish society, as in other European countries, have brought more and more women into formal employment and partly transformed the traditional household division of labour, which typically had involved mothers doing the bulk of housework. Over two-thirds of the overall sample of 446 children had mothers in employment. Many children noted how they returned from school to homes devoid of adults and hence had to fend for themselves. For example, some children outlined how they routinely made their own meals or often started dinner for their family because the school day was shorter than the adult working day. Older children took on 'adult' roles in their engagement with younger siblings. Some collected younger siblings from school, made snacks and ensured younger siblings commenced their homework, with many indicating that they actively drew on their more mature educational knowledge to help with homework. Some mothers were employed on flexible labour contracts and often were not entitled to sick pay. In these cases, sometimes older children were kept off school to look after younger children when they were sick, on the basis that the child missing a day of school was preferable to the mother losing a day's pay or potentially risking termination of an already precarious flexible employment contract.

Intra-generational factors impacted on the allocation of household tasks. In the majority of cases, girls performed more housework than boys and this was particularly revealing in households where male and female siblings were close in age, but where gender rather than age acted as the core device for adults' justification around who should do what. Some girls complained about having to do more housework than older male siblings because of dominant gendered expectations in their families and communities. For many Irish families, it remains the case that mothers do the lion's share of domestic work and hence children were presented with a model based on a highly gendered division of labour. However, while some children accepted this arrangement, others negotiated and contested the dominant gendered expectations within their families. Data from a sub-sample of 94 girls revealed that more than three-quarters perceived the allocation of domestic work within their households as unfair. They were adamant that they would not replicate this pattern if and when they formed their own households. While there was no follow-up study, nonetheless there was evidence of an erosion of taken-for-granted assumptions regarding traditional gender roles and duties, with children questioning rather than passively replicating existing household norms.

For the overall sample, responsibility for housework became a site of inter-generational and intra-generational negotiation. While the majority of children indicated that a level of compulsion and persuasion initiated by parents provoked their participation in housework, reasons were additionally punctuated by notions of mutual reciprocity and interdependency to characterise their intergenerational relationships within the household. Involvement in household chores was an ongoing negotiated and renegotiated process between household members.

For the most part, children saw their positioning within the household through the triple lens of autonomy, dependency and interdependence. At times, they carried out tasks allocated by parents without protest and, at other times, they resisted and avoided household chores. Non-compliance went beyond merely refusing to do household tasks and potentially incurring coercive responses from parents. Rather, children actively employed a range of tactics to avoid responsibility for household tasks. For example, some children were aware of the importance that parents placed on education and pretended that they had additional homework as a ruse to avoid household chores. In this way, they drew on dominant narratives around their positioning as 'human becomings' and played on the importance of education for their future career prospects as a way of avoiding participation in housework. Hence, they were able to actively exploit their childhood positioning in terms of knowing how to play on parents' dreams and ambitions for their future. Others persuaded and bribed siblings to undertake their chores. Sometimes children deliberately messed up tasks to avoid future participation. In this way, they actively and tactically brought together past, present and future in their performance of household tasks. Doing a bad job in the present would create a past memory in the minds of parents which could prevent future involvement in order not to repeat poor performance. Hence, children actively employed a range of strategies to avert responsibility for household chores.

At the same time, many children participated in household chores from a sense of moral responsibility and awareness of the interconnectedness of relationships within the household. Knapp (1999) suggests that parent–child relationships should be reformulated to take account of the fundamental moral responsibility each has for the other. Knapp argues that agency falsely implies autonomy and this model breaks down when applied to the real world of households where individual agents are located within collective units. In his view, it is problematic to consider family relationships in terms of actors operating as autonomous, rational selves. Rather, he suggests a model based on 'moral responsibility' (Knapp, 1999: 69), in turn based on the moral relationships in which the child is embedded. While Knapp argues that these relationships exist prior to the exercise of rational choice, it is more accurate to view these moral relationships as co-existing with rational choice and self-interest, so that family relationships function simultaneously as sites of cooperation and sites of resistance. In this example, inter-generagency and intra-generagency are practised through a range of negotiated interactions between adults and children and across children within households.

Project C was concerned with documenting the extent and significance of term-time employment among a sample of 545 15–16-year-olds; 47% had a current or previous term-time job. While newspaper delivery and babysitting emerged as the two most common types of paid child employment, children worked in a range of enterprises, including shops, cafes, pubs, offices and building sites. Participation differed along gender lines, with newspaper delivery being the most common type of job undertaken by males, while babysitting was the most common type of term-time work undertaken by females. The overall research themes were wide-ranging and included examining children's experiences of specific types of child employment such as newspaper delivery (Leonard, 2002) and their attitudes to and experiences of existing child labour legislation and their articulation of the right to work (Leonard, 2004a). But, for the purposes of this chapter, I want to draw on the inter-generational and intra-generational dimensions of child employment.

Many children felt that having a term-time job was the first step towards achieving adult status and moving away from parental control and interference. Having an income rather than pocket money gave children much more independence and autonomy over how this money was spent. Some children contributed to the household and their earnings enhanced the economic viability of their households. Others spent money on personal items and stated that because they had earned this money, their parents gave them independent control over spending earnings. Hence, term-time employment challenges taken-for-granted assumptions and dominant frameworks that locate school pupils as dependents within the household. Access to term-time employment enabled some children to achieve an element of independence within relationships that simultaneously remained dependent. Their relationships with adults within the household became less clear cut and more open to negotiation and renegotiation. Both children and adults could become accustomed to the shifting boundaries that were gradually emerging between childhood and adulthood.

Term-time employment also brought children into contact with a range of adults outside the household and positioned them as employees, co-workers and consumers. As in Project A, children who babysat often did so for relatives or friends of their parents, but some forged their own independent relationships with adults in their community not known by their parents. While of course one could argue that this enhances child risk, some children stated how they would vet prospective customers and then convince parents of their credibility. In this way, children developed their own adult networks independent of their parents' existing circles. Hence, their strategies reveal more complex patterns of ties between parents and children, whereby, at times, they drew on parents' social circles, while, at other times, they demonstrated agency in forging their own networks as sources of income. Many children suggested that their parents saw them as more responsible and self-reliant as a result of their capacity to earn an independent income.

While work and education are often seen as mutually incompatible in the lives of school pupils, children demonstrated an ability to make reasoned judgements in achieving a complementary balance between the two. This brought to the fore intergenerational relationships with parents and to a lesser extent with teachers. Children had to engage in a range of negotiations with these adults regarding the extent of their participation in paid employment. Children were aware of the importance parents placed on education and several discussed how parental permission was dependent on their ability to convince and prove to parents that grades would not be affected. But some children also demonstrated adherence to the importance of education in enhancing their future prospects. Hence, children themselves addressed the common fear expressed by adults that employment may have a negative impact on education. Some children gave up their term-time job or decided not to seek term-time work and gave an inability or unwillingness to reconcile the demands of studying while working as a core reason for leaving or deciding not to enter employment. Hence, children practised agency in weighing up the pros and cons associated with term-time employment, and for some deciding not to work was as much an active choice as deciding to take on a term-time job. A minority of children from disadvantaged economic backgrounds revised their educational intentions as a result of their participation in routine, mundane, repetitive work and suggested that these experiences had encouraged them to rethink their future career options, including staying on at school and obtaining a set of qualifications that would enable them to avoid permanent low-skilled jobs. While wider structural disadvantages may of course mitigate against the realisation of these re-evaluations, nonetheless these wider macro forces did not passively determine these working-class children's future employment intentions.

In relation to intergenerational relationships with teachers, many term-time workers felt that their participation in paid employment would not meet with teachers' approval. Indeed, in the majority of both the middle-class and working-class schools visited, study time was prioritised and term-time employment was actively discouraged. Only 16% of child workers felt that teachers would approve of their employment. Indeed, 68% of term-time workers indicated that teachers were unaware of their term-time jobs. Hence, children dealt with the perceived objections of teachers by not informing them that they worked outside school hours. Moreover, children actively sought a level of autonomy from the teacher's gaze and felt that their lives outside school were their own affair and should not be subject to the prying eyes of teachers. Hence, their silence regarding their term-time jobs enabled them to locate school and work as separate spheres. While accepting that the structure of school resulted in a lack of power, in this instance it also provided children with opportunities to demonstrate power through the withholding of information.

Child employment also enabled children to extend their relationships and interactions with adults beyond the commonly considered spheres of home and school. Children interacted with adults as employers and co-workers. Four out of five working pupils felt that they had a supportive relationship with their adult employers. They expressed similar attitudes to adult co-workers. Children felt that their relationships were less hierarchal than in other spheres of their everyday lives and some felt empowered by being considered as serious, valid workers. Of course, aspects of their working lives and conditions were far from ideal. Several were paid below the minimum wage and were aware that their capacity to provide cheap employment made them an attractive option to employers. Moreover, they had few employment rights and no trade union to argue on their behalf. Nonetheless, several considered their employment in positive terms and felt they were able to negotiate a more individualised conception of themselves as co-workers or employees, rather than as children.

The job search strategies of children drew on their intra-generational relationships. Children formed alliances with other children. Peer groups were an important source of information about jobs. Some children found out about jobs through their peer networks rather than through formal advertising or adult contacts. Often, jobs such as newspaper delivery work were passed on from older to younger children. Many children, in different types of jobs, recommended friends to employers. In all these ways, children brought their social ties into the labour market and, at times, created obligations between themselves and the children they recruited. The money earned from employment gave some children additional resources that could be used to fit in with more affluent peers. Children could buy into global teen culture through the independence given to them by their parents, enabling them to make autonomous decisions on how to spend earnings. While one could argue that global teen culture could also be viewed as a determining constraint of the wider social structure in that children could be coaxed by the industry to buy certain products, nonetheless, as outlined in Chapter 4, children's purchasing power also actively shapes this industry. The lens of generagency enables the interpenetration and dynamic interplay between structure and agency to come to the fore.

Conclusion

The concept of generagency brings together core themes that emerged within and across these three projects. In all three projects, children were located as dependents within their households, but they actively reworked this dependency through their involvement in a range of formal and informal work practices and strategies. The lens of generagency provides a tighter overall framework that brings more fully to the fore the extent to which agency can be considered as part of children's relationships with adults and with each other. I must admit that my original writing output on these projects did not develop in any significant way the interplay between structure and agency and how this plays out within and across generations. Yet, this framework was implicit and indeed explicit when the findings were considered. Revisiting this work through the lens of generagency brings more coherence to the overall findings and provides an effective lens to enable these relationships to be more adequately understood and theorised. It locates children's interactions with adults within a multitude of dynamic cross-cutting relationships. Children are simultaneously members of families, school pupils and workers, and these varying identities impact on their interactions with adults and peers. The structure and dynamics of each relationship may impact on other relationships and underscore the need to contextually place children within multiple settings. Across these varying spheres, children faced various contradictions and ambiguities in their interactions with adults.

Generagency and its offshoots of inter-generagency and intra-generagency act as potentially useful tools to enable childhood researchers to more effectively understand and illuminate the complexity of children's relationships with adults and with each other. This conceptualisation brings to the fore how in their everyday relationships with adults, engagement with the adult world and with each other, children demonstrate a range of competencies, choosing to accept, resist, modify and transform the often taken-for-granted assumptions on which adulthood and childhood are based. While the model uses existing concepts such as generation, structure and agency, it brings them together within an improved framework for highlighting connections between the three. Using this framework makes it possible to identify a rich variety of dynamic relationships between adults and children and within children's peer relationships. These collective encounters render the relationship between structure and agency as messy, blurred and full of internal complexities and contradictions. At the same time, I do not want to over-claim that this conception resolves the ongoing tensions between structure, agency and generation. Such tensions are unlikely to be resolved, and remain a defining element within childhood studies and a difficult endeavour in sociological analyses of the relationship between the child and society. This issue will be returned to in the final chapter.

QUESTIONS FOR DISCUSSION

1. Does Qvortrup offer a convincing explanation of why generation is so important for understanding contemporary childhood?
2. Outline and critically evaluate the extent to which children can be seen as active agents.
3. How useful is the concept of generagency in explaining how structure and agency impact on children's everyday lives?
4. Using examples, outline how inter-generagency and intra-generagency illuminate children's relationships with adults and with each other.

Recommended Reading

Alanen, L. (2011) 'Generational Order', in Qvortrup, J., Corsaro, W. A. and Honig, M. (eds) *The Palgrave Handbook of Childhood Studies*, London: Palgrave Macmillan.

King, M. (2007) 'The Sociology of Childhood as Scientific Communication: Observations from a Social Systems Perspective', *Childhood*, 14, 2, 193–213.

Narvanen, A. and Nasman, E. (2004) 'Childhood as Generation or Life Phase?', *Young*, 12, 1, 71–91.

Qvortrup, J. (2011) 'Childhood as a Structural Form', in Qvortrup, J., Corsaro, W. A. and Honig, M. (eds) *The Palgrave Handbook of Childhood Studies*, London: Palgrave Macmillan, pp. 21–33.

Valentine, K. (2011) 'Accounting for Agency', *Children and Society*, 25, 347–58.

7

CONCLUSIONS: BLURRED BOUNDARIES

The core aim of this book has been to highlight the significant contribution that sociology has made to the increasingly diverse field of childhood studies. As a 'magpie subject' (Blakemore, 2003: 3), childhood studies adopt concepts and approaches from a range of diverse disciplines, so much so that the ensuing hotch-potch of ideas creates confusion around different ways of knowing and the ontological basis on which they rest. Sociology has made a highly significant con-tribution to childhood studies; indeed it could be argued that many core themes in childhood studies reflect a parasite adoption of core sociological concepts. One of the enduring, central themes underpinning contemporary sociology is to under-stand, illuminate and bridge the divide between structure and agency. The relationship between structure and agency remains an ongoing conundrum and continues to exert a significant influence on current work within sociology, and how this impacts on the sociology of childhood has been demonstrated throughout the chapters in this book. The dichotomous association between structure and agency was viewed as a starting point for bringing to the fore and exploring other dichotomies as they apply to children and childhood. These include the gulf between childhood and adulthood, the disjunction between psychological and sociological approaches to understanding the connection between the biological and the social, the separation between traditional and 'new' sociological approaches to childhood and the chasm between macro and micro processes affecting both childhood and children. These dichotomies were challenged and were seen as blurred, overlapping, interdependent and messy, but they were used as a framework to demonstrate the tensions and contradictions that both adults and children must confront and negotiate.

In Chapter 2, I outlined how traditional psychological and sociological approaches to children and childhood position them as non-agents. These approaches tend to locate children in terms of their future potential, in terms of what values need to be transmitted for children to become well-adjusted adults, and in the process, children's lives in the here and now are marginalised, along with their perspectives on what socialisation and development mean to them as they go about their everyday lives. 'New' sociologists of childhood outline and demonstrate how children respond to this positioning and the active ways in which they accept, reject and modify their location as passive recipients of wider societal structures, processes and relationships. Yet, it is fair to say that an unresolved dualism continues to exist between structure and agency, and the increasing incorporation of children into the frameworks underpinning core theoretical debates does little to resolve ongoing tensions. In Chapters 3 and 4, I tried to achieve a balance between understanding childhood as a structural phenomenon and recognising children as meaning makers actively involved in constructing and reconstructing their everyday lives. As already outlined, the focus on children as active agents has been one of the most significant contributions of the 'new' sociologists of childhood. Drawing largely on Giddens' notion of structuration, structure and agency were viewed as mutual processes rather than disconnected entities. This means that structures are not just constraining but enabling and indeed inherently transformable. However, it remains unclear which holds the most weight. Does structure impact on the individual or structurally located group (i.e. children) more than the capacity to practise agency either individually or collectively, or does agency either individually or collectively impact on structure? Alternatively, have both equal weight and, if so, does either then have any explanatory value? I argued that one of the inherent weaknesses in accounts of children's agency is the seeming lack of transformative capacity of their actions. This calls into question children's agency in terms implied by Giddens (1984: 14), who states:

> To be an agent is to be able to deploy ... a range of causal powers, including that influencing those deployed by others. Action depends on the capability of the individual to make a difference to a pre-existing state of affairs or course of events.

While Chapter 4 outlined myriad ways in which children have a sense of agency, the practice of their agency suggests an ongoing thorny relationship between the outworking of this agency and its impact on a macro level, which remains muted. Willmott (1999) argues that accounts which give primacy to structure over agency fall short in capturing the scope for manoeuvre that differentially placed agents have over structure. On the other hand, accounts which emphasise agency over structure 'end up with agency being accorded an inordinate degree of interpretative freedom and the capacity to effect structural change as and when such change is desired' (1999: 8). The impasse for Qvortup (2009: 2) is that

> the point is not the classical argument about striking a balance between socio-economic circumstances and human agency; it is rather that the human interventions that make observable *societal changes* are adults'

rather than children's interventions. I do not by that say that children do not make a difference, but their activities do not count much among purposive changes at a societal level.

Hence to Qvortrup, while change is an ever-present possibility, generational differences between adults and children, their differential access to wider resources and distinct power bases, seem remarkably durable. The ongoing relevance of adult generational privilege was clearly evident in Chapter 5 where the CRC was highlighted as improving substantially the position of children in modern society, providing policy makers and others with renewed impetus to reshape what it means to be a young person. Yet, despite widespread advances, many children continue to live in poverty, do not have the vote, are restricted from various choices on the basis of age and are reliant on well-meaning adults to articulate their rights and needs. Moreover, the chapter used various examples to show that where adults' and children's interests clash, adults have the power and resources to hierarchically intervene. This reminds us that agency should not simply refer to the capacity for action but should include the capacity to have influence over the conditions that shape the context for action.

So where does this leave us in relation to the subtle interplay between structure and agency? At one level, Qvortrup is right in identifying childhood as an ongoing structural component of modern 'western' societies, and indeed the bulk of the material covered in this book outlines the limited capacity for children's agency to have a transformative impact on childhood's overall structural dimensions. Despite multiple accounts of children's agency, wider societal institutions continue to position children differently from adults. Adult-dominated political, educational and legal systems continue to have a profound impact on children. This is why, then, it is important to locate children's agency within generational relationships.

However, a number of qualifications are then necessary. Relationships between adults and children are co-dependent and interdependent. They are not mutually exclusive. Adulthood and childhood are mutually interactional processes and indeed only make sense relationally. Agency emerges from within these relationships. Agency is a practice, not a possession. One cannot be said to possess agency. Agency has to be enacted. At its most basic level, agency is often referred to as purposive human action, but this is too general and too narrow a definition. One could reduce almost every action to purposive action, and using this definition, then, to agency. So, for example, if I want to lift a pen off the table so that I can write a note, I am engaging in purposive action. My purpose is to lift the pen and begin writing. The pen has little part to play in this process. It cannot resist my attempts to lift it from the table. In this way, I have agency over the pen. I possess agency to interact with the pen, with the purpose of removing the pen from the table. But the social world is very different from this engagement with inanimate objects (although, as pointed out in Chapter 6, some recent sociological work – Lee and Motzkau, 2011; Prout, 2005 – makes interesting connections between the inanimate and social worlds). The social world engages us with other members of that world. If I go back to the pen example, another person could have prevented me, for one reason or another, from removing the pen from the table or could have assisted me by removing the pen and then passing it to me. Most of our everyday actions are practised in interaction with other individuals. Children, like adults, live their daily lives in a variety of different settings and take part in a range of activities within and across these varying locations. It is within these relationships that children's agency needs to be anchored and contextualised. It is individuals' collective engagement with others that provides the opportunities, constraints and locations in which agency emerges and takes shape.

But this throws up another issue. To view children as fully agentic beings within these relationships is clearly problematic. Their agency emerges from and operates within generational relationships. These relationships are a central component of macro structures of childhood. Adults and children are positioned differently within this generational order. Power and resources are differentially distributed between adults and children, and this impacts on each group's ability to exercise agency. This is not to suggest that adulthood and childhood will be experienced in a uniform way, as within each category additional variables such as class, gender and ethnicity may structure the options available. However, generation remains a significant structural variable that needs to be taken into account alongside these other variables.

At the same time, to portray children as lesser agents is equally problematic. Children do not fit passively into adult constructions of childhood. The supposed characteristics of immaturity and incompetency are not inherent childhood traits but emerge and are rendered significant within specific discourses and interactions. The meaning and experience of childhood are constantly negotiated and renegotiated between adults and children. In the process, children 'help constitute their own reality' (Shanahan, 2007: 419). They reproduce, undermine and reconfigure stereotypical understandings of childhood and indeed adulthood. Children perform childhood within the generational structuring of adult–child relationships, but these offer different opportunities and constraints for confirming, negotiating, contesting and reformulating what it means to be a child in different contexts. In this vein, agency is something that is achieved rather than existing at the outset. By taking part in specific temporal, social and relational interactions, children accomplish agency. Because these situations are different and the interactional contexts may be variable, agency may fluctuate from one location to another so that the child could be agentic in one setting and less agentic in another. The core point here is that agency is not something that one can achieve in isolation. Agency, for the most part, cannot be achieved solely by any agent, rather it is something that emerges from and within interactions with others.

I introduced the concept of generagency in an attempt to merge the structural positioning emanating from generation with the capacity of members of each generation to practise agency. My aim was to demonstrate how adults and children are members of different collectives and, hence, their agency emerges from within these collectives and varies from one context to another. Generagency acknowledges both the structural nature of childhood and the capacity for children to practise agency within this location. Hence, the model attempts to provide a conceptual framework for bringing together what are often seen as oppositional positions. For example, I illustrated in Chapter 6 how dependency and agency are not mutually exclusive concepts. Rather, dependency and agency are parallel and interconnecting processes. If we look at family life as an example, where children are often located in mainstream discourses as dependent, Bjerke's (2011: 101) observations are relevant in that

> agency and dependency are not necessarily seen in opposition to each other but are a part of the interconnected nature of relationships between children and adults, where children can express their agency, yet also continue to be dependent on nurturance, support or regulation from adults.

Children are dependent on adults in multiple ways and this dependency is shaped by wider structural processes and policies. Children's dependence is part of a wider generational order which often creates and produces hierarchal relationships, but within this framework children have the ability to, at the very least, influence the structures around them and the relationships that emanate from them. This reflects Mayall's (1994) work, which cautions against seeing children's relationships with adults as one consistent set of relationships. Children's relationships with adults reflect dependence, independence, interdependence, autonomy and connectivity, as they move within and across different social settings. Generagency sheds light on the ways in which children are involved in complex and ever-changing intergenerational relationships and practices.

In suggesting that the concept of generation remains useful for understanding the context within which structure and agency are practised, I also sub-divided generagency into two components – inter-generagency and intra-generagency. These two interrelated components represent structured but also dynamic relationships between adults and children and between children themselves. They provide a platform for examining the structural–social dimensions of childhood and how children engage with each other and with adults within this broader framework, with generation acting as an overall filter. While these concepts do not represent a paradigm shift, nonetheless they provide a conceptual tool for thinking about the continuities, challenges and changes that impact on how childhood is lived and experienced. I applied this conceptualisation to my previous research on children and work to demonstrate how using this construction facilitates a better understanding of how children shape and are shaped by current childhood discourses and processes. The model sheds light on how adults and children draw on different resources to enable them to respond to, shape and create everyday lives within the wider context of generational relationships. The resulting social positions stemming from generational positions are complex and fragmented. Inter-generagency reflects Waksler's (1991: viii) notion of children 'inhabiting two worlds: that of adults and that of children'. However, these worlds are not separate but interrelated. Children interact with adults to produce negotiated outcomes. They make sense of and interpret their everyday interactions with adults. Within these interactions with more powerful social actors, children strive to achieve elements of social control over their daily environment. While many children recognise and accept that their agency is constrained, they nonetheless see themselves as having the capacity to act autonomously within largely dependent relationships. I used Moosa-Mitha's (2005) notion of 'differently equal' to acknowledge how children are positioned differently in the wider social order, but noted that this should not detract from their ability not only to have an impact on their own lives, but also to exert an element of influence on the lives of powerful others. Relationships between generations are multi-layered, dynamic and often messy. Relationships between adults and children generate fields of negotiation and renegotiation where norms and expectations are actively challenged and modified. Children adopt a host of multiple strategies in their dealings with adults, at times complying with or resisting adult control over their daily lives.

This focus also necessitates revisiting structured power relationships between adults and children. These relationships are asymmetrical. Children lack a range of legal, economic and political resources and this places them at a structural disadvantage. For the most part, the wider structural positions that adults occupy within society and ongoing various contemporary discourses and practices continue to locate them in a hierarchal position. Hence, power is situated and temporal, but it is also relational. Power is only realised (or not) through action, and within their relationships with others, children have varying degrees of power to make and shape decisions about their everyday lives. Their agency is enmeshed within myriad generational relationships that demonstrate the need to move beyond a narrow and superficial notion of adults having power over children. Power, like agency, also has to be negotiated in daily interactions. Children are aware of their less powerful status but respond to this positioning in diverse and strategic ways. Within each of these micro interactions, the possibility always exists to produce new realities. Power, like agency, has to be performed to be realised. At times, children accept adult authority but this acceptance should be seen as active rather than passive. Here, I introduced the notion of moral agency. Social actors are also moral actors who make moral judgements about how others exercise agency. In revisiting my earlier work, I gave examples of where children's acquiescence to adult demand was influenced by their judgements of fairness. Children and adults, at times, demonstrated shared moralities but these were not universal or predetermined. Sometimes children evaded, challenged and subverted adult demands. They appropriated and reworked moral and cultural values. Agency was embedded within and accorded meaning within past, present and future anticipated relationships. As children pass through time, their agency fluctuates as they negotiate the varying levels of openings and limitations available to them. In myriad ways, these examples illustrate how power is activated, practised and accomplished within and across the minutiae of children's everyday interactions with adults (Foucault, 1982).

Hence, power should not just be seen vertically. Its horizontal dimensions also need to be considered. The notion of intra-generagency pays attention to the differing structural locations of childhood rather than reduce this to an undifferentiated, unitary, all-encompassing category. Hence, age, gender, class and ethnicity present children with different opportunities and constraints around practising agency so that agency is likely to be variable rather than uniform. In other words, hierarchal relationships do not just permeate adult–child relations but also impact on relationships between children. Within these positionings, children reproduce structure but simultaneously practise agency, although again from differing structural positions. Hence, children do not have the same capacity for practising agency. Other factors such as age within childhood, gender, ethnicity and class will impact on the choices and constraints that individual children face in practising agency. Moreover, as outlined above, children live their lives in multiple contexts and hence express their agency within multiple contexts, and this may result in children having more agency in some contexts than in others. Thus far, the ability of the same children to express agency across a variety of different contexts has been under-researched.

Through the concepts of inter-generagency and intra-generagency, I have attempted to introduce a tool for articulating how children may practise agency across the broad dimensions of childhood and adulthood, and how children may practise agency in their relationships with each other. This model of inter-generagency and intra-generagency provides an overarching conceptual framework that enables us to understand agency as something accomplished rather than something possessed. It enables us to view agency as a form of dynamic co-existence that is practised in diverse ways and across dispersed settings. Agency involves the capacity to make a difference and can be located across and within a continuum which reveals various cross-cutting dimensions of power. Children develop a range of tactics and strategies (de Certeau, 1988) in their dealings with each other and with adults. These tactics and strategies are not universally applied but rather applied specifically within different contexts and across and between different groupings of adults and children. In the process, childhood and adulthood are actively co-produced. Applying this model to specific groups of children, such as younger children, those from ethnic minority backgrounds and children with disabilities, could provide a fruitful context for examining the networks of inter- and intra-relationships that characterise their everyday lives and the form which their agency takes within and across these multiple settings.

Agency is ever-present but subject to systematically different levels of structural constraint and possibilities, producing contradictions, ambiguities and inconsistencies throughout the life course. At the same time, it is still the case that adults' agency may have more convertibility, and the unpacking of agency needs to continue to pay attention to the limits to children's agency at the macro level. While some optimistic commentators would argue that the recurring micro acts of agency practised by children, over time, may create a shift in relational power, thus far there has been limited evidence of children's capacity to transform wider structures. But this should not divert attention from recognising that agency remains imprecise and ambiguous. At a basic level, agency concerns the capacity to make a difference, and numerous examples were presented throughout the book which amply suggest that children can and do make a difference. Children are engaged in ongoing processes of interpretation and reinterpretation as they move within the different arenas of their social worlds, through their engagement with each other and a wide array of adults in everyday life. They are co-creators of generational relationships. Their active contributions are evident in their daily life practices.

But, while agency derives from relationships between actors and is practised in multiple settings, the positions that actors occupy in the wider social structure still need to be factored into the equation, demonstrating that linking relational agency in micro settings to relational agency at the macro level continues to reflect wider generational privileges and to impact on opportunities and constraints open to children in relation to possibilities for transformation. At the same time, power is not exclusively hierarchal, and various examples were presented throughout the book to indicate that both power and agency are not attributes of individual actors but are located in and practised within interdependent social relationships. This reworking of the traditional relationship between structure and agency and the reformulation of underlying taken-for-granted assumptions through the concept of generagency provide a useful overarching conceptual framework for exploring ongoing connections and disconnections between children, childhood and generation – the three central concepts on which this book is based.

BIBLIOGRAPHY

Alanen, L. (1988) 'Rethinking Childhood', *Acta Sociologica*, 31, 1, 53–67.

Alanen, L. (1994) 'Gender and Generation: Feminism and the "Child Question"', in Qvortrup, J., Bardy, M., Sgritta, G. and Wintersberger, H. (eds) *Childhood Matters: Social Theory, Practice and Politics*, Aldershot: Avebury.

Alanen, L. (2001) 'Explorations in Generational Analyses', in Alanen, L. and Mayall, B. (eds) *Conceptualizing Adult–Child Relations*, London: Routledge.

Alanen, L. (2011) 'Generational Order', in Qvortrup, J., Corsaro, W. A. and Honig, M. (eds) *The Palgrave Handbook of Childhood Studies*, London: Palgrave Macmillan.

Alanen, L. (2012) 'Disciplinarity, Interdisciplinarity and Childhood Studies', *Childhood*, 19, 4, 419–22.

Alderson, P. (2000) 'School Students' Views on School Councils and Daily Life at School', *Children and Society*, 14, 121–34.

Alderson, P. and Goodwin, M. (1993) 'Contradictions within Concepts of Children's Competence', *The International Journal of Children's Rights*, 1, 303–13.

Alderson, P. and Montgomery, J. (1996) *Health Care Choices: Making Decisions with Children*, London: Institute for Public Policy Research.

Alderson, P., Hawthorne, J. and Killen, M. (2005) 'Are Premature Babies Citizens with Rights? Provision Rights and the Edges of Citizenship', *Journal of Social Sciences*, 9, 71–81.

Alexander, J. (1992) 'Some Remarks on "Agency" in Recent Sociological Theory', *Theory Section Newsletter, American Sociological Association*, 15, 1–4.

Alexander, J. (1993) 'More Notes on the Problem of Agency: A Reply', *Revue Suisse de Sociologie*, 19, 501–6.

Allison, A. (2006) *Millennial Monsters: Japanese Toys and the Global Imagination*, Berkeley, CA: University of California Press.

Althusser, L. (1988) *On Ideology*, London: Verso.

Ambert, A. (1986) 'Sociology of Sociology: The Place of Children in North American Sociology', in Adler, P. and Adler, P. (eds) *Sociological Studies of Child Development*, 1, 11–31.

Archard, D. (1993) *Children: Rights and Childhood*, London: Routledge.

Archard, D. and Skivenes, M. (2009) 'Balancing a Child's Best Interests and a Child's Views', *The International Journal of Children's Rights*, 17, 1–21.

Aries, P. (1962) *Centuries of Childhood*, London: Jonathan Cape.

Backett-Milburn, K. and Harden, J. (2004) 'How Children and their Families Construct and Negotiate Safety and Danger', *Childhood*, 11, 4, 429–47.

Bacon, K. and Frankel, S. (2014) 'Rethinking Children's Citizenship: Negotiating Structure, Shaping Meanings', *The International Journal of Children's Rights*, 22, 21–42.

Baraldi, C. (2008) 'Promoting Self-Expressions in Classroom Interactions', *Childhood*, 15, 2, 239–57.

Baraldi, C. (2010) 'Children's Citizenships: Limitations and Possibilities of Childhood Sociology in Italy', *Current Sociology*, 58, 2, 272–91.

Bartholet, E. (2011) 'Ratification by the United States of the Convention on the Rights of the Child: Pros and Cons from a Child's Rights Perspective', *The Annals of American Political and Social Science*, 633, 80–101.

Bass, L. (2010) 'Childhood in Sociology and Society: The US Perspective', *Current Sociology*, 58, 2, 335–50.

Beck, U. (1992) *Risk Society: Towards a New Modernity*, London: Sage.

Beck, U. and Beck, E. (1995) *The Normal Chaos of Love*, Cambridge: Polity Press.

Becker, S., Aldridge, J. and Dearden, C. (1998) *Young Carers and their Families*, Oxford: Blackwell.

Berger, P. L. and Berger, B. (1991) 'Becoming a Member of Society: Socialization', in Berger, P. L. and Berger, B. (eds) *Studying the Social Worlds of Children: Sociological Readings*, London: Falmer.

Bernardi, F., Gonzalez, J. and Requena, M. (2006) 'The Sociology of Social Structure', in Bryant, C. D. and Peck, D. L. (eds) *21st Century Sociology*, Thousand Oaks, CA: Sage.

Besen, Y. (2006) 'Exploitation or Fun? The Lived Experience of Teenage Employment in Suburban America', *Journal of Contemporary Ethnography*, 35, 3, 319–40.

Besson, S. (2005) 'The Principal of Non-Discrimination in the Convention on the Rights of the Child', *The International Journal of Children's Rights*, 13, 4, 433–61.

Bjerke, H. (2011) '"It's the Way they Do it": Expressions of Agency in Child–Adult Relations at Home and School', *Children and Society*, 25, 93–103.

Blakemore, K. (2003) *Social Policy: An Introduction*, 2nd edition, Buckingham: Open University Press.

Bluebond-Langner, M. (1978) *The Private Worlds of Dying Children*, Princeton, NJ: Princeton University Press.

Bohman, J. (2011) 'Children and the Rights of Citizens: Nondomination and Intergenerational Justice', *The Annals of the American Political and Social Science*, 633, 128–40.

Bourdieu, P. (1977) *Outline of a Theory of Practice*, Cambridge: Cambridge University Press.

Bourdieu, P. (1986) 'The Forms of Capital', in Richardson, J. (ed.) *Handbook of Theory and Research for the Sociology of Education*, New York: Greenwood Press.

Bowles, B. and Gintis, H. (1976) *Schooling in Capitalist America: Educational Reform and the Contradictions of Economic Life*, London: Routledge.

Boyden, J. (1997) 'Childhood and the Policy-makers: A Comparative Perspective on the Globalisation of Childhood', in James, A. and Prout, A. (eds) *Constructing and Reconstructing Childhood: Contemporary Issues in the Sociological Study of Childhood*, London: Falmer.

Bradley, H. (1996) *Fractured Identities: Changing Patterns of Inequality*, Cambridge: Polity Press.

Brannen, J. (1995) 'Young People and their Contributions to Household Work', *Sociology*, 29, 2, 317–38.

Brannen, J. and O'Brien, M. (eds) (1996) *Children in Families: Research and Policy*, London: Falmer Press.

Brownlie, J. (2001) 'The "Being Risky" Child: Governing Childhood and Sexual Risk', *Sociology*, 35, 2, 519–37.

Buhler-Niederberger, D. (2010) 'Introduction: Childhood Sociology – Defining the State of the Art and Ensuring Reflection', *Current Sociology*, 58, 2, 155–64.

Burman, E. (2008) 'Beyond "Women vs. Children" or "Women and Children": Engendering Childhood and Reformulating Motherhood', *The International Journal of Children's Rights*, 16, 177–94.

Byrne, B. and Lundy, L. (2015) 'Reconciling Children's Policy and Children's Rights: Barriers to Effective Government Delivery', *Children and Society*, 29, 4, 266–76.

Cairns, L. (2006) 'Participation with a Purpose', in Tisdall, K., Davis, J., Hill, M. and Prout, A. (eds) *Children, Young People and Social Exclusion: 'Participation for What?'* Bristol: Polity Press.

Chin, E. (2001) 'Feminist Theory and the Ethnography of Children's Worlds: Barbie in New Haven, Connecticut', in Schwartzman, H. (ed.) *Children and Anthropology: Perspectives for the 21st Century*, London: Bergen and Garvey.

Clarke, J. (2004) 'Histories of Childhood', in Wyse, D. (ed.) *Childhood Studies: An Introduction*, Oxford: Blackwell.

Cockburn, T. (1998) 'Children and Citizenship in Britain: A Case for a Socially Interdependent Model of Citizenship', *Childhood*, 5, 1, 99–117.

Cockburn, T. (2005) 'Children's Participation in Social Policy: Inclusion, Chimera or Authenticity', *Social Policy and Society*, 4, 2, 109–19.

Cockburn, T. (2012) *Rethinking Children's Citizenship*, London: Palgrave MacMillan.

Cody, K. (2012) '"BeTween Two Worlds": Critically Exploring Market Segmentation and Liminal Consumers', *Young Consumers*, 13, 3, 284–302.

Cohen, E. (2005) 'Neither Seen nor Heard: Children's Citizenship in Contemporary Democracies', *Citizenship Studies*, 9, 2, 221–40.

Coleman, J. (1988) 'Social Capital in the Creation of Human Capital', *American Journal of Sociology*, 94 (Supplement), S95–S120.

Connolly, P. (1998) *Racism, Gender Identities and Young Children*, London: Routledge.

Connolly, P. (2004) *Boys and Schooling in the Early Years*, London: Routledge/Falmer.

Cook, D. (2000) 'The Other "Child Study": Figuring Children as Consumers in Market Research, 1910s–1990s', *The Sociological Quarterly*, 41, 3, 487–507.

Corsaro, W. A. (1985) *Friendship and Peer Culture in the Early Years*, Norwood, NJ: Ablex.

Corsaro, W. A. (1997) *The Sociology of Childhood*, Thousand Oaks, CA: Pine Forge.

Corsaro, W. A. (2015) *The Sociology of Childhood*, 4th edition, London: Sage.

Croll, P., Attwood, G. and Fuller, C. (2010) *Children's Lives, Children's Futures: A Study of Children Starting Secondary School*, London: Continuum.

Cross, G. (2004) *The Cute and the Cool: Wondrous Innocence and Modern American Children's Culture*, Oxford: Oxford University Press.

Cross, G. (2010) 'Children and the Market: An American Historical Perspective', in Marshall, D. (ed.) *Understanding Children as Consumers*, London: Sage.

Cunningham, H. (1991) *The Children of the Poor: Representations of Childhood Since the Seventeenth Century*, Oxford: Blackwell.

Cunningham, H. (1995) *Children and Childhood in Western Society Since 1500*, London: Longman.

Cunningham, H. (1996) 'Combatting Child Labour: The British Experience', in Cunningham, H. and Viazzo, P. (eds) *Child Labour in Historical Perspective 1800–1985 – Case Studies from Europe, Japan and Colombia*, Florence, Italy: UNICEF Child Development Centre.

Cunningham, H. (2012) 'Saving the Children, c.1830–c.1920', in Morrison, H. (ed.) *The Global History of Childhood Reader*, London: Routledge.

Cunningham, H. and Viazzo, P. (eds) (1996) *Child Labour in Historical Perspective 1800–1985 – Case Studies from Europe, Japan and Colombia*, Florence, Italy: UNICEF Child Development Centre.

Daly, M. and Leonard, M. (2002) *Against All Odds: Family Life on a Low Income*, Dublin: Combat Poverty Agency.

Davey, C. and Lundy, L. (2011) 'Towards Greater Recognition of the Right to Play: An Analysis of Article 31 of the UNCRC', *Children and Society*, 25, 3–14.

Davies, J. M. (2007) 'Analysing Participation and Social Exclusion with Children and Young People: Lessons from Practice', *International Journal of Children's Rights*, 15, 1, 121–46.

Davies, L. (2000) 'Researching Democratic Understanding in Primary School', *Research in Education*, 61, 39–48.

De Certeau, M. (1988) *The Practice of Everyday Life*, Berkeley, CA: University of California Press.

De Herdt, R. (1996) 'Child Labour in Belgium: 1800–1914', in Cunningham, H. and Viazzo, P. (eds) *Child Labour in Historical Perspective 1800–1985 – Case Studies from Europe, Japan and Colombia*, Florence, Italy: UNICEF Child Development Centre.

Denniss, R. (2005) 'Young People's Attitudes to Workplace Bargaining', *Journal of Australian Political Economy*, 56, 145–155.

Denscombe, M. (1985) *Classroom Control: A Sociological Perspective*, London: Allen and Unwin.

Devine, D. (2002) 'Children's Citizenship and the Structuring of Adult–Child Relations in the Primary School', *Childhood*, 9, 3, 303–20.

Devine, D. (2009) 'Mobilising Capitals? Migrant Children's Negotiation of their Everyday Lives in School', *British Journal of Sociology of Education*, 30, 5, 521–35.

Dockett, S. (2004) 'Researching with Children: Insights from the Starting School Project', Paper presented at the Australian Institute of Family Studies, Melbourne, 11 November.

Dotson, H., Vaquera, E. and Cunningham, S. A. (2015) 'Sandwiches and Subversion: Teachers' Mealtime Strategies and Preschoolers Agency', *Childhood*, 22, 3, 362–76.

Earls, F. (2011) 'Children: From Rights to Citizenship', *The Annals of the American Academy of Political and Social Science*, 633, 6–16.

Edwards, R. and Alldred, P. (2000) 'A Typology of Parental Involvement in Education Centring on Children and Young People: Negotiating Familialisation, Institutionalisation and Individualisation', *British Journal of Sociology of Education*, 21, 3, 435–55.

Einarsdottir, M. (2014) *Paid Work of Children and Teenagers in Iceland*, University of Iceland: Faculty of Social and Human Sciences.

Ekstrom, K. (2010) 'Consumer Socialisation in Families', in Marshall, D. (ed.) *Understanding Children as Consumers*, London: Sage.

Elkind, D. (2001) *The Hurried Child*, Cambridge, MA: Perseus.

Emirbayer, M. and Mische, A. (1998) 'What is Agency?', *American Journal of Sociology*, 103, 4, 962–1023.

Firth, R. (1971) *Elements of Social Organisation*, London: Routledge.

Foucault, M. (1982) 'The Subject and Power', *Critical Inquiry*, 8, 777–95.

Franklin, B. and Petley, J. (1996) 'Killing the Age of Innocence: Newspaper Reporting of the Death of James Bulger', in Pilcher, J. and Wagg, S. (eds) *Thatcher's Children? Politics, Childhood and Society in the 1980s and 1990s*, London: Falmer Press.

Freeman, M. (1983) *The Rights and Wrongs of Children*, London: Frances Pinter.

Freeman, M. (1996) *Children's Rights: A Comparative Perspective*, Aldershot: Dartmouth.

Freeman, M. (1997) *The Moral Status of Children*, The Hague: Martinus Nijhoff.

Freeman, M. (2000) 'The Future of Children's Rights', *Children and Society*, 14, 277–93.

Freeman, M. (2006) 'What's Right with Rights for Children?', *International Journal of Law in Context*, 2, 1, 89–98.

Freeman, M. (2007) *A Commentary on the United Nations Convention on the Rights of the Child*, The Hague: Martinus Nijhoff.

Fuchs, S. (2001) 'Beyond Agency', *American Sociological Association*, 19, 1, 24–40.

Gallacher, L. and Gallagher, M. (2008) 'Methodological Immaturity in Childhood Research? Thinking through Participatory Methods', *Childhood*, 15, 4, 499–516.

Giddens, A. (1979) *Central Problems in Social Theory*, Berkeley, CA: University of California Press.

Giddens, A. (1984) *The Constitution of Society: Outline of the Theory of Structuration*, Cambridge: Polity Press.

Giddens, A. (1991) *Modernity and Self Identity*, Cambridge: Polity Press.

Giddens, A. (1998a) *The Third Way: The Renewal of Social Democracy*, London: Polity Press.

Giddens, A. (1998b) 'The Scope of Sociology', in Giddens, A. (ed.) *Sociology: Introductory Readings*, Cambridge: Blackwell.

Grytnes, R. (2011) 'Making the Right Choice! Inquiries into the Reasoning behind Young People's Decisions about Education', *Young*, 19, 3, 333–51.

Hansen, D., Mortimer, J. and Kruger, H. (2001) 'Adolescent Part-time Employment in the United States and Germany: Diverse Outcomes, Contexts and Pathways', in Mizen, P., Pole, C. and Bolton, A. (eds) *Hidden Hands: International Perspectives on Children's Work and Labour*, London: RoutledgeFalmer.

Hanson, K. and Vandaele, A. (2003) 'Working Children and International Labour Law: A Critical Analysis', *The International Journal of Children's Rights*, 11, 73–146.

Harden, J., Backett-Milburn, K., Scott, S. and Jackson, S. (2000) '"Scary Faces, Scary Places": Children's Perceptions of Risk and Safety', *Health Education Journal*, 59, 1, 12–22.

Hardman, C. (2001) 'Can There Be an Anthropology of Children?', *Childhood*, 8, 4, 501–17.

Hendrick, H. (1990) 'Constructions and Reconstructions of British Childhoods: An Interpretative Survey 1800 to the Present', in James, A. and Prout, A. (eds) *Constructing and Reconstructing Childhood*, Bristol: Falmer Press.

Hendrick, H. (1994) *Child Welfare: England 1872–1989*, London: Routledge.

Hitlin, S. and Elder, G. (2007) 'Time, Self and the Curiously Abstract Concept of Agency', *Sociological Theory*, 25, 2, 170–91.

Hobbs, S. and McKechnie, J. (1997) *Child Employment in Britain*, Edinburgh: The Stationery Office.

Hobbs, S., McKechnie, J. and Anderson, S. (2007) 'Making Child Employment in Britain More Visible', *Critical Social Policy*, 27, 3, 415–25.

Hockey, J. and James, A. (1993) *Growing Up and Growing Old: Ageing and the Life Course*, London: Sage.

Hoggett, P. (2001) 'Agency, Rationality and Social Policy', *Journal of Social Policy*, 30, 1, 37–56.

Holt, J. (1975) *Escape from Childhood*, New York: Penguin.

Hood-Williams, J. (1990) 'Patriarchy for Children: On the Stability of Power Relations in Children's Lives', in Chisholm, L., Buchner, P., Kruger, H. and Brown, P. (eds) *Childhood, Youth and Social Change*, London: Falmer.

Howieson, C., McKechnie, J and Semple, S. (2006) *The Nature and Implications of the Part-time Employment of Secondary School Pupils*, Edinburgh: Department of Enterprise, Transport and Lifelong Learning.

Hungerland, B., Liebel, M., Milne, B. and Wihstutz, A. (2007) *Working to be Someone: Child Focused Research and Practice with Working Children*, London: Jessica Kingsley Publishers.

Ingelby, D. (1986) 'Development in a Social Context', in Richards, M. and Light, P. (eds) *Children of Social Worlds*, Cambridge: Polity Press.

Ingenhorst, H. (2001) 'Child Labour in the Federal Republic of Germany', in Mizen, P., Pole, C. and Bolton, A. (eds) *Hidden Hands: International Perspectives on Children's Work and Labour*, London: RoutledgeFalmer.

James, A.L. (2010) 'Competition or Integration? The Next Step in Childhood Studies?' *Childhood*, 17, 4, 485–99.

James, A. (2013) *Socialising Children*, London: Palgrave Macmillan.

James, A. (2011) 'To Be (Come) or Not to Be (Come): Understanding Children's Citizenship', *The Annals of the American Academy of Political and Social Science*, 633, 167–79.

James, A. and James, A. (2001) 'Tightening the Net: Children, Community and Control', *British Journal of Sociology*, 52, 2, 211–28.

James, A. and James, A. (2004) *Constructing Childhood, Theory, Policy and Social Practice*, London: Palgrave Macmillan.

James, A. and Prout, A. (eds) (1997) *Constructing and Reconstructing Childhood: Contemporary Issues in the Sociological Study of Childhood*, London: Falmer Press.

James, A., Jenks, C. and Prout, A. (1998) *Theorising Childhood*, Cambridge: Polity Press.

Jamieson, L. (1999) 'Intimacy Transformed? A Critical Look at the "Pure Relationship"', *Sociology*, 33, 3, 477–94.

Jenks, C. (1982) *The Sociology of Childhood: Essential Readings*, London: Batsford.

Jenks, C. (1996) *Childhood*, London: Routledge.

Jensen, A. (1994) 'The Feminisation of Childhood', in Qvortrup, J., Bardy, M., Sgritta, G. B. and Winterberger, H. (eds) *Childhood Matters: Social Theory, Practice and Politics*, Aldershot: Avebury.

Jensen, A. (2008) 'Children's Welfare in Ageing Europe: Generations Apart?', in Leira, A. and Saraceno, C. (eds) *Childhood: Changing Contexts, Comparative Social Research*, Vol. 25, Bingley: JAI Press/Emerald Group.

Jensen, A. (2011) 'Pluralisation of Family Forms', in Qvortrup, J., Corsaro, W. and Honig, M. (eds) *The Palgrave Handbook of Childhood Studies*, London: Palgrave Macmillan.

John, D. R. (1999) 'Through the Eyes of a Child: Children's Knowledge and Understanding of Advertising', in Macklin, M. C. and Carlson, L. (eds) *Advertising to Children: Concepts and Controversies*, Thousand Oaks, CA: Sage.

Johnson, H. B. (2001) 'From the Chicago School to the New Sociology of Children: The Sociology of Children and Childhood in the United States, 1990–1999', in Hofferth, S. and Owens, T. (eds) *Advances in Life Course Research, Vol. 6: Children at the Millennium – Where Have We Come From, Where Are We Going?* New York: JAI Press.

Kaltenborn, K. (2001) 'Individualization, Family Transitions and Children's Agency', *Childhood*, 8, 4, 463–98.

Katz, E. (2013) 'Domestic Violence, Children's Agency and Mother–Child Relationships: Towards a More Advanced Model', *Children and Society*, 1–11.

Kehily, M. J. (2008) 'Understanding Childhood', in Kehily, M. J. (ed.) *An Introduction to Childhood Studies*, 2nd edition, Maidenhead: Open University Press/McCraw.

Kieser, E. (1999) 'Comparing Varieties of Agency Theory in Economics, Political Science and Sociology: An Illustration from State Policy Implementation', *Social Theory*, 17, 146–70.

King, M. (2007) 'The Sociology of Childhood as Scientific Communication: Observations from a Social Systems Perspective', *Childhood*, 14, 2, 193–213.

King, P. and Howard, J. (2014) 'Children's Perceptions of Choice to their Play at Home, in the School Playground and at the Out-of-school Club', *Children and Society*, 28, 2, 116–27.

Kjorholt, A. (2013) 'Children as Social Investment, Rights and the Valuing of Education', *Children and Society*, 27, 4, 245–57.

Kline, S. (1993) *Out of the Garden*, London: Verso.

Kline, S. (2010) 'Children as Competent Consumers', in Marshall, D. (ed.) *Understanding Children as Consumers*, London: Sage.

Knapp, S. J. (1999) 'Facing the Child: Rethinking Models of Agency in Parent–Child Relations', in Berardo, F. M. and Shehan, C. L. (eds) *Through the Eyes of the Child: Revisioning Children as Active Agents of Family Life – Contemporary Perspectives on Family Research, Vol. 1*, Stamford, CT: JAI Press.

Krappmann, L. (2010) 'The Weight of the Child's View (Article 12 of the Convention on the Rights of the Child)', *The International Journal of Children's Rights*, 18, 501–13.

Kuczynski, L. (2003) 'Beyond Bidirectionality: Bilateral Conceptual Frameworks for Understanding Dynamics in Parent–Child Relations', in Kuczynski, L. (ed.) *Handbook of Dynamics in Parent–Child Relations*, Thousand Oaks, CA: Sage.

Kuhn, T. (1962) *The Structure of Scientific Revolutions*, Chicago, IL: Chicago University Press.

Lanas, M. and Corbett, M. (2011) 'Disaggregating Student Resistances: Analysing What Students Pursue with Challenging Agency', *Young*, 19, 4, 417–34.

Lancaster, Y. and Broadbent, V. (2003) *Listening to Young Children*, Maidenhead: Open University Press.

Langer, B. (2005) 'Research Note: Consuming Anomie – Children and Global Commercial Culture', *Childhood*, 12, 2, 259–71.

Lansdown, G. (2001) *Promoting Children's Participation in Democratic Decision Making*, Florence, Italy: Innocenti Research Centre, Innocenti Insight 6.

Lansdown, G. (2005) *The Evolving Capacities of the Child*, Florence, Italy: Innocenti Research Centre, Innocenti Insight 11.

Lareau, A. (2003) *Unequal Childhoods: Class, Race and Family Life*, Berkeley, CA: University of California Press.

Lavalette, M. (1999) *A Thing of the Past? Child Labour in Britain in the Nineteenth and Twentieth Centuries*, Liverpool: Liverpool University Press.

Lee, J. A. (1982) 'Three Paradigms of Childhood', *Canadian Review of Social Anthropology*, 19, 591–608.

Lee, N. (1998) 'Towards an Immature Sociology', *The Sociological Review*, 46, 3, 458–81.

Lee, N. (2001) *Childhood and Society: Growing Up in an Age of Uncertainty*, Buckingham: Open University Press.

Lee, N. and Motzkau, J. (2011) 'Navigating the Bio-politics of Childhood', *Childhood*, 18, 1, 7–19.

Leonard, M. (1994) *Informal Economy Activity in Belfast*, Aldershot: Avebury.

Leonard, M. (1998) 'Children's Contribution to Household Income: A Case Study from Northern Ireland', in Pettitt, B. (ed.) *Children and Work in the UK: Reassessing the Issues*, London: Child Poverty Action Group.

Leonard, M. (2002) 'Working on Your Doorstep: Child Newspaper Deliverers in Belfast', *Childhood*, 9, 2, 190–204.

Leonard, M. (2003) 'Children's Attitudes to Parents', Teachers' and Employers' Perceptions of Term-Time Employment', *Children and Society*, 17, 349–60.

Leonard, M. (2004a) 'Children's Views on Children's Right to Work: Reflections from Belfast', *Childhood*, 11, 1, 45–61.

Leonard, M. (2004b) 'Teenage Girls and Housework in Irish Society', *Irish Journal of Sociology*, 13, 1, 1–13.

Leonard, M. (2005) 'Children, Childhood and Social Capital: Exploring the Links', *Sociology*, 39, 4, 605–22.

Leonard, M. (2006) 'Segregated Schools in Segregated Societies: Issues of Safety and Risk', *Childhood*, 13, 4, 145–64.

Leonard, M. (2009) 'Helping with Housework: Exploring Teenagers' Perceptions of Family Obligations', *Irish Journal of Sociology*, 17, 1, 1–18.

Lewis, J. (2006) *Children, Changing Families and Welfare States*, Cheltenham: Edward Elgar.

Liebel, M. (2004) *A Will of their Own: Cross-Cultural Perspectives on Working Children*, London: Zed Books.

Lister, R. (2007) 'Why Citizenship: Where, When and How Children?', *Theoretical Inquiries in Law*, 8, 2, 693–718.

Lollis, S. (2003) 'Conceptualizing the Influence of the Past and the Future in Present Parent–Child Relationships', in Kuczynski, L. (ed.) *Handbook of Dynamics in Parent–Child Relations*, Thousand Oaks, CA: Sage.

Loudoun, R. and McDonald, R. (2014) 'The Impact of Employment-Level Characteristics on Work–Life Interference in School-Aged Children', *Journal of Industrial Relations*, 56, 4, 508–26.

Luhmann, N. (1995) *Social Systems*, Stanford, CA: Stanford University Press.

Mackay, R. W. (1991) 'Conceptions of Children and Models of Socialization', in Waksler, F. C. (ed.) *Studying the Social Worlds of Children: Sociological Readings*, London: Falmer Press.

Mannheim, K. (1952) *Essays on the Sociology of Knowledge*, London: Routledge.

Mansurov, V. (2001) 'Child Labour in Russia', in Mizen, P., Pole, C. and Bolton, A. (eds) *Hidden Hands: International Perspectives on Children's Work and Labour*, London: RoutledgeFalmer.

Marshall, D. (2010) *Understanding Children as Consumers*, London: Sage.

Marshall, T. H. (1950) *Citizenship and Social Change*, London: Pluto.

Marx, K. (1974) 'The Eighteenth Brumaire of Louis Bonaparte', in Fernbach, D. (ed.) *Karl Marx: Surveys from Exile*, New York: Vintage Books.

Mason, J. and Tipper, B. (2008) 'Being Related: How Children Define and Create Kinship', *Childhood*, 15, 4, 441–60.

Mayall, B. (1994) *Children's Childhoods: Observed and Experienced*, London: Falmer Press.

Mayall, B. (2013) *A History of the Sociology of Childhood*, London: Institute of Education Press.

Mayall, B. and Zeiher, B. (eds) (2003) *Children in Generational Perspective*, London: Institute of Education.

Mayo, E. and Nairn, A. (2009) *Consumer Kids*, London: Constable Robinson.

McDonald, H. (2013) 'Abortion Refusal Death: Hindu Woman told Ireland "is a Catholic country"', *The Guardian*, 8 April.

McDonald, P., Bailey, P., Price, R. and Pini, B. (2012) 'School-aged Workers: Industrial Citizens in Waiting?', *Journal of Sociology*, 50, 3, 315–30.

McGillivray, A. (1994) 'Why Children Do Have Equal Rights: In Reply to Laura Purdy', *The International Journal of Children's Rights*, 2, 243–58.

McKechnie, J. and Hobbs, S. (2000) 'Child Employment: Filling the Research Gaps', *Youth and Policy*, 66, 19–33.

McKechnie, J., Hobbs, S., Simpson, A., Anderson, S., Howieson, C. and Semple, S. (2010) 'School Students' Part-time Work: Understanding What They Do', *Journal of Education and Work*, 23, 2, 161–75.

Mead, G. H. (1934) *Mind, Self and Society: From the Standpoint of a Social Behaviourist*, Chicago, IL: University of Chicago Press.

Middleton, S. and Loumidis, J. (2001) 'Young People, Poverty and Part-time Work', in Mizen, P., Pole, C. and Bolton, A. (eds) *Hidden Hands: International Perspectives on Children's Work and Labour*, London: RoutledgeFalmer.

Mitchell, J. (1971) *Woman's Estate*, Harmondsworth: Penguin.

Mitchell, R. and McCusker, S. (2008) 'Theorising the UN Convention on the Rights of the Child within Canadian Post-Secondary Education: A Grounded Approach', *The International Journal of Children's Rights*, 16, 159–76.

Mizen, P., Pole, C. and Bolton, A. (2001) 'Why Be a School Aged Worker?', in Mizen, P., Pole, C and Bolton, A. (eds) *Hidden Hands: International Perspectives on Children's Work and Labour*. London: RoutledgeFalmer.

Moosa-Mitha, M. (2005) 'A Difference-Centred Alternative to Theorization of Children's Citizenship Rights', *Citizenship Studies*, 9, 4, 369–88.

Moran-Ellis, J. (2010) 'Reflections on the Sociology of Childhood in the UK', *Current Sociology*, 58, 2, 186–205.

Moran-Ellis, J. (2013) 'Children as Social Actors, Agency and Social Competence: Sociological Reflections for Early Childhood', *Neue Praxis*, 4, 323–38.

Morrow, V. (1996) 'Rethinking Childhood Dependency: Children's Contribution to the Domestic Economy', *The Sociological Review*, 44, 1, 58–77.

Mortimer, J. (2003) *Working and Growing Up in America*, Cambridge, MA: Harvard University Press.

Nairn, A. (2010) 'Children and Brands', in Marshall, D. (ed.) *Understanding Children as Consumers*, London: Sage.

Narvanen, A. and Nasman, E. (2004) 'Childhood as Generation or Life Phase?', *Young*, 12, 1, 71–91.

Neale, B. and Flowerdew, J. (2007) 'New Structures, New Agency: The Dynamics of Child–Parent Relationships after Divorce', *International Journal of Children's Rights*, 15, 1, 25–42.

Nixon, E., Greene, S. and Hogan, D. (2013) '"It's What's Normal for Me": Children's Experiences of Growing up in a Continuously Single-Parent Household', *Journal of Family Issues*, 20, 10, 1–19.

Oakley, A. (1974) *The Sociology of Housework*, London: Martin Robertson.

O'Connell, R. and Brannen, J. (2014) 'Children's Food, Power and Control: Negotiations in Families with Younger Children in England', *Childhood*, 21, 1, 87–102.

O'Donnell, C. and White, L. (1998) *Invisible Hands: Child Employment in North Tyneside*, London: Low Pay Unit.

Oldman, D. (1994) 'Adult–Child Relations as Class Relations', in Qvortrup, J., Bardy, M., Sgritta, G. B. and Winterberger, H. (eds) *Childhood Matters: Social Theory, Practice and Politics*, Aldershot: Avebury.

Oswell, D. (2013) *The Agency of Children: From Family to Global Human Rights*, Cambridge: Cambridge University Press.

Parsons, T. (1954) *Essays in Social Structure*, Glencoe, IL: Free Press.

Pearson, G. (1983) *Hooligan: A History of Respectable Fears*, London: Macmillan.

Percy-Smith, B. (2006) 'From Consultation to Social Learning in Community Participation with Young People', *Children, Youth and Environments*, 17, 1, 136–47.

Piaget, J. (1932) *The Moral Judgement of the Child*, London: Routledge and Kegan Paul.

Piaget, J. (1936) *Origins of Intelligence in the Child*, London: Routledge and Kegan Paul.

Piaget, J. (1957) *Construction of Reality of the Child*, London: Routledge and Kegan Paul.

Pollard, A. and Filer, A. (2007) 'Learning, Differentiation and Strategic Action in Secondary Education', *British Journal of Sociology of Education*, 28, 4, 441–58.

Pollock, L. (1983) *Forgotten Children: Parent–Child Relations from 1500 to 1900*, Cambridge: Cambridge University Press.

Postman, N. (1982) *The Disappearance of Childhood*, London: W. H. Allen.

Prout, A. (2000) *The Body, Childhood and Society*, London: Palgrave Macmillan.

Prout, A. (2005) *The Future of Childhood*, London: RoutledgeFalmer.

Prout, A. and James, A. (1997) 'A New Paradigm for the Sociology of Childhood? Provenance, Promise and Problems', in James, A. and Prout, A. (eds) *Constructing and Reconstructing Childhood: Contemporary Issues in the Sociological Study of Childhood*, London: Falmer Press.

Purdy, L. (1994) 'Why Children Shouldn't Have Equal Rights', *The International Journal of Children's Rights*, 2, 223–41.

Putnam, R. (1995) 'Bowling Alone: America's Declining Social Capital', *Journal of Democracy*, 6, 1, 64–78.

Quennerstedt, A. (2010) 'Children, but not Really Humans? Critical Reflections on the Hampering Effect of the "3 P's"', *The International Journal of Children's Rights*, 18, 619–35.

Qvortrup, J. (1987) 'Introduction to Sociology of Childhood', *International Journal of Sociology*, 17, 3, 3–37.

Qvortrup, J. (1994) 'From Useful to Useful: The Historical Continuity of Children's Constructive Participation', *Sociological Studies of Children*, 7, 49–76.

Qvortrup, J. (1995) 'From Useful to Useful: The Historical Continuity of Children's Constructive Participation', in Ambert, A. (ed.) *Sociological Studies of Children*, Vol. 7. Greenwich, CT: JAI Press.

Qvortrup, J. (1999) *Childhood and Societal Macrostructures: Childhood Exclusion by Default, Working Paper No. 9*, Odense, Denmark: Odense University, Department of Contemporary Cultural Studies.

Qvortrup, J. (2001) 'School Work, Paid Work and the Changing Obligations of Childhood', in Mizen, P., Pole, C. and Bolton, A. (eds) *Hidden Hands: International Perspectives on Children's Work and Labour*, London: RoutledgeFalmer.

Qvortrup, J. (2009) 'The Development of Childhood: Change and Continuity in Generational Relations', in Qvortrup, J. (ed.) *Sociological Studies of Children and Youth, Vol. 12: Structural, Historical and Comparative Perspectives*, Bingley: Emerald.

Qvortrup, J. (2011) 'Childhood as a Structural Form', in Qvortrup, J., Corsaro, W. A. and Honig, M. (eds) *The Palgrave Handbook of Childhood Studies*, London: Palgrave Macmillan.

Raby, R. (2008) 'Frustrated, Resigned, Outspoken: Students' Engagement with School Rules and Some Implications for Participatory Citizenship', *The International Journal of Children's Rights*, 16, 77–98.

Raby, R. and Pomerantz, S. (2013) 'Playing it Down/Playing it Up: Girls' Strategic Negotiations of Academic Success', *British Journal of Sociology of Education*, 1–19.

Rehfeld, A. (2011) 'The Child as Democratic Citizen', *The Annals of American Academy of Political and Social Science*, 633, 141–66.

Renold, E. and Allan, A. (2006) 'Bright and Beautiful: High Achieving Girls' Ambivalent Femininities and the Feminisation of Success', *Discourse: Studies in the Cultural Politics of Education*, 27, 4, 547–73.

Reynaert, D., Bourverne-de-Bie, M. and Vandevelde, S. (2009) 'A Review of Children's Rights Literature since the Adoption of the United Nations Convention on the Rights of the Child', *Childhood*, 16, 4, 518–34.

Roche, J. (1999) 'Children: Rights, Participation and Citizenship', *Childhood*, 6, 4, 475–93.

Rousseau, J. (2003 [1762]) *Emile: or Treatise on Education* (trans. Payne, W. H.), New York: Prometheus Books.

Ruckenstein, M. (2010) 'Toying with the World: Children, Virtual Pets and the Value of Mobility', *Childhood*, 17, 4, 500–13.

Ruckenstein, M. (2013) 'Spatial Extensions of Childhood: From Toy Worlds to Online Communities', *Children's Geographies*, 11, 4, 476–89.

Russell, R. and Tyler, M. (2002) 'Thank Heaven for Little Girls: "Girl Heaven" and the Commercial Context of Feminine Childhood', *Sociology*, 36, 3, 619–37.

Russell, R. and Tyler, M. (2005) 'Branding and Bricolage: Gender, Consumption and Transition', *Childhood*, 12, 2, 221–37.

Rutter, M. (1982) *Fifteen Thousand Hours: Secondary Schools and their Effects on Children*, Cambridge, MA: Harvard University Press.

Ryan, K. W. (2012) 'The New Wave of Childhood Studies: Breaking the Grip of Bio-social Dualism', *Childhood*, 19, 4, 439–52.

Ryan, P. J. (2008) 'How New is the "New" Social Study of Childhood? The Myth of a Paradigm Shift', *Journal of Interdisciplinary History*, XXXVIII, 4, 553–76.

Samuelsson, T. (2007) 'Out of Place? Children's Ideas on Work', in Engwall, K. and Soderlind, I. (eds) *Children's Work in Everyday Life*, Stockholm: Institute for Future Studies.

Samuelsson, T. (2008) *Children's Work in Sweden*, Linkoping: Linkoping University Press.

Saporiti, A. (1994) 'A Methodology for Making Children Count', in Qvortrup, J., Bardy, M., Sgritta, G. and Wintersberger, H. (eds) *Childhood Matters: Social Theory, Practice and Politics*, Aldershot: Avebury.

Schoenhals, M., Tienda, M. and Schneider, B. (1998) 'The Educational and Personal Consequences of Adolescent Employment', *Social Forces*, 77, 723–62.

Schor, J. (2004) *Born to Buy*, New York: Schribners.

Seiter, E. (2004) 'The Internet Playground', in Goldstein, J., Buckingham, D. and Brougere, G. (eds) *Toys, Games and Media*, London: Lawrence Erlbaum.

Sgritta, G. B. (1994) 'The Generational Division of Welfare: Equity and Conflict', in Qvortrup, J., Bardy, M., Sgritta, G. B. and Winterberger, H. (eds) *Childhood Matters: Social Theory, Practice and Politics*, Aldershot: Avebury.

Shanahan, S. (2007) 'Lost and Found: The Sociological Ambivalence Towards Childhood', *Annual Review of Sociology* 33, 407–28.

Shilling, C. (1992) 'Reconceptualising Structure and Agency in the Sociology of Education: Structuration Theory and Schooling', *British Journal of Sociology of Education*, 13, 69–87.

Sirota, R. (2010) 'French Childhood Sociology: An Unusual, Minor Topic or Well-Defined Field?', *Current Sociology*, 58, 2, 250–71.

Skelton, C., Francis, B. and Read, B. (2010) 'Brains Before Beauty? High Achieving Girls, School and Gender Identities', *Educational Studies*, 36, 2, 185–94.

Slevin, J. (2000) *The Internet and Society*, Cambridge: Polity Press.

Smith, K. (2011) 'Producing Governable Subjects: Images of Childhood Old and New', *Childhood*, 19, 1, 24–37.

Sommer, D. (2012) *A Childhood Psychology: Young Children in Changing Times*, London: Palgrave Macmillan.

Speier, M. (1976) 'The Child as a Conversationalist', in Hammersley, M. and Woods, P. (eds) *The Process of School*, London: Routledge and Kegan Paul.

Spyrou, S. (2000) 'Education, Ideology and the National Self: The Social Practice of Identity Construction in the Classroom', *The Cyprus Review*, 12, 1, 61–81.

Stasiulis, D. (2002) 'The Active Child Citizen: Lessons from Canadian Policy and the Children's Movement', *Citizenship Studies* 6, 4, 507–38.

Strandell, H. (2010) 'From Structure-Action to Politics of Childhood: Sociological Childhood Research in Finland', *Current Sociology*, 58, 2, 165–85.

Taylor, N., Smith, A. B. and Gollop, M. (2008) 'New Zealand Children and Young People's Perspectives on Citizenship', *International Journal of Children's Rights*, 16, 195–210.

Thomas, N. (2012) 'Love, Rights and Solidarity: Studying Children's Participation using Honneth's Theory of Recognition', *Childhood*, 19, 4, 453–66.

Thornberg, R. (2009) 'The Moral Construction of the Good Pupil Embedded in School Rules', *Education, Citizenship and Social Justice*, 4, 3, 245–61.

Thornberg, R. and Elvstrand, H. (2012) 'Children's Experiences of Democracy, Participation and Trust in School', *International Journal of Educational Research*, 53, 44–54.

Thorne, B. (1987) 'Revisioning Women and Social Change: Where are the Children?', *Gender and Society*, 1, 1, 85–109.

Thorne, B. (1993) *Gender Play: Girls and Boys in School*, New Brunswick, NJ: Rutgers University Press.

Thorne, B. (2007) 'Editorial: Crafting the Interdisciplinary Field of Childhood Studies', *Childhood*, 14, 2, 147–52.

Tisdall, K. (2008) 'Conclusion: Is the Honeymoon Over? Children and Young People's Participation in Public Decision-Making', *International Journal of Children's Rights*, 16, 419–29.

Tisdall, K. and Davis, J. (2004) 'Making a Difference? Bringing Children and Young People's Views into Policy-making', *Children and Society*, 18, 131–42.

Torney-Purta, J. and Amadeo, J. (2011) 'Participatory Niches for Emergent Citizenship in Early Adolescence: An International Perspective', *The Annals of the American Association of Political and Social Science*, 633, 180–200.

Tufte, B. and Rasmussen, J. (2010) 'Children and the Internet', in Marshall, D. (ed.) *Understanding Children as Consumers*, London: Sage.

Twiner, A., Littleton, K., Coffin, C. and Whitelock, D. (2013) 'Meaning Making as an Interactional Accomplishment: A Temporal Analysis of Intentionality and Improvisation in Classroom Dialogue', *International Journal of Educational Research*, 63, 94–106.

Valentine, G. (1996) '"Children Should be Seen and Not Heard": the Production and Transgression of Adults' Public Space', *Urban Geography*, 17, 205–20.

Valentine, G. (1997) 'A Safe Place to Grow Up: Parenting, Perceptions of Children's Safety and the Rural Idyll', *Journal of Rural Studies*, 13, 137–48.

Valentine, K. (2011) 'Accounting for Agency', *Children and Society*, 25, 347–58.

Vandenbroeck, M. and Bouverne-De-Bie, M. (2006) 'Children's Agency and Educational Norms', *Childhood*, 13, 1, 127–43.

Van Krieken, R. (2010) 'Childhood in Australian Sociology and Society', *Current Sociology*, 58, 2, 232–49.

Veerman, P. (2010) 'The Ageing of the UN Convention on the Rights of the Child', *International Journal of Children's Rights*, 18, 585–618.

Vygotsky, L. (1962) *Thought and Language*, Cambridge, MA: MIT Press.

Waksler, F. C. (1991) *Studying the Social Worlds of Children: Sociological Readings*, London: Falmer Press.

Walkerdine, V. (1984) 'Developmental Psychology and the Child-Centred Pedagogy: The Insertion of Piaget into Early Education', in Henriques, J., Hollway, W., Urwin, C., Venn, C. and Walkerdine, V. (eds) *Changing the Subject: Psychology, Social Regulation and Subjectivity*, London: Methuen.

Walkerdine, V., Lucey, J. H. and Melody, J. (2001) *Growing up Girl: Psychosocial Explorations of Gender and Class*, Basingstoke: Palgrave.

Wall, J. and Dar, A. (2011) 'Children's Political Representation: The Right to Make a Difference', *The International Journal of Children's Rights*, 19, 595–612.

White, B. (1996) 'Globalisation and the Child Labour Problem', *Journal of International Development*, 8, 6, 829–39.

Williams, S. and Williams, M. (2005) 'Space Invaders: The Negotiation of Teenage Boundaries through the Mobile Phone', *The Sociological Review*, 53, 2, 315–30.

Willmott, R. (1999) 'Structure, Agency and the Sociology of Education: Rescuing Analytical Dualisms', *British Journal of Sociology of Education*, 20, 1, 5–21.

Wilson, A. (1980) 'The Infancy of the History of Childhood: An Appraisal of Philippe Aries', *History and Theory*, 19, 2, 132–53.

Woodhead, M. (1997) 'Psychology and the Cultural Construction of Children's Needs', in James, A. and Prout, A. (eds) *Constructing and Reconstructing Childhood: Contemporary Issues in the Sociological Study of Childhood*, London: Falmer Press.

Woodhead, M. (1999) 'Reconstructing Developmental Psychology: Some First Steps', *Children and Society*, 13, 1, 3–19.

Woodhead, M. (2011) 'Child Development and the Development of Childhood', in Qvortrup, J., Corsaro, W. A. and Honig, M. (eds) *The Palgrave Book of Childhood Studies*, Basingstoke: Palgrave Macmillan.

Woodhead, M. and Faulkner, D. (2000) 'Subjects, Objects or Participants? Dilemmas of Psychological Research with Children', in Christensen, P. and James, A. (eds) *Research with Children, Perspectives and Practices*, London: Falmer Press.

Wrong, D. (1961) 'The Over-socialized Conception of Man in Modern Sociology', in Coser, L. A. and Rosenberg, B. (eds) *Sociological Theory*, London: Collier Macmillan.

Wyness, M. (1999) 'Childhood, Agency and Educational Reform', *Childhood*, 6, 3, 353–68.

Wyness, M. (2014) 'Children, Family and the State: Revisiting Public and Private Realms', *Sociology*, 48, 1, 59–74.

Wyness, M. (2015) *Childhood*, Cambridge: Polity Press.

Zeiher, H. (2010) 'Childhood in German Sociology and Society', *Current Sociology*, 58, 2, 292–308.

Zelizer, V. (1985) *Pricing the Priceless Child: The Changing Social Value of Children*, Princeton, NJ: Rutgers University Press.

INDEX

Made in the USA
Middletown, DE
25 August 2017